# Lecture Notes
# in Business Information Processing · 383

More information about this series at http://www.springer.com/series/7911

Viktoria Stray · Rashina Hoda ·
Maria Paasivaara · Philippe Kruchten (Eds.)

# Agile Processes
# in Software Engineering
# and Extreme Programming

21st International Conference
on Agile Software Development, XP 2020
Copenhagen, Denmark, June 8–12, 2020
Proceedings

*Editors*
Viktoria Stray
University of Oslo
Oslo, Norway

Maria Paasivaara
IT University of Copenhagen
Copenhagen, Denmark

Rashina Hoda
Monash University
Clayton, VIC, Australia

Philippe Kruchten
University of British Columbia
Vancouver, BC, Canada

ISSN 1865-1348     ISSN 1865-1356   (electronic)
Lecture Notes in Business Information Processing
ISBN 978-3-030-49391-2     ISBN 978-3-030-49392-9   (eBook)
https://doi.org/10.1007/978-3-030-49392-9

This Springer imprint is published by the registered company Springer Nature Switzerland AG
The registered company address is: Gewerbestrasse 11, 6330 Cham, Switzerland

# Preface

This volume contains the research papers of the 21st International Conference on Agile Software Development (XP 2020), planned to be held June 8–12 at the IT University of Copenhagen, Denmark. However, due to the COVID-19 pandemic, the conference was held online.

XP is the premier agile software development conference combining research and practice. It is a unique forum where agile researchers, practitioners, thought leaders, coaches, and trainers get together to present and discuss their most recent innovations, research results, experiences, concerns, challenges, and trends. XP conferences provide an informal environment to learn and trigger discussions and welcome both people new to agile and seasoned agile practitioners.

XP 2020 marked the 21st edition of the "First Conference in Agile." Agile continues to advance, and the focus of the XP conference program has expanded over the years. While the first XP conference focused on eXtreme Programming and predated the "Agile Manifesto," XP 2020 solicited contributions that address all modern agile approaches, as well as the application of agile to areas including but not limited to FinTech, AI/ML, IoT, and other mission-critical systems with global reach.

The XP 2020 conference invited submissions on 12 tracks, including research papers, research workshops, experience reports, industry and practice, doctoral symposium, education and training, on-site research, journal first, diversity and inclusion, leadership, agile games, and lightning talks. In total, across all submission types, we received over 300 proposals, which demonstrates that the XP community is growing and active.

The research paper track invited submissions of unpublished high-quality research papers, full and short, related to agile and lean software development. Submissions addressing topics across the full spectrum of agile software development, broadly on agile, on issues of concern to researchers or practitioners or both were welcomed.

The XP 2020 research paper track received 46 submissions. After the first screening by the track chairs, 37 submissions were sent for peer review. Each paper was reviewed by three members of the Program Committee. Based on the reviewer comments, 12 full and 4 short papers were accepted for publication in these proceedings. The papers contribute to the literature on agile research and experience, addressing a wide range of topics, including distributed development, large-scale transformation, ethics, leadership, user-centered design, and test-driven development.

We would like to extend our sincere thanks to all the people who contributed to XP 2020: the authors, reviewers, sponsors, chairs, and volunteers. Finally, we would like to express our gratitude to the XP Conference Steering Committee and the Agile Alliance for their ongoing support.

April 2020

Viktoria Stray
Rashina Hoda
Maria Paasivaara

# Organization

## Conference Chair

Maria Paasivaara         Technical University of Denmark, Denmark

## Program Co-chairs

Viktoria Stray         University of Oslo, SINTEF, Norway
Rashina Hoda         Monash University, Australia

## Publication Chair

Philippe Kruchten         The University of British Columbia, Canada

## Program Committee

| | |
|---|---|
| Noura Abbas | Colorado Technical University, USA |
| Scott Ambler | SA+A, Canada |
| Craig Anslow | Victoria University of Wellington, New Zealand |
| Hubert Baumeister | Technical University of Denmark, Denmark |
| Marthe Berntzen | University of Oslo, Norway |
| Jan Bosch | Chalmers University of Technology, Sweden |
| Frank Buschmann | Siemens AG, Germany |
| Fabio Calefato | University of Bari, Italy |
| Daniela S. Cruzes | SINTEF, Norway |
| Torgeir Dingsøyr | Norwegian University of Science and Technology, Norway |
| Yael Dubinsky | StepAhead, Israel |
| Jutta Eckstein | IT Communication, Germany |
| Neil Ernst | University of Victoria, Canada |
| Steven Fraser | Innoxec, USA |
| Juan Garbajosa | Universidad Politécnica de Madrid, Spain |
| Eduardo Guerra | National Institute of Space Research, Brazil |
| Orit Hazzan | Technion – Israel Institute of Technology, Israel |
| Helena H. Olsson | University of Malmö, Sweden |
| Philippe Kruchten | The University of British Columbia, Canada |
| Kati Kuusinen | Technical University of Denmark, Denmark |
| Casper Lassenius | Aalto University, Finland |
| Ville Leppänen | University of Turku, Finland |
| Lech Madeyski | Wroclaw University of Science and Technology, Poland |
| Michele Marchesi | Cagliari University, Italy |

# Contents

# Agile Adoption

# Agile Implementation and Expansive Learning: Identifying Contradictions and Their Resolution Using an Activity Theory Perspective

Pritam Chita[(✉)] [ID], Peter Cruickshank [ID], Colin Smith [ID], and Kendall Richards [ID]

Edinburgh Napier University, Edinburgh, UK
p.chita@napier.ac.uk

**Abstract.** A key challenge organisations face when transitioning to agile delivery methods is that of quickly and effectively learning new ways of working. This study posits that fundamental historical, cultural and behavioural aspects affect the transition and contribute to the poor performance of many agile implementations. In order to address such factors, this study applies a modified Activity Theory (AT) based framework to a case study agile implementation within a large public sector organisation. An activity is closely defined, and six generic activities associated with all agile implementations are identified. These are validated against the agile maturity model literature and a set of evaluation criteria of contradictions, congruences and collaboration is established. Evidence is gathered from participant interviews and the framework is used to surface learning and development obstacles and issues within an expansive learning cycle. The study argues that analysis via this modified AT framework brings original insight. Initial findings indicate that there are relatively few learning and development issues associated with the use of agile tools and techniques themselves and that most problems arise at the interface where the "changed" (more agile) delivery teams meet the organisation's behavioural norms and practices.

**Keywords:** Organisational learning · Activity Theory · Expansive learning · Contradictions · Congruences

## 1  Introduction

Understanding the difficulties and issues associated with agile implementations has been problematic [8] with many varied perspectives [26], organisational settings and approaches [18]. Previous studies [11] have highlighted the need to consider environmental, behavioural and cultural dimensions when studying software development and a recent study [10] suggested an organisational learning perspective with Activity Theory as a useful lens for examining these elements when implementing and adapting agile delivery practices. This paper adds to the discussion by applying an Activity Theory (AT) based framework to evaluate organisational learning, cultural problems and issues when implementing and adapting agile practices. It addresses the following research questions:

© The Author(s) 2020
V. Stray et al. (Eds.): XP 2020, LNBIP 383, pp. 3–19, 2020.
https://doi.org/10.1007/978-3-030-49392-9_1

*RQ1:*   How can Activity Theory provide a structured framework to understanding learning & development issues when implementing an agile approach?

*RQ2:*   What insights does AT give into the learning & development issues that predominate when an organisation transitions to an agile mode of delivery.

An Activity Theory based framework is applied to a large case study organisation text implementing an agile approach and the focus is Engestrom's notion of expansive learning whereby learning and development within organisations progresses by resolution of contradictions and frictions [13]. Consequently, the development and successful take-up of agile practices will only occur as the organisation progresses through a sequence of identification, consideration and subsequent resolution of multiple contradictions. This paper posits that the identification of these contradictions and their approaches to resolution within an expansive learning cycle provides a useful structured framework that facilitates an original insight into the obstacles and issues that impact agile implementations.

To achieve this objective, this paper defines an activity within an Activity Theory context and then hierarchically deconstructs agile development activities from Agile Manifesto principles to propose a set of six key activities that encompass agile delivery activity. This framework is used to examine the issues that an organisation encounters as it adopted agile delivery practices. This study uses the identification of contradictions, their types and occurrences as well as their resolution and collaborative activity as a structured and progressive indicator of the nature and type of learning and development issues that organisations face in implementing agile approaches. This paper is organized as follows. Section 2 develops an Activity Theory based framework of six generic agile activities. Section 3 outlines the case study organisation and the research method adopted. Section 4 details the study findings in terms of identified contradictions, congruences and collaborative interactions that take place within the agile activities. Section 5 discusses the results and concludes the paper.

## 2   Background and Related Work

Originating within the Cultural-Historical Analytical Theory (CHAT) domain, Activity Theory (AT) provides a framework to examine many aspects of work activity and especially highlights frictions and tensions when new initiatives are developed. Chita [10] provides a fuller account of the learning cycle within an agile development environment. From a learning perspective, Activity Theory helps to focus on the important influence of the environmental mix such as culture, procedures, roles, peers, policies and artifacts.

### 2.1  Activity Theory Based Framework

Engestrom [13] sees the unit of analysis as collective rather than individual activity [25] and argues that the collective perspective is a useful tool for studying organisational change and learning. Engestrom's approach is illustrated in Fig. 1. Generic delivery activity of a project team is shown with the focus or purpose of the activity, represented

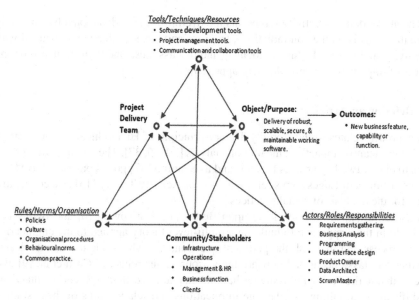

**Fig. 1.** Example Project Delivery Activity (after Engestrom, [13])

by the horizontal line through the middle of the triangle from the Project Delivery Team node (also known as Subject node) to the Object/Purpose node.

This delivery activity both mediates and is mediated (affected/influenced) by the node representing Tools/Techniques/Resources (e.g. a story board or a work package) which might be used as part of the activity, as well as by the Community/Stakeholders (e.g. clients or management) context node within which the delivery activity takes place.

The relationship between the Project Delivery Team node and the Community/Stakeholders node is mediated by the Rules/Norms/Organisation node and also the relationship between the Community/Stakeholders node and the Object/Purpose is mediated by the Actor/Roles/Responsibilities node that reflects how work and responsibilities are divided and allocated. According to Engestrom [15] there will be contradictions and friction within and between these nodes and also between discrete organisational activities. Allen et al. [1] taking a holistic activity system perspective, define "contradiction" as anything that opposes the overall motive of the activity and the individual or collective aims that the subjects (activity actors) are striving for. These contradictions occur in a progression as the activity evolves and changes through an expansive learning process which occurs as a series of progressive series of contradictions are resolved. The cycle starts with *Primary Contradiction* that emerges as an initial trigger point from within one of the above six nodes. A *Secondary Contradiction* leads to a deeper analysis by the subjects (activity actors) with more detailed questioning and is likely to emerge between two nodes. A *Tertiary Contradiction* emerges as the now evolved or changed activity clashes with the older more established mode of operation [30]. Finally, a *Quaternary Contradiction* occurs when the newly organised or more advanced activity comes up against other organisational activities which are still expecting the interaction to be with the previous older version of the activity.

The above delivery activity represents the overall framework adopted by this study where the focus is on the contradictions, frictions and tensions that are associated with the activity. and this study aims to identify and discuss these and their influence on the process of implementing agile delivery approaches.

## 2.2 Defining an Activity

This approach relates to the Activity Theory principle of Hierarchical Decomposition which significantly impacts on the unit of analysis [30, 35, 37]. The AT literature mostly refers to one or two key articles [13, 14] and as Sannino [37] points out there have been various critiques of Engestrom's representation of Activity Theory [13] as a conceptual model for the analysis of social practices.

Cash et al. [9] draw extensively upon Bedny and Karwowski [6] and Bedny and Harris [5] in their approach to building a multi-level theory applied to the engineering design process and they ask the pertinent question, "At what scale do distinct design activities and tasks occur and how are the various scales related?" Cash et al. [9] also indicate that in the design field, studies have taken place at different levels and that there are difficulties in pulling together the implications and relationships of these studies. This could also be said to be true of studies in IS/IT where there are extensive articles on methods and processes as well as programming and interface design [8, 32, 38, 39] but little that actually pulls them together into a coherent whole. Cash et al. [9] state that "as with any technical system, the ability to describe behaviours and properties of the system across multiple scales is essential for generating deep scientific understanding," and borrowing from Bedny and Karwowski [6] they arrive at an Activity → Task → Action decomposition that differs from the conventional Activity Theory structure of Activity → Action → Operation.

Bedny and Harris [5] identify the production process as a *sequence* of transformations of raw material into a finished product and Cash et al. [9] apply this to the design process and arrive at an illustrative diagram which has been modified below (Fig. 2) to start at

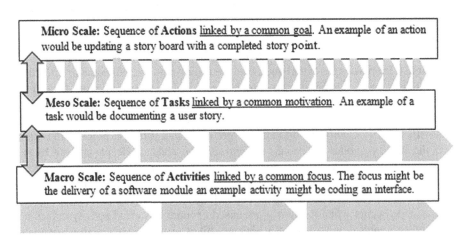

**Fig. 2.** Cash et al. [9] framework adapted for an agile environment.

the lowest level (Actions) to arrive at Activities at the highest level and is applied to the agile delivery process.

For gathering research data and analytical purposes, this represents a more granular approach to the application of AT rather than an approach that envisions the whole of the software development process as a single activity. Applying this approach to a traditional delivery lifecycle, one could classify each stage of the cycle as a specific activity. Such a linear approach might well fit some development lifecycles, but most are likely to have more than one activity either taking place simultaneously or across multiple stages.

## 2.3   Activities in Agile Delivery

Identification of a generic and widely applicable set of agile delivery activities was pursued by re-visiting the twelve agile principles on which much of current agile development activity and practice is founded. What constitutes a "principle" is open to interpretation and general definitions of a principle vary from "a fundamental truth or proposition that serves as the foundation for a system of belief or behaviour or for a chain of reasoning" to "a fundamental source or basis of something" as well as "a general scientific theorem or law" [33].

Meyer [28] posits his own set of principles which he calls a "usable list", divided into two groups, Organisational and Technical. This consolidates the rationale and core concepts behind the Agile Manifesto Principles into a logical, granular and discrete list. Supporting these principles, Meyer [29] identifies several practices that he regards as the regular "almost ritual" activities that must be undertaken in order to be able to conform with and apply the agile principles. Amending Meyer's list with additional elements (Requirements Gathering and Learning and Development) we can derive a coherent set of agile activities that cater for the concepts underpinning the Agile Manifesto Principles and which should support all agile delivery approaches, and which can be identified as constituting activities within an AT context. These defined activities are depicted in Table 1 below.

**Table 1.**  Generic agile activities and tasks

| Agile activity | Description | Example tasks |
| --- | --- | --- |
| Development (Dev) | Simple and incremental design; coding standards and shared coding | Deploying coding standards Pair programming; Refactoring |
| Release Management (RM) | Planning, Continuous Integration and Configuration Management | Estimation tasks Frequent/small releases Configuration Management |
| Testing and Quality (T&Q) | Test driven development and all aspects of assuring software capability | TDD; Unit testing Defect analysis |

*(continued)*

**Table 1.** (*continued*)

| Agile activity | Description | Example tasks |
|---|---|---|
| Requirements Engineering (RE) | Customer focus, gathering and developing user stories, use cases etc. | Customer collaboration. Manage changing requirements. User story development |
| Learning and Development (L&D) | Retrospectives for incremental improvement | Sprint retrospectives; Training Project retrospectives |
| Governance and Support (G&S) | Incorporates Meyer's management practices and other organisational support elements | Daily stand-ups Self-organised/teams Development environment |

This identified set of activities was assembled in a draft paper and circulated amongst senior Agile coaches and consultants within the financial services, public sector and consulting domains in the Edinburgh (Scotland, United Kingdom) area and the feedback to date has been positive and in general agreement with the set.

Having arrived at a defined set of activities and tasks, the initial requirement is to evaluate these suggested activities according to published literature to provide a wider appraisal and comparison with other perspectives that address agile delivery activities and practices. These perspectives are most likely to be addressed in agile maturity model literature, as it aims to align agile processes[1] and practices/activities either within the traditional maturity model approaches [26] or those that define separate agile maturity models [18]. A recent study by Fontana et al. [17] aims to evaluate "currently proposed agile maturity models" and the authors identified 14 papers that were considered important for their analysis.

This study adopted these same 14 articles as representative of the wider context and perspectives of all elements that make up agile activities and practices and compares them with the proposed set of generic agile activities in Table 1 above. The generic activities were found to map well to all indications of agile activities and practices mentioned within the 14 articles. Given the wide variety of likely organisational situations, and an Activity Theory based approach that progresses bottom up from Actions → Tasks → Activity to arrive at an activity that consists of a number of conceptually linked tasks with a common focus, these agile activities represent a logical, distinct and comprehensive set. Within each of these agile activities and tasks, expansive learning will occur as organisations and delivery teams face contradictions and obstacles within these activities/tasks and either adopt additional practices to resolve them or perhaps pursue them in different ways. Therefore, each organisation will have its own view and/or hybridized version of tasks and artifacts within each of the above six activities.

---

[1] This study views a process as a sequence of activities/practices.

## 2.4　Congruences and Collaborative Activity

In their analysis of technology-mediated organisational change, Allen et al. [1] introduce the concept of "congruences" which they see as "temporary stabilization" or stabilizing forces within an activity system, which they regard as a development that leads to balance rather than precipitating change. In this analysis, it is important to recognize elements that promote reproduction as well as those that give rise to change as that whilst there will be tensions that provoke change, there are also issues related to the development of congruences.

Through their analysis of primary and secondary contradictions, Allen et al. [1] argue that these sources of tension give rise to an advanced form of the activity as a result of greater congruencies within the work activity. Their analysis of case studies revealed contradictions being offset by congruencies and through a process of feedback and action, the contradictions were transformed into congruencies [1]. Dennehy and Conboy [12] take up this point and note that the congruence of contradictions within and between activities will act as drivers of change giving rise to several levels of congruency between the different elements. The authors quote Allen et al. [2] who indicate that these congruencies can be immediate where things work better within an activity or give rise to longer term congruencies. The authors [12] argue that it is the congruence of contradictions that is important in explaining the evolution and development of an activity.

Hasan and Banna [20] indicate that innovation and the resolution of a contradiction has to take place at the social level and cannot happen at the individual level. They point to Bodker's [7] work in HCI who indicates that there has to be close collaboration and cooperation to deliver better design. Engestrom [15] and Bardram [3] have also considered this element in their examination of collaborative activity. Engestrom et al. [16] identified a progression of three levels of collaborative activity taking place.

Co-ordination is the "normal scripted flow of interaction" [16, p. 372] where individuals will focus on their own assigned roles, objects and actions. The script may consist of written rules and unwritten traditions and participants within the activity are coordinated without question or discussion. In the context of a software development environment, Barthelmess and Anderson [4] indicate that there is a lack of a community concept in this type of collaborative activity and it may be noted that in the context of organisational process or practice this level of activity might be that which is typically incorporated into a traditional maturity model perspective. Progression to the co-operation level of collaborative activity, involves actors that will instead of focusing on their assigned roles will focus on a shared problem or object in order to find an agreed solution. Actors (subjects) will move beyond the confines of a script but will not explicitly question or reinterpret it. According to Bardram [3] the important difference between coordinated and co-operative work is a shared objective and the actors have to balance their own actions with those of their activity partners to achieve a common goal.

Finally, to achieve the co-construction level of collaborative activity, actors will reconceptualize their roles and interactions with the shared object or problem. According to Bardram [3] the objective (motive) of the work is not stable and has to be collectively constructed which he calls "co-construction". According to Engestrom et al. [16] the script may be re-conceptualised as well as the individual's interactions with each other.

Actors will pose questions such as "What is the meaning of this problem in the first place? Why are we trying to solve it - and who benefits from its solution? How did the problem emerge?" [3: 9].

Barthelmess and Anderson [4] indicate that there is a close interplay between these different levels as they are all part of "collaborative activity" and that a pattern of dynamic transformations between these levels can be observed. To illustrate using a software development example, writing software might occur in a coordinated way and a developer might encounter a problem perhaps with a specification or a tool (contradiction). This might then become a collaborative activity as the developer and business analyst collaborate with regards to problem resolution and once resolved activity returns to a coordinated state. Alternatively, it might be a serious problem that requires a more considered approach that involves re-thinking practice in which case the activity becomes a co-constructive effort at which point practice is questioned and re-conceptualized and expansive learning takes place as contradictions are resolved. The activity then returns to the coordinated state.

In the case study organisation below, the different types and details of contradictions within the agile implementation are identified in order to determine the learning and development issues that the organisation encounters when implementing an agile approach. The occurrence of different types of collaborative activity as pre-cursors to expansive learning are also examined.

## 3   Case Organisation and Study Design

This research focuses on a single case study organisation with the intention to identify the nature and type of contradictions, congruences and collaborative activity that has occurred within the organisation during its adoption of the Structured Agile Framework (SAFe) method. According to Runeson and Host [36] the case study methodology is well suited to software engineering research and provides a deeper understanding of the phenomena under study. The case study organisation is a large public sector body that delivers a broad range of services. As a single body employing over 3500 people, the organisation leverages efficiencies of scale and reduced infrastructure costs in the delivery of its services for which the demand has grown rapidly creating many challenges which led to the creation of the Change Programme which ran from May 2017 to April 2019.

The Programme was initiated by senior management and the IT and Programme Support functions decided to adopt and use agile approaches in a very short space of time leading to the rapid deployment of the SAFe framework. This represented a major change from the waterfall and PRINCE2 based approaches previously deployed. Given the starting point, scale, speed of implementation and the requirement to urgently deliver value in the complex public sector environment, the Change Programme had many significant learning and development issues. Over the two-year duration of the Change Programme, a core group of around 100 people were involved but intermittently this grew to nearly 200 people, divided into twelve delivery streams.

This paper presents the initial results from an analysis of semi-structured interviews conducted so far with 13 delivery managers involved in the programme. The hour-long interviews were with senior managers responsible for delivery streams and took place in the period immediately after the programme ended in April through to September 2019. The interview questions were derived from a series of previous papers that have applied Activity Theory to case study organisations [21–23, 27, 31, 34]. Thirty-seven interview questions were derived and were designed to be as widely applicable as possible. In addition, illustrative diagrams were used to guide the interviewees. The NVivo (v12) qualitative data analysis tool was used to code the interview transcripts for the occurrences of contradictions, congruences and collaborative activity. Interview transcripts were also examined for statements indicating problems & issues related to the Change Programme's agile approach.

The interviews were conducted immediately after the Change Programme had finished and so individual's perspectives were current and relevant. Interviewees were forthright and open in their responses and were keen to divulge their views and perspectives. As the interviews were conducted at the delivery manager level, the results are likely to reflect broader issues that concern delivery managers rather than immediate software development and build issues. Consequently, identified contradictions and congruences such as those relating to Governance & Support, Learning & Development activities are likely to predominate. With the programme having terminated and with over 100 core personnel involved having returned to their core functions there was little opportunity to engage in observational research to enable the collected data to be triangulated.

## 4   Findings

The findings are structured into three sections related to contradictions, congruences and indications of collaborative interactions. For contradictions, the type and levels were identified and for congruences only levels could be established. For collaborative interactions, attention focused on instances of co-operation and co-construction.

### 4.1   Contradictions

Instances of the four types of contradictions across all six generic agile activities are depicted in Table 2 below; the last column indicates the number of mentions and discussions of discrete elements within the interview transcripts.

**Table 2.** Contradiction frequency

| Contradiction | Description | Mentions |
|---|---|---|
| Primary | Occur within the six nodes | 51 |
| Secondary | Occur between the six nodes | 318 |
| Tertiary | Occur between the activity and an advanced form | 20 |
| Quaternary | Occur between the activity and neighbouring activities | 53 |

The nodes in Table 2 relate to the six points of the Activity Triangle in Fig. 1 and the "advanced form" relates to an improved version of the activity. There are few initial tensions and contradictions within individual nodes as indicated by the relatively few *Primary Contradictions*. This indicates that individuals do not experience many issues or tensions or difficulties within nodes such as the delivery teams or the tools and techniques per se used when implementing agile methods. The large number of *Secondary Contradictions* indicate by a significant margin that most of the frictions and tensions occur between nodes as the delivery activities evolve and more questions are being asked. A summary of these secondary contradictions is displayed below in Table 3.

**Table 3.** Secondary contradictions analysis

| Secondary contradiction | Example description | No. |
|---|---|---|
| Subject – Artefact | Use of agile tools and techniques by delivery team | 77 |
| Subject – Rules & Norms | Delivery team practices and norms | 19 |
| Subject – Div. of Labour | Allocation of roles and work within delivery team | 20 |
| Community – Artefact | Use of agile tools and techniques by other stakeholders with an interest in the activity | 24 |
| Community – Rules & Norms | Organisation wide practices and norms | 150 |
| Community – Div. of Labour | Division of labour within the other stakeholders | 14 |

Within the project delivery teams most issues revolved around the use of the agile tools and approaches (77). Typical issues related to the understanding and deployment of agile techniques and the mixed level of training that was provided as was illustrated by one delivery stream manager.

*"I think it would have been better if I had been trained and knew how the organisation wanted to implement it. But I had other people, like I know that other people received really good support and back-up"*

To a much lesser extent, the delivery team came up against issues regards adopting agile practice and norms compared to existing team delivery practices as illustrated by another delivery stream manager.

*"we had real difficulties because solution architects their job and title is thinking about solutions. But of course, when you are running in an agile way you are kind of solution agnostic until the point you have gathered all your engineering requirements"*

By far the most prevalent secondary contradictions (150) occurred beyond the delivery team, within the area involving the wider organisational groups who had a vested interest in the delivery activity and who interfaced with the activity in terms of the organisational rules, procedures and normal practices that were deployed. The magnitude of the issue is illustrated by one delivery stream manager.

*"Very simply we work in an organisation of three and a half thousand people and there was only 200 people on an agile programme so we're not, we're not going to change the way those two or two strands run in the organisation for 200 people.*

The existing organisational structure continued to pose issues throughout for the whole programme There were few *Tertiary Contradictions* (20) which indicates that either there were not many tensions and frictions with moving to a more evolved version of the agile activities and an overall willing preparedness to embrace newer approaches. Alternatively, it could mean that the agile activities are not yet evolved to a point that demanded the older ways needed to be abandoned. Typically, the main difficulty centered around individuals reverting to previous ways of working as was mentioned by the programme director.

*"And then what happens is that, if you get people joining a team, they don't get the proper training, and then if they've got five things to manage, it's easier for them to default to their existing ways of working. So, I think that's been an issue with [...], and I would say generally an issue with SAFe and Scrum, is if you don't have dedicated resources, it's really hard to make it stick, because people just get pulled back into, you know...if the environment doesn't change, you get pulled back into the same ways of working"*

There were far more *Quaternary Contradictions* (53) that occurred, and one delivery stream manager put it rather tersely: *"We clashed with probably every part of the organization"*. Others indicated the repetitive nature of continually having to engage with and educate multiple organisational elements.

*"it's harder to control because you're bringing in business units and they've got their old ways of working and they're not necessarily motivated because they've not been in the programme for a year and getting used to ways of Agile and all that kind of thing. And so, you felt that you were having to start again, and then again in the next increment, and again as soon as another service came on"*

From the above it is apparent that different people that are engaged in different activities are facing a variety of learning and development issues all at various stages of the expansive learning cycle as the programme engages with a different way of working. The least problematic area is overcoming the reluctance of individuals and organisational units to let go of older approaches (*Tertiary*). The introduction and use of new tools and techniques (*Primary*) and the interface that an evolved new activity (*Quaternary*) has with the rest of the organisation is slightly more problematic but by far most of the tensions and frictions and therefore learning and development opportunities relate to where the change programme's developing and evolving activities interface with the rest of the organisation's existing norms and practices (*Secondary*).

**Table 4.** Generic agile activities and contradictions frequency

| Generic agile activity | No. |
|---|---|
| Governance and Support (G&S) | 80 |
| Release Management (RM)l | 40 |
| Learning and Development (L&D) | 57 |
| Requirements Engineering (RM) | 14 |
| Testing and Quality (T&Q) | 2 |
| Building and Coding (B&C) | 4 |
| **Stream** – contradictions affecting whole stream | 108 |
| **Programme -** contradictions affecting whole programme | 179 |

Of these evolving and developing activities the occurrences of tensions and frictions is not evenly distributed across all the generic activities as illustrated in Table 4 above. This shows programme wide contradictions dominate followed by those affecting a single stream and then those that affect the Governance and Support (G&S) generic agile activity. However, this may well reflect the perspectives of the senior management individuals interviewed so far. This would also explain why Building and Coding (B&C) and Testing and Quality (T&C) are so low.

### 4.2   Congruences and Stabilizations

The following table details the occurrences of Congruences and Stabilizations within the analysis conducted so far (Table 5).

**Table 5.** Congruences and stabilizations occurrences

| Congruences and stabilizations | No. |
|---|---|
| Primary – within a node | 21 |
| Secondary – between nodes | 61 |
| Tertiary – between an activity and an advanced version | 11 |
| Quaternary – between activity and an adjacent activity | 34 |

As can be seen the most common occurrences of congruences are the congruences that relate to secondary contradictions. Given that secondary contradictions emerged as the most common in the previous analysis then the higher number of secondary congruences is indicative of substantial efforts to address the contradictions. The following quote from a delivery stream manager is indicative.

*"All of the scrum event planning, retros, reviews and scrum they help support the team. We knew we had to go to those we did go to those, they supported us, they allowed openness so the events themselves worked very well for us. Helped knowledge management and sharing. In relation to capacity and estimation that was really, really good because for the first time probably we weren't just assuming that everybody was there all the time"*

## 4.3  Collaborative Activity

Co-ordination activities are prevalent all the time and have not been identified as they are not indicative of any progression towards expansive learning activity.

**Table 6.** Collaborative activity

| Congruences and stabilizations | No. |
| --- | --- |
| Co-ordination – not looked for | N/A |
| Co-operation | 36 |
| Co-construction | 6 |

Table 6 provides a high-level perspective indicating the presence of substantial levels of co-operative activity which is a significant pre-cursor to expansive learning taking place [16]. There were many illustrative examples of this such as the following:

*"So, what I think it did is, the hand raisers found themselves in it and what it did is it raised an awareness of what was possible, let's look, here's a way of working. And I was one of them, I didn't raise my hand to be in it but I found myself or the universe found me in it, and I think it raised a kind of oh this is what's possible, this is really exciting."*

Examples of co-construction were very limited but there were indicators of a supportive environment that would facilitate such activity.

*"I think all my people, regardless of age or inclination, are probably full of good ideas, but they all require different ways of getting those ideas to come out of their mouths, so Agile will help some of them"*

Identifying examples of collaborative activity simply shows at a very high level the propensity or potential of the individuals and organisational units to make progress along the expansive learning cycle. With the interview transcripts analysed so far, it's not been possible to link collaborative activity to the different levels of contradictions and congruences, but this is a later aim of this study.

## 5  Discussion and Conclusion

Focusing on the learning and development aspects, this study proposes an alternative structured approach that is granular and progressive, and which helps to identify and understand the issues that an organisation encounters when implementing agile. When they examined the challenges facing organisations implementing agile, Gregory et al. [19] identified seven major themes and twenty-seven sub-themes in the data collected. The highly diverse themes ranged from organisational elements to cultural aspects to sustainability elements to business value. Whilst a very useful list of elements there is little likelihood of identifying inter-relationships or connective elements perhaps precisely due to the wide diversity of the issues identified.

The analytical approach taken in the paper of viewing the issues identified within an Activity Theory framework has been shown to provide an inter-connected context which places these issues in a useful progressive framework. For example, anything to do with teams whether it is team practices or recruitment relates to the subject node and issues with teams themselves constitutes a primary contradiction. Team practices using new approaches constitute a secondary contradiction. Organisational culture elements and business value aspects can relate to Rules & Norms node and Distributed Teams relates to the Division of Labour nodes. Primary contradictions will relate to issues within teams and once they are resolved then attention will turn to secondary contradictions that occur beyond the subject or team nodes. This offers a form of a progression of issues and the value of the Activity Theory framework is that it places these issues within a structure where resolution of contradictions & congruences leads onto the next step in the Expansive Learning Cycle. This Activity Theory based framework identifies contradictions at particular levels to provide a useful insight and understanding in terms of locating where the major issues are in a progressive cycle compared to simply identifying a list of different types of issues that the organisation faces without any context of importance or contribution regards progress towards an organisation successfully transitioning to an agile mode of delivery.

As evidenced by the number of occurrences of *Primary Contradictions,* this study indicates that in this case, most issues do not relate to the actual use of agile tools and techniques or even a reluctance to let go of previous ways of working as evidenced by the relatively few occurrences of *Tertiary Contradictions*. The location of these contradictions within the six generic agile activities facilitates a more structured and granular approach to locating specific issues. In this study the contradictions have been mostly concentrated around the Governance & Support tasks, though this is likely to reflect the focus of the delivery managers interviewed. As indicated by the large number of *Secondary Contradictions*, the major tensions and frictions relate to the interface between the delivery team and the rest of the organisation and its practices and behavioural norms. This is consistent with the findings of other authors such as Gregory et al. [19] and Kuusinen et al. [24]. These issues extended beyond specific agile activities and most affected the whole programme and many related to individual delivery streams.

The findings indicate that the agile activities that experienced substantial issues were related to Governance and Support (G&S) as well as Learning and Development (L&D) activities. The G&S activity would be expected to be significant due to the large number of contradictions identified that related to the interface between the delivery team and the rest of the organisation. It could also be indicative of the management level of individuals who have been interviewed so far. The L&D contradictions seem to be derived partially from the mixed levels of formal training and development that was made available to the participants although there is also evidence of substantial provision of mentoring and support provided throughout. This presents an area for further analysis within this study, for instance examining the reasons the organisation is less willing to fund formal training but is willing to spend on mentoring and coaching and whether this relates to budget holders or funding cycles.

The distribution of congruences broadly follows that of the contradictions which is indicative of significant attempts to address and resolve the occurring contradictions. The occurrence of collaborative interactions particularly in terms of co-construction is extremely limited and is perhaps indicative of the limited opportunity for individuals to reconceptualize their roles and interactions. With regards to the second research question, this approach could indicate where learning and development issues predominate when implementing agile an agile approach. The findings point to specific areas for further research, particularly in the area of the impact of organisational practices and norms as well as individual attitudes and autonomy. This study is confined to delivery managers and further research could consider interviewing delivery personnel as well obtaining perspectives from business units benefiting from the change initiative as well as business functions supporting the initiative such as finance and HR.

This study has provided a framework to map defined Activity Theory concepts to agile delivery processes. It has used the concepts of contradictions, congruences and collaborative interactions to suggest a structured framework to view obstacles to learning & development encountered by organisation. With regards to the first research question this structured, granular, generic and scalable approach provides a framework that moves beyond a checklist approach of issue identification and the study findings should complement existing approaches of both academics & practitioners as they examine the issues and difficulties of implementing agile delivery methods.

# References

1. Allen, D.K., Brown, A., Karanasios, S., Norman, A.: How should technology-mediated organizational change be explained? A comparison of the contributions of critical realism and activity theory. MIS Q. **37**(3), p835–p854 (2013)
2. Allen, D.K., Karanasios, S., Norman, A.: Information sharing and interoperability: the case of major incident management. Eur. J. Inf. Syst. **23**(4), 418–432 (2014). https://doi.org/10.1057/ejis.2013.8
3. Bardram, J.: Designing for the dynamics of cooperative work activities. In: Proceedings of the 1998 ACA4 Conference on Computer Supported Cooperative Work, Seattle Washington (1998)
4. Barthelmess, P., Anderson, K.M.: A view of software development environments based on activity theory. Comput. Support. Coop. Work **11**, 13–37 (2002). https://doi.org/10.1023/A:1015299228170
5. Bedny, G.Z., Harris, S.R.: The systemic-structural theory of activity: applications to the study of human work mind. Cult. Act. **12**(2), p128–p147 (2005)
6. Bedny, G.Z., Karwowski, W.: Activity theory as a basis for the study of work. Ergonomics **47**(2), p134–p153 (2004)

7.   Bodker, S.: Activity theory as a challenge to systems design. in information system research: contemporary approaches and emergent traditions. In: Sanstrom, G., Nissen, H.E. (eds.) Proceedings of the IFIP TC 8/WG 8.2 Working Conference. Elsevier

8.   Boehm, B., Turner, R.: Management challenges in implementing agile processes in traditional development organisations. IEEE Softw. **22**, 30–39 (2005)

9.   Cash, P., Hicks, B., Culley, S.: Activity theory as a means of multi-scale analysis of the engineering design process a protocol study of design in practice. Des. Stud. **38**, 1–32 (2015)

10.  Chita, P.S.: Agile Software Development – Adoption & Maturity. in Agile Processes in Software Engineering and Extreme Programming. XP2018

11.  Dennehy, D., Conboy, K.: Going with the flow: an activity theory analysis of flow techniques in software development. J. Syst. Softw. **133**, 160–173 (2017)

12.  Dennehy, D., Conboy, K.: Breaking the flow: a study of contradictions in information systems development (ISD). Inf. Technol. People **33**(2), 477–501 (2019)

13.  Engestrom, Y.: Learning by Expanding: An Activity-Theoretical Approach to Developmental Research. Cambridge University Press, Cambridge (1987)

14.  Engestrom, Y.: Activity theory as a framework for analyzing and redesigning work. Ergonomics **43**(7), 960–974 (2000)

15.  Engestrom, Y.: Expansive learning at work: towards an activity theoretical reconceptualization. J. Educ. Work **14**(1), p133–p156 (2001)

16.  Engestrom, Y., Brown, K., Christopher, L.C., Gregory, J.: Co-ordination, cooperation and communication in the courts: expansive transitions in legal work. In: Mind, Culture and Activity: Seminal papers from the Laboratory of Comparative Human Cognition, p. 239 (1997)

17.  Fontana, R.M., Albuquerque, R., Luz, R., Moises, A.C., Malucelli, A., Reinehr, S.: Maturity models for agile software development: what are they? In: Larrucea, X., Santamaria, I., O'Connor, Rory V., Messnarz, R. (eds.) EuroSPI 2018. CCIS, vol. 896, pp. 3–14. Springer, Cham (2018). https://doi.org/10.1007/978-3-319-97925-0_1

18.  Fontana, R.M., Fontana, I.M., Garbuio, P.A., Reinehr, S., Malucelli, A.: Processes versus people: how should agile software development maturity be defined? J. Syst. Softw. **97**, 140–155 (2014)

19.  Gregory, P., Barroca, L., Sharp, H., Deshpande, A., Taylor, K.: The challenges that challenge: Engaging with agile practitioners' concerns. Inf. Softw. Technol. **77**, p92–p104 (2016)

20.  Hasan, H., Banna, S.: The unit of analysis in IS theory: the case for activity. In: The Fifth Biennial ANU Workshop on Information Systems Foundations. pp. 1–8. ANU, Canberra (2010)

21.  Jonassen, D.H., Rohrer-Murphy, L.: Activity theory as a framework for designing constructivist learning environments. Educ. Technol. Res. Dev. **47**(1), 61–79 (1999). https://doi.org/10.1007/BF02299477

22.  Kaptelinin, V., Nardi, B., Macaulay, C.: The Activity Checklist: A Tool for Representing the "Space" of context. Interactions July/August (1999)

23.  Korpela, M., Activity Analysis and Development in a nutshell. Handout Version 2 (1999)

24.  Kuusinen, K., Gregory, P., Sharp, H., Barroca, L.: Strategies for doing agile in a non-agile environment. In: Proceedings of the 10th ACM/IEEE International Symposium on Empirical Software Engineering and Measurement, pp. 1–6 (2016)

25.  Leoniev, A.N.: Activity, Consciousness and Personality. Prentice-Hall, Englewood Cliffs (1978)

26.  Maier, A.M., Moultrie, J., Clarkson, P.J.: Assessing organizational capabilities: reviewing and guiding the development of maturity grids. IEEE Trans. Eng. Manage. **59**(1), 138–159 (2012)

27. Martins, L.E.G., Daltrani, B.M.: An approach to software requirements elicitation using precepts from activity theory. In: 14 IEEE International Conference on Automated Software Engineering, pp. 15–23 (1999)

28. Meyer, B.: Agile!: The Good, the Hype and the Ugly. Springer, Heidelberg (2014). https://doi.org/10.1007/978-3-319-05155-0

29. Meyer, B.: Agile Software Development. Online EDX course. https://www.edx.org/course/agile-software-development. Accessed 18 Sept 2018

30. Mursu, A., Luukkonen, I., Toivanen, M., Korpela, M.: Activity theory in information systems research and practice: theoretical underpinnings for an information systems development model. Inf. Res. Inte. Electron. J. **12**, 3 (2007)

31. Mwanza, D.: Where theory meets practice: a case for an activity theory based methodology to guide computer systems design. In: Proceedings of Interact 2001: Eighth IFIP TC 13 Conference on Human-Computer Interaction, Tokyo, Japan (2001)

32. Newell, S., Galliers, R.D.: Facilitating – or inhibiting – knowing in practice. Eur. J. Inf. Syst. **15**, p441–p445 (2006)

33. Oxford dictionaries. https://en.oxforddictionaries.com/definition/principle

34. Quek, A., Shah, H.: A comparative survey of activity-based methods for information systems development. ICEIS **5**, 221–232 (2004)

35. Roth, W.M.: On the inclusion of emotion, identity and ethico-moral dimensions of actions. In: Sannino, A., Daniels, H., Gutierrez, K. (eds.) Learning and Expanding with Activity Theory. Cambridge University Press, Cambridge (2009)

36. Runeson, P., Host, M.: Guidelines for conducting and reporting case study research in software engineering. Empir. Softw. Eng. **14**, 131 (2009). https://doi.org/10.1007/s10664-008-9102-8

37. Sannino, A.: Activity theory as an activist and interventionist theory. Theory Psychol. **21**(5), p571–p597 (2011)

38. Sauer, C., Horner, B.H.: Rethinking IT project management: evidence of a new mindset and its implications. Int. J. Project Manage. **27**, 182–193 (2009)

39. Uden, L., Valderas, P., Pastor, O.: An activity theory based model to analyse web application requirements. Inf. Res. **13**(2), 13–24 (2008)

# Onboarding: How Newcomers Integrate into an Agile Project Team

Peggy Gregory[1]([✉]) [iD], Diane E. Strode[2] [iD], Raid AlQaisi[3], Helen Sharp[4] [iD], and Leonor Barroca[4] [iD]

[1] University of Central Lancashire, Preston, UK
ajgregory@uclan.ac.uk
[2] Whitireia Polytechnic, Wellington, New Zealand
diane.strode@whitireia.ac.nz
[3] Independent Researcher, Glasgow, UK
r.alqaisi@gmail.com
[4] The Open University, Milton Keynes, UK
{helen.sharp,leonor.barroca}@open.ac.uk

**Abstract.** Although a stable team is deemed optimal for agile project success, new team members need to join ongoing agile projects. Newcomers must rapidly assimilate into the organisational and project environment while learning how to contribute effectively to the project and integrate into the team without seriously interrupting project progress. This paper addresses how newcomers integrate into an established agile project team and the challenges newcomers and the team face during this process. This paper is a single case study of a co-located agile project team in a large IT department who regularly onboard inexperienced newcomers. We found a mixture of traditional onboarding practices and specific agile practices contribute to the onboarding process. Onboarding challenges include empowerment and mindset change, accommodating part-timers, conveying agile principles, and adjusting to changes in team composition.

**Keywords:** Agile team onboarding · Onboarding · Newcomers · Scrum · Self-organizing team onboarding

## 1 Introduction

Software development is a knowledge-intensive activity that relies on people with advanced technical knowledge, skills, experience, and domain knowledge. To organise software development, the commonly accepted approach is to adopt the mindset, process, and practices of agile software development. Agile software development is currently used in co-located, distributed, and large-scale systems development projects [1, 2], and within these environments, agile development optimally occurs in self-organising teams that are autonomous, cross-functional, and self-improving [3]. Newcomers to these environments face challenges in becoming fully integrated and productive team members. The challenges involve acquiring organisational knowledge, project knowledge, product

© The Author(s) 2020
V. Stray et al. (Eds.): XP 2020, LNBIP 383, pp. 20–36, 2020.
https://doi.org/10.1007/978-3-030-49392-9_2

and domain knowledge, knowledge of the technical environment, as well as understanding and becoming proficient in the agile approach used by the team, and undergoing socialization into a self-organising team environment [4].

Onboarding is the term used to describe new employees joining and integrating into an organisation. There is extensive literature on onboarding in organisations extending back to the 1970s [5, 6], and significant research into onboarding in Open Source Software Development projects [7, 8], as well as literature on onboarding in software development organisations [9]. There is a dearth of research into onboarding into co-located agile software development project teams with a single paper indicating that certain agile practices contribute to onboarding [4]. Onboarding was raised as a concern by practitioners in an international research-practitioner workshop in 2019 [10]. Practitioners are also concerned with sustaining successful agile project teams [11], and integrating newcomers is a factor in achieving long-term sustainability.

We expect onboarding into agile project teams will be similar in some respects to organisational onboarding in general, but also different to traditional onboarding because of the need for newcomers to understand the agile mindset, process, and practices and to effectively integrate into projects where self-organising teamwork is the norm. Therefore, we sought to understand the onboarding experiences of newcomers and their colleagues, into an ongoing co-located agile software development project team, how newcomers are integrated and how they learn the unique agile approach of the team. This study addresses the question: *How do newcomers integrate into an ongoing agile project team and learn the agile approach?* To address this question, we undertook a single case study of a co-located agile project team in a large IT department who regularly onboard inexperienced newcomers. We found a mixture of traditional onboarding practices and specific agile practices contribute to the onboarding process and several challenges occur for newcomers and established team members.

This paper is organised as follows. We first review pertinent literature on onboarding and describe Bauer's framework [12], which we used to frame our analysis. Our case study method is described followed by our findings. The findings include a description of the agile project team, an analysis of the onboarding practices both agile-related and traditional, and an analysis of the key issues in onboarding for this team. A discussion of our contributions follows with a conclusion that includes ideas for future work.

## 2  Background

*"Organizational socialization, or onboarding, is a process through which new employees move from being organizational outsiders to becoming organizational insiders. Onboarding refers to the process that helps new employees learn the knowledge, skills, and behaviors they need to succeed in their new organizations"* [5, p. 51].

In onboarding, a central idea is that of the *newcomer.* A newcomer is a new staff member joining an organisation. Newcomers also include people moving within the organisation, for example from one department to another or from one team to another. These people are organisational insiders, although not yet team insiders.

Onboarding literature emerged in the field of organisation studies in the 1970s when Maanen and Schein [6] defined the concepts of organisational socialisation, newcomers, insiders, and outsiders. Their idea was that organisations have functional, hierarchical, and inclusionary boundaries that newcomers cross as they are socialized from being outsiders to become insiders. Socialisation has six inter-related dimensions [6, p. 37] (the comments in brackets are our explanations).

1. Collective vs. individual socialization processes (join as a group or individually)
2. Formal vs. informal socialization processes (formal training or experiential learning)
3. Sequential vs. random steps in the socialization process (formal hierarchy of achievements or ad hoc, ambiguous achievement requirements)
4. Fixed vs. variable socialization processes (timetabled steps or no scheduled steps)
5. Serial vs. disjunctive socialization processes (role models or no role models)
6. Investiture vs. divestiture socialization processes (build on a person's skills, values, attitudes or rebuild the person to fit the organisation)

Onboarding in commercial software development organisations was studied by Sharma and Stol [9]. After a review of empirical studies, these authors found nine studies of onboarding in software development organisations. They developed and tested a theoretical model of the relationship between onboarding activities (orientation, training, and support), onboarding success, organisational fit (job satisfaction and workplace relationship quality) and turnover intention. One key result was that orientation and support are strongly related to onboarding success.

Britto, Cruzes, Smite and Sablis [13] report a study of onboarding in three cases of globally distributed legacy software development, using the onboarding framework of Bauer [12] (described below). One key finding was that the greatest challenge was onboarding remote developers to an ongoing project when agile methods were followed because of the minimal documentation and the need for continuous dialogue with mentors to understand the project.

Onboarding in co-located agile project teams is addressed by Buchan, MacDonell, and Yang [4]. From an initial systematic literature survey, they identified 11 goals in the general software development literature that they determined were also relevant for agile onboarding (adapted from [4, p.3]).

- Understand and fit with company culture
- Understand and fit with team norms
- Understand and meet others' expectations and one's own role's responsibilities.
- Understand the responsibilities, expertise and authority of other team members
- Understand what work to do and when
- Understand how to code and test to the team's expectations
- Understand the team's standards of team quality
- Understand and adopt the agile mindset
- Know how to use agile artefacts and techniques used by the rest of the team
- Understand the short, medium and long-term work structures, aims and implications
- Understand the product/project domain knowledge and terminology

This research reported 24 techniques for onboarding [4] and found that, among many traditional onboarding techniques such as access to formal training and access to online communities, the following agile practices contributed to onboarding: simple task, pair programming, retrospectives, and stand-up meetings. Due to the small number of research participants, 11 interviews in different organisations in New Zealand, these researchers acknowledged their list of onboarding techniques is unlikely to be exhaustive.

## 2.1 Bauer's Onboarding Framework

To frame the onboarding processes discussed in this paper we used the six functions described in Bauer's framework for successful onboarding [5, 12]. Bauer's framework is generic to all onboarding environments and situations. We selected this framework to structure our study because it is empirically based, highly cited in many fields, and currently no substantial framework or model exists for agile software development project team onboarding. The six functions in Bauer's framework [12] are as follows:

- *Recruiting process* – The process that provides information to newcomers and helps them form realistic expectations of the organisation and their role. The recruiting process can be separate from the onboarding process but has been shown to be more effective if integrated into onboarding.
- *Orientation* – The process of helping newcomers to understand the important aspects of their jobs and of the organisation including the organisation's culture, values, goals, history, and power structure. Orientation includes formal face-to-face, written guidelines, and online programmes for providing key information to newcomers. Orientation includes socialization, which involves making newcomers feel welcome by introducing them to co-workers and other people in the organisation.
- *Support tools and processes* – Support tools include a written onboarding plan for newcomers that includes timelines, goals, responsibilities, support systems, and how to access assistance. Attending regular meetings with a variety of stakeholders within the organisation is a mechanism for support of newcomers. Online support tools are another mechanism for onboarding but have been shown to be somewhat less effective than regular face-to-face orientation sessions.
- *Coaching and support* – Coaching, mentoring, and having role models are mechanisms for helping newcomers learn about the organisation and their role, and to navigate the social and political aspects of the organisation. Coaching and mentoring can be external or internally sourced. Using mentors is shown to improve newcomer knowledge of the organisation.
- *Training* – Training includes learning hard, soft, and onboarding skills. Training can be informal (learning-on-the-job) or formal (mandatory scheduled courses).
- *Feedback tools* – Feedback and guidance provide newcomers with information on progress, strengths, and weaknesses. Feedback can be formal (e.g. performance appraisals) and informal (e.g. the newcomer is proactive in asking questions about the expectations and evaluations of co-workers and supervisors).

Bauer's [12] framework also includes adjustments that newcomers move through during onboarding. These adjustments are self-efficacy, role clarity, social integration, and knowledge of the culture. We have restricted our study to the six features in the framework because evaluating adjustments requires longitudinal research.

## 3  Method

An organisation approached our research group and asked for assistance in identifying how to help new team members shift from an individual view of working to a team-oriented view of working when they joined an agile team for the first time. A single case study was selected as an appropriate method for addressing the research question with the unit of analysis being the co-located agile software development team [14]. The University of Central Lancashire gave ethical approval for the research.

The data was collected primarily by interviews. All people in the project team were asked if they would agree to be interviewed and were provided with an information sheet about the research. More than half of the project team were interviewed. The set of interviews covers a range of newcomers – new hires and those who had worked for up to a year in the project team – and insiders – established team members who had worked for 1 year or more in the project team and included the Team Lead/Scrum master – who had the longest experience in the project team.

Initial meetings and observations occurred in October 2018 followed by interviews and observations of the workplace in November and December 2018. Two researchers carried out the interviews. The interviews were semi-structured and followed an interview schedule, but the interviewers strived to remain open to new ideas and probed for additional information when necessary or relevant to the topic. All interviews were transcribed, and then analysed using the NVIVO tool. Table 1 shows the profile of the interviewees.

Observations of daily work and specific meetings were undertaken to get to know team members, observe how the team worked and aspects of team culture, and to identify problems. Observations were recorded with field notes during and immediately following the observation session.

The interview transcripts were initially coded by the first author for themes related to onboarding approaches, practices and challenges, following the coding guidelines of Saldana [15]. The data was also analysed to understand the team's history, work practices (both social practices and agile practices), and the organisation and team culture. Once this was complete the first and second author mapped the onboarding approach and practice themes to the six functions in Bauer's framework [12], described in Sect. 2.1. The second author then further analysed the themes to separate agile-related and traditional approaches. All authors reviewed the final analysis, and a draft of the paper was shared with the research participants for review and discussion before submission.

**Table 1.** Profile of interviewees

| | Role and code name | Work Mode | Duration in role | Experience |
|---|---|---|---|---|
| 1 | Team lead; Scrum master [TL] | FT Perm | 10 years | Degree; Certified Scrum Master Prior development and agile experience |
| 2 | Assistant project manager [PM] | FT Perm | 6 years | Degree 4.5 yr as a student then employed FT No prior agile experience |
| 3 | Software developer 1 [SD1] | FT Perm | 5 years | Degree 4 yr as a student then employed FT No prior agile experience |
| 4 | Software developer 2 [SD2] | FT Perm | 1 year | Degree 3.5 years prior development experience Prior agile experience |
| 5 | Software developer 3 [SD3] | FT Perm | 1 year | Degree Prior development experience prior agile experience |
| 6 | Apprentice developer [NC1] | PT Temp | 8 months | Studying No prior development experience No prior agile experience |
| 7 | Student developer [NC2] | PT Temp | 4 months | Studying Minimal prior development experience No agile experience |
| 8 | Software developer [NC3] | PT Temp | 3 months | Degree prior agile and development experience 3 yrs at the university in another section |
| 9 | Conversation specialist [NC4] | PT Temp | 3 months | Degree No prior development experience No prior agile experience |

## 4   Findings

### 4.1   The History and Nature of the Agile Team

The agile software development team was a unit based in a UK university within the IT services section (ISS). Over six years, the unit increased from two members at inception to 15 at the time of the study. During the case study, the unit acted as a single team following a whole-team approach regardless of how many staff they had. The unit's remit was to develop mobile applications for the university and investigate ideas and technology for future innovation. The unit worked on new projects and maintained deployed apps and systems.

Team membership and size changed depending on workload, consisting of full-time, part-time, experienced, inexperienced, student, and apprentice members. At the time of this study, there were 6 full-time staff, 3 apprentices and 6 part-time staff. Of the part-time staff 3 had full-time roles within the university and were part-time in this team. The team lead was full-time and had a duel role as Scrum Master and line manager. Apprentices worked full-time for most weeks but attended block courses, typically for one week per month, at their home institute. Student team members usually studied at the university while working part-time on the project team, typically for 2 or 3 mornings or afternoons per week. Most of the team were in their 20 s with little or no previous work experience except the Scrum Master, Product Owner and Conversation Specialist who were in the 35–55 age group and had a range of previous experience. Many of the full-time staff had started as part-time students and gained full-time posts as new graduates. There was regular staff turnover as students and apprentices left after graduating, and full-time staff were often attracted by jobs outside Higher Education.

The team developed their use of agile methods over time. In the early days, agile use was not systematic *"when I first started work, we were quite a small team, and we didn't follow any methodology strictly, it was a bit ad hoc almost. We did follow the idea of sprints and some tokens of agile but not the sort of full beast that it is. It's only once the team has grown that we have scaled up our utilisation of agile" [SD1].*

The team worked in an open-plan office space with an adjacent meeting room. The developers used a hot-desk system and often changed the configuration of their desks to suit themselves. The team used a Scrum approach, running two-week sprints, with the last Friday a non-Sprint day used to complete other work. The team had daily stand-ups, sprint planning, sprint refinement, sprint review, and retrospective meetings, product demos and used a Scrum wallboard. The Team Lead held weekly one-to-one meetings with staff if they wanted it. The team was functioning well. The general feeling among the team was stated by a staff member who had been with the team for a year, *"Personally, I love it. It's very relaxed. It's quite dynamic, the way we do things. It's just a nice workplace" [SD1].*

### 4.2   Onboarding Practices

The team's onboarding practices are described in the following sections, organised according to Bauer's framework [12]. Note that all names are pseudonyms.

**Recruiting Process**

The recruitment process was formal and standardized for all staff who join the organisation. The process is mandated by the organisation and requires a job description, person specification, and advertisement. The process differs for full-time (usually permanent) and part-time (usually temporary students and apprentices) newcomers. The recruitment of full-time staff is formal and requires a trained balanced panel of interviewers, applications are evaluated using a scoring mechanism, and applicants are interviewed using standard interview questions. All applicants are expected to show evidence of creativity, enthusiasm, and hard work. Experience and technical knowledge are expected of full-time applicants whereas for student and apprentice applicants this is not expected. Once hired, full-time members get an institutional induction. Both full-time and part-time members get a personal welcome from the Team Leader and are assigned a mentor. There is also a Scrum Coach to help newcomers.

*Long-term recruitment:* The unit had a long-term recruitment approach that involved hiring temporary students and apprentices who would work within the team as part-time employees whilst completing their studies. In some cases, these people would finish their degree and then become full-time permanent staff members on the project. This approach provided permanent staff who required minimal onboarding because they had a pre-existing good team fit, and understood the organisation, the unit's goals, products, technologies, stakeholders, and the teams' agile approach.

*Onboarding during recruitment:* During recruitment interviews, newcomer's knowledge gaps began to be identified. "One *of the things I do is in the interviews when we take people on, I try to understand what their understanding of agile is, to see how much of a gap there is …" [TL].*

**Orientation**

*"New staff" pack:* This document described things that new employees need to know and was given to all newcomers. This was described by one team member, *"Here's everything you need to know about the team," [PM].* The lack of detail about the team's approach to agile was acknowledged as a missing element *"… there's no formal element. There should be. I'll hold my hands up and go, there should be." [PM].*

*"How our team works" pack:* This document is given to newcomers. The document describes the project team members and explains what newcomers need to sign up to, how to get into TFS (Team Foundation Server™) and explains how the team works.

*"How our team works with the client" pack:* This document is sent to clients before they work with the team. The document explains how the team writes user stories, what client communication the team expects, and how the team tests and signs-off products. This document is also given to newcomers to provide an overview of team practices.

*Agile method pack:* The Team Lead informed the newcomers about agile practices by sending them a guide, *"New team members, I now send them a guide, the principles behind it. A Scrum Guide. I talk about the fact that this is what they do" [TL].*

*Socialising:* The project team made efforts to socialise with and get to know one another because they found this helped newcomers to trust the team and be more confident in interacting and communicating with one another. *"For example, practices that we've encouraged in our full-time team meeting, we'll say 'what can you present to the team that you think is valuable or about yourself?', you know breaking down those barriers, it could be about anything. So [a team member] recently did one about e-capture and [another team member] did one about his passion for Rubik's Cubes" [TL].* The whole team was invited to social events, *"the different team members will often be going for lunch, that sort of thing. The odd evening here or there, we'd be going for drinks in town or we do our own team Christmas thing..." [SD3].*

**Support Tools and Processes**

*Information radiator*: The project team used a Scrum/Kanban wallboard with physical and virtual versions, although they tended to prefer the physical board. The established members saw the physical board as useful also for newcomers, *"Sometimes the team don't necessarily engage quite as much with a digital thing as with a physical thing, it seems to be a bit more natural...I think it helps [the newcomers] as well because it's a more instantaneous way to look and see where things are."[SD1].* The wallboard was viewed by one newcomer as useful for developers but not for him as an architect, *"it's all development tasks that are on the board... now. But then, my work is stuff that just supports all of that, and sometimes it's like, I want to write a story that is... 'As an architect, I want'"* [NC3].

*Communication tools:* The team used communication tools including Teams, Slack, TFS, and email. These tools helped the part-time newcomers to some extent, although there was often quite a lot of missing information to catch up on during an absence, so part-timers also walked around the room to talk to people.

**Coaching and Support**

*Mentoring*: Mentoring was viewed as an important part of the onboarding experience for most newcomers. The Team Lead was frequently mentioned as a mentor but he also recognised the mentoring role of the established team members, *"from my perspective the mentoring aspect of things, it helps both with the integration into the unit, the integration with the technology stack and the integration into the agile way, and it's kind of almost subliminal. The messages come across from the team members rather than from me, which, I hope, [the newcomer] would learn better because of that" [TL].*

*Role modelling*: The more experienced team members noted that role modelling desired behaviours was beneficial for the newcomer and the established staff, *"I try and get rid of the stigma ... and set an example, and the rest of the team will realise that it's fine to say 'I don't know how to do that. I don't know what this is or that is, or I need help with this'" [SD3].* Another type of role modelling was shown by the continuous self-learning of new technologies by the established staff, *"I do a lot of learning outside of work at the moment, especially with all the new stuff that we're doing" [PM].*

*Ceremonies:* As part of the immersion approach, ceremonies were explained to newcomers the first time they attended. For example, just before the stand-up meeting, a newcomer would have the process explained so they knew what they were expected to do, *"they were very good at explaining everything they did, explaining why they had stand-ups in the morning, and explain the meetings, you know, before and the end of the sprints. They explained that before they happened" [NC4].*

*Encouraging teamwork:* The established team members encouraged knowledge sharing and helping behaviours among the team, *"everyone is very friendly, and ask if you want anything and yeah, you are encouraged to talk to people." [NC3].* The level of trust between newcomers and established staff was perceived as good, *"There's a lot of trust... especially with the student developers as well, there's a lot of trust for them to do work, ... once they're part of the team, and they fit and work as part of the team, we trust them to do work"*. *"Everyone is very helpful, very friendly... it feels very inclusive, very inclusive, it's not sort-of developers and non-developers" [NC3]*.

*Encouraging learning*: One newcomer appreciated being encouraged to try new things, *"[The TL] is very good at encouraging you to take on more challenging things. ... He'll suggest, why doesn't [Sally] do that, why don't you do that [Sally]? Initially, I'll go ohhh (shouting in confusion and panic!) and then... But in a good way, it is good to push your staff, isn't it? It is good to learn new things and yeah. Yeah, it is good. Scary but good. Good scary" [NC3]*.

*Empathy:* Because some established team members had previously been student members in the team, they could still recall their own experiences and this helped them to understand newcomers issues, *"I'd like to think anyway, that we treat the students, especially with my background as a student developer, that we're all treated as equals. We don't really have the junior developer syndrome that some teams suffer from where they're handed lesser tasks or things like that. ...Sometimes if a part-time student is only in for 3 h or something, then there might be a situation where we might suggest things for them, just to maximise that time that they have. But it's more for their benefit because I know how frustrating it is to get into a piece of work and then have to down tools and go to lectures" [SD1]*.

*Pair programming:* The Team Lead recognised that pair programming was useful to support newcomers. *"When they first come in, I pair them up with a full-time member ... the same full-time member for about 2 to 3 weeks until we then release them to work on their own on a particular area." [TL]*. Pairing was also used to learn new technologies, *"Where we want skills on a particular technology or something like that we'll pair up, or equally if we want to teach someone something we'll pair up" [SD1]*.

*Reimagining yourself:* The Team Lead encouraged the newcomers to reimagine themselves in their new role, *"when I've taken students on and they've transitioned to being full-time members of staff, I've tried to coach them to say you need to reimagine yourself in the new role. So [newcomer]..., she was an administrator but now she's a, well technically her title is [new role], but that's actually different to what she does and she's had to reimage herself in those new roles because she's no longer doing the roles that she was doing earlier on" [TL]*.

*Daily stand-up meetings:* These meetings were held sometimes twice a day for the benefit of the part-time staff. One developer, with one year of experience on the team, saw the stand-ups as useful for understanding the project status and as a time for getting help, *"If you're stuck on something, don't know how to do something or you're just lost, then it's a good place to air that and usually, somebody will, oh I'll help you with that." [SD3]*. One newcomer noted that she did not yet understand the language, *"If I understood their language, then I would probably understand more" [NC3]*. Established members also saw that stand-ups helped newcomers. *"A lot of the communication comes at the stand-up in the morning... We also have another, sometimes, in the afternoon if someone's come in just to get them on board. So we might have two stand-ups" [SD2]*.

*Co-location:* Co-location made asking for help and sharing knowledge easier, *"...look at this code, or something like that but also, just asking the person you're sat next to... If you don't know something, there's a good chance the person next to you does" [SD3].* Co-location allowed for conversations to be overheard, which helped newcomers, *"It does [give a] general sense of what other people doing, even if it's just overhearing them have, talking between themselves" [NC1].*

*Signalling:* To signal availability and issues the team had developed methods of communicating so members could understand who could be interrupted and who preferred to focus on their work, or if there was an important issue for the team to address. *"Sometimes members of the team will wear headphones when they're really concentrating so you know to stay clear, or you just from intuition just by knowing each other...And I think we're all accessible to part-time students as well". "if it's a particular barrier in terms of the project, then we have little red notices that go on the Kanban board...so that everyone knows there is a barrier and if anyone has a solution ... we can discuss and try to break that barrier down" [SD1].*

### Training

*Formal training:* No formal training was available for full-time members of staff due to budget restrictions. In addition, most of the project team were not able to attend Agile Conferences or other external events due to the heavy workload. No formal courses were mentioned, but students and apprentices already attended formal courses of study.

*Immersion: (or experiential learning)* Newcomers started working in the team from their first day and much of the learning and socialisation was accomplished by being a productive member of the team. For example, two of the established members described the process in a similar way as, *"Generally we try to let them get their hands into a piece of work, learn literally on the job, so we give them a sort of induction into what their sort of expectations are in the team, what they can do to get support and all that kind of stuff and just let them loose and fit right in" [PM].* A newcomer's perception reinforced this, *"I was very much thrown in at the deep end, "Here are some meetings. Yeah, let's go ahead with it," and very much learning on a day-to-day basis with the team how they do it". "it's really largely practice, or very practical, with some explanations when necessary... before we went into the meeting and we were voting with our animal cards and things, that was explained to me before we went in, we do this, so... I got in there and wasn't surprised by what happened" [NC3].*

*Self-study:* Newcomers who were not aware of agile methods were asked to read about it before starting with the team and were given links to online resources. *"In the interviews, we tend to ask them if they have any experience of agile, and if they say no, we say, 'That's fine, but we recommend you look into it'" [PM].* The existing project team expected newcomers to self-learn and would request them to do so, *"when we took him on, we said 'you need to do some learning outside of work if you want to continue with the team'" [TL].* For some newcomers, the self-study was self-motivated, *"I did a lot of background work ...I did lots of reading [about Alexa] on the internet... A couple of courses on Udemy ...At home, I am doing Python and Excel, I am doing a course on Excel. And ... I have just signed up for, ... user stories" [NC4].*

## Feedback Tools

_One-to-Ones_: Full-time members of the team had regular, often weekly, one-to-one meetings with the team lead. This gave team members a chance to receive guidance about technical issues and reflect on their work practice.

_Immediate feedback:_ The team was able to provide face-to-face feedback, as a newcomer explained after the testing of her work, _"people do point things out, but in an ok way... but it is always nicely done"._ [NC3].

_Meetings:_ Meetings were used to communicate university, department, and team knowledge and concerns. _"everyone gets to say something in there. That's working quite well. It's nice and relaxed. It's breaking down some barriers. People are understanding people better, and new learning is coming into the team."_ [TL]

_Code reviews:_ Code reviews were used for providing feedback, _"We do a group code review each week to see what we've been going over, to learn off each other. That meeting is primarily just for the programmers and the apprentices"_ [SD2]. A newcomer, who had not yet presented at a code review, thought the code reviews useful, _"At the moment I don't quite understand everything. But it is useful because it can be quite scary to have a look at the [code], it makes it a bit more familiar"_ [NC1].

_Testing:_ Unit tests were viewed as a feedback mechanism and some test-driven development was used during pair programming to assist newcomers, _"We do try pair programming, especially with the students... so, when [Martin] started, we actually added some testing-driven development with him to introduce him to what we're working on, how we work"_ [SD2]. A newcomer explained, _"which is really good, because that extra bit of testing is, and then I can see whether it does what I hoped it will do and if it works"_ [NC3].

_Retrospectives_: Retrospectives were used to adjust and improve the agile process, the established team members viewed them as a valuable feedback tool. _"We do it at the retrospectives or we give feedback on how we did, what we liked, what we'd improve. So that's more feedback as a team"_ [SD2].

_Sprint review:_ Feedback at the sprint review was concerned with the technical matters, _"Feedback's generally kept back for the sprint review, so before a retro, we do a review session where we demo the build. Hopefully, it works and we can celebrate, or there will be some critique about the way it's been implemented or the design choices, or that kind of stuff"_ [SD1].

_Sprint refinements:_ The team used these sessions to discuss and refine user stories before sprint planning sessions. _"We have Sprint refinements before we do a planning, where we go through each of the work items and ask a lot of questions"_ [SD3].

_Small tasks:_ Smaller tasks were given to part-time newcomers for practical reasons. _"We'll give smaller tasks to the students because there's just not enough time... if we've got a small user story, say, getting the next timetable event from an API, that's something that we could see a student doing"_ [SD2]. Minor bug fixes were often an entry point for newcomers, _"I'll have like a list of bugs that need fixing because generally, we don't want to pull the full-timers out of sprint."_ [PM].

_Task allocation:_ A mixture of self-selection and supervisor selection was used for task allocation. Considerations of expertise were a factor in allocating tasks. _"On the bigger tasks, sometimes [TL] will delegate who to do that ... But usually, we just pick_ *up the next task on the board. If there's no task on the board, then we have to ask [the administrator] or [TL] to bring it in or liaise with the product owner..." [SD2].*

*Product demo:* Feedback on the product was given by Product Owners to the team, *"Other bits [of feedback] will be demos to the business. So, as developers, we try to talk to the actual product owners quite regularly" [SD1].*

The findings from the analysis are summarised in Table 2.

**Table 2.** Summary of findings

| Onboarding | Traditional | Agile-related |
|---|---|---|
| Recruiting process | Follow legal recruitment requirements<br>Long-term recruitment | Evaluate agile knowledge and give resources |
| Orientation | Provide new staff pack<br>Provide teamwork pack<br>Socialise with newcomers | Provide agile fundamentals pack |
| Support tools and processes | Introduce all communication tools | Introduce and use an information radiator |
| Coaching and support | Mentoring<br>Role-modelling<br>Encourage learning<br>Empathy<br>Reimaging | Ceremonies – explain just prior<br>Encourage teamwork<br>Pair programming<br>Stand-ups<br>Co-locate<br>Signalling |
| Training | Offer formal courses, training, and conferences on relevant topics | Immersion from day one<br>Self-study |
| Feedback tools | One-on-ones with senior staff<br>Immediate feedback during immersion<br>Meetings – encourage staff to speak<br>Small tasks | Code reviews<br>Testing<br>Retrospectives<br>Sprint review<br>Sprint refinements<br>Task allocation |

### 4.3   Onboarding Challenges for the Newcomers and the Agile Project Team

Onboarding challenged newcomers and established team members. Challenges identified in the analysis included empowerment, mindset change, accommodating part-timers, conveying agile principles, and adjusting to changes in team composition.

Empowerment: was a constant issue within the team. The Team Lead identified a difficulty with onboarding younger newcomers who had never worked in a self-organising empowered team. He thought they needed to be helped, *"when they're just out of university and they've come from an academic background that doesn't teach team work very well, doesn't teach about empowerment ... sometimes in conversations, they may turn to me in terms of a position of authority and I'm like, no you go and do that, so I've tried to set up things where they have their own meetings and they run their own meetings so I may well initiate something and step out and say well there you go, you don't need to talk to me anymore, just sort it out yourselves." [TL].* However, at times of pressure, a command-and-control approach did emerge, *"and then I'll pull someone out of sprint and go, "This needs fixing," or I'll say, "This will be fixed at the end of the sprint, depending on how urgent it is" [PM].*

Mindset change: Project team members tended to rely on senior staff to maintain their agile processes, *"If me or [the TL] aren't in the office, stand-ups don't happen, and so we're really trying to encourage, 'This is your meeting, this is for you to help each other'" [PM].* A constant effort was made to empower newcomers, *"We try to leave it down to them what they want to do" [SD1].* Related to the issue with empowerment, is the problem of perfectionism. Newcomers found it hard to adopt an experimental mindset, *"Because they're so new, they also don't understand how to tackle problems. It's a case of, 'well just start, just get started it doesn't matter if you throw it all away' ... it's a mindset thing about trying to find the perfect solution the first time you do it" [TL].*

Accommodating part-timers: A recurrent theme among the team was connecting with, and sharing knowledge with, the part-time newcomers. Both established members and part-time newcomers saw this as an issue, *"...for part-time members or [those] who can't attend, and it's probably trying to find ways of bridging the gap in the communications that occur. So, it's kind of every time we've had a retro everyone has said, communications need to improve. It's like you've said it, but you're not actually doing it." [TL].* A part-time newcomer commented on the difficulty of finding out what had happened in the project after an absence, *"because they'll just talk to each other and just figure something out, and then you won't find it documented anywhere, or it won't even be in the [TFS]" [NC3].*

Conveying agile principles: The established members had high expectations of newcomers and struggled to convey agile principles. *"And we now have a very high bar of workforce that are now the team, are highly motivated and through that, there's an expectation that you have to fit into that kind of ethos as well, and that becomes a barrier for recruiting new students because the bar is so high." [TL].* The Team Lead thought the main onboarding issue was integrating relatively young and inexperienced part-time newcomers, *"It's just them being immersed in it, and for part-time that's hard, because up to 15 h a week, whilst doing other learning, and whilst you're young and having a social life, and everything else. Finding space in their brain for this is hard, and it's being able to get over the principles and culture, which is what I want to focus on" [TL].*

Adjusting team composition: Over time the team evolved to consist of more established members and fewer newcomers. This balance improved their ability to continuously improve. *"We've been through a lot of iterations of how we approach our work, and I think we're hitting a sweet spot of getting things done, ...with having more full-time members we thought there was value in doing those [sprint refinements]" [SD1].*

## 5  Discussion

This study explored the onboarding of newcomers into a co-located agile software development project team because of its interest to practitioners who want to sustain their teams over the long term. We addressed the question of how newcomers integrate into ongoing teams and learn the agile approach. Analysing our single case study using Bauer's onboarding framework [12], we found that onboarding combines traditional and agile-related techniques (see Table 2). Agile-related techniques include self-study of agile fundamentals, information radiators, introducing ceremonies prior to experiencing the ceremony, pair programming, immersion for experiential learning, code reviews, testing, retrospectives, sprint reviews, sprint refinement sessions, and flexible task allocation. In our case, we also found onboarding issues. The issues included supporting newcomers to act in an empowered agile manner and approach the work with an experimental mindset, being flexible to support inclusiveness of part-time staff, that conveying agile principles is a challenge, and the proportion of established to newcomer staff affects continuous improvement.

Our findings support those of [4, 9], and [13], however, ours are based on an in-depth contextual study of onboarding practices in an agile team and provide more nuance than those prior studies. We identify additional agile practices that support onboarding and show the extensive use of coaching and feedback processes in agile onboarding. In addition, our study identifies specific onboarding challenges for newcomers and teams. The challenge not identified in these earlier studies is empowerment, more specifically, how to encourage newcomers to act in an empowered way.

Our study contributes to practice by providing guidance for agile project teams who want to better understand the role of specific agile practices in supporting onboarding, and which traditional onboarding techniques to use alongside these agile practices to provide comprehensive onboarding support. We provide three recommendations for agile practitioners 1) incorporate the agile-relate practices shown in Table 2 that support onboarding, 2) use a long-term recruitment approach such as hiring placement students and apprentices and hire from this pool to ensure good staff 'fit', and 3) focus on training, explaining, and modelling empowerment when onboarding staff.

For theory, our study supports traditional onboarding knowledge, as it is an example of the use of Bauer's framework, and extends that framework to, at least partially, account for onboarding in co-located agile software development project teams.

Our study has limitations. Our findings are based on a single case study with a limited number of interviews, and we acknowledge our findings are of limited transferability to other settings. In addition, we did not interview the whole team, so some perceptions are missing. We did get insights from a range of people, from very new staff, staff with 1 year of experience, to long-established staff. Thus we achieved some triangulation of data sources [16]. We also carried out a member check by providing a report to the project team summarising our findings and asking for confirmation and feedback.

# 6  Conclusion

In this paper, we claimed that onboarding newcomers to co-located agile software development projects might differ from onboarding in general. We found traditional onboarding practices are used in agile project teams and that certain agile practices taught using immersive learning also support onboarding. We also identified challenges in onboarding to an agile project team.

This paper makes three contributions 1) provides in-depth insights into onboarding in an established co-located agile project team and specifies agile and other practices that support onboarding including challenges faced, 2) shows that Bauer's [12] onboarding framework is appropriate in a software engineering context, and 3) provides recommendations for practitioners as to those agile practices that support onboarding.

In future work, we recommend research to develop a comprehensive onboarding model that fully elaborates the factors in agile onboarding. That research should encompass onboarding in all agile environments, co-located, distributed and large-scale.

**Acknowledgements.** We acknowledge the contributions of the research participants, and the co-funding provided by the Agile Business Consortium (ABC Ltd.) for the Agile Research Network.

# References

1. Stavru, S.: A critical examination of recent industrial surveys on agile method usage. J. Syst. Softw. **94**, 87–97 (2014)
2. VersionOne: The 13th Annual state of agile report, pp. 1–15. VersionOne Inc. (2019)
3. Hoda, R., Murugesan, L.K.: Multi-level agile project management challenges: a self-organizing team perspective. J. Syst. Softw. **117**, 245–257 (2016)
4. Buchan, J., MacDonell, S.G., Yang, J.: Effective team onboarding in agile software development: techniques and goals. In: ACM/IEEE International Symposium on Empirical Software Engineering and Measurement (ESEM), pp. 1–11. IEEE (2019)
5. Bauer, T.N., Erdogan, B.: Organizational socialization: The effective onboarding of new employees. In: Zedeck, S. (ed.) APA Handbook of Industrial and Organizational Psychology, vol. 3, pp. 51–64. American Psychological Association, Washington, DC (2011)
6. Van Maanen, J.E., Schein, E.H.: Toward a theory of organizational socialization. MIT, Massachusetts Institute of Technology (1977)
7. Fagerholm, F., Guinea, A.S., Borenstein, J., Münch, J.: Onboarding in open source projects. IEEE Softw. **31**, 54–61 (2014)
8. Steinmacher, I., Gerosa, M.A.: How to support newcomers onboarding to open source software projects. In: Corral, L., Sillitti, A., Succi, G., Vlasenko, J., Wasserman, Anthony I. (eds.) OSS 2014. IAICT, vol. 427, pp. 199–201. Springer, Heidelberg (2014). https://doi.org/10.1007/978-3-642-55128-4_29
9. Sharma, G.G., Stol, K.-J.: Exploring onboarding success, organizational fit, and turnover intention of software professionals. J. Syst. Softw. **159**, 1–16 (2020)
10. Moe, N.B., Stray, V., Hoda, R.: Trends and updated research agenda for autonomous agile teams: a summary of the second international workshop at XP2019. In: Hoda, R. (ed.) XP 2019. LNBIP, vol. 364, pp. 13–19. Springer, Cham (2019). https://doi.org/10.1007/978-3-030-30126-2_2

11. Barroca, L., Gregory, P., Kuusinen, K., Sharp, H., AlQaisi, R.: Sustaining agile beyond adoption. In: 44th Euromicro Conference on Software Engineering and Advanced Applications (SEAA), 29–31 August 2018, pp. 22–25. IEEE, Prague (2018). https://doi.org/10.1109/seaa.2018.00013
12. Bauer, T.N.: Onboarding New Employees: Maximizing Success. The Society for Human Resource Management Foundation (SHRM), VA, USA (2010)
13. Britto, R., Cruzes, D.S., Smite, D., Sablis, A.: Onboarding software developers and teams in three globally distributed legacy projects: a multi-case study. J. Softw. Evol. Process **30**, 1–17 (2018)
14. Yin, R.K.: Case Study Research and Applications: Design and Methods. Sage Publications, Thousand Oaks (2018)
15. Saldaña, J.: The Coding Manual for Qualitative Researchers. Sage, London (2016)
16. Shenton, A.K.: Strategies for ensuring trustworthiness in qualitative research projects. WI **22**, 63–75 (2004)

# Agile Practices

# Combining User-Centered Design and Lean Startup with Agile Software Development: A Case Study of Two Agile Teams

Ingrid Signoretti, Larissa Salerno, Sabrina Marczak$^{(\boxtimes)}$, and Ricardo Bastos

MunDDoS Research Group, School of Technology, PUCRS,
Porto Alegre, RS, Brazil
{ingrid.manfrim,larissa.salerno}@acad.pucrs.br,
{sabrina.marczak,ricardo.bastos}@pucrs.br

**Abstract.** The combined use of User-Centered Design and Lean Startup with Agile Development has been pointed out by the literature as a manner to boost software development. User-Centered Design principles focus on providing tools for developers to better explore user needs and seek for a fitter solution. Lean Startup, on the other hand, supplements the triad combination by bringing the Build-Measure-Learn cycle and the concept of pivoting, either the problem understanding or the proposed solution. This paper reports on a case study of two software teams that have been undergoing the changes and impacts of such combined adoption. We investigated these teams for six months, from the moment that team members were trained on the job to grasp the essence of using the integrated approach inspired on Pivotal Labs proposal to the time they were considered mature enough to share their experiences with others within the organization. Through our in-depth study, we illustrate how this adoption promotes changes regarding to mindset, activities, practices, and techniques. We also report on the 'team rhythm' (or work flow) as experienced by the two teams. The paper contributes to current knowledge on the topic reporting on the changes and impacts that teams observed during the combined approach adoption.

**Keywords:** User-Centered Design · Lean startup · Agile Development · Transformation · Case study

## 1 Introduction

Agile methods are defined by flexibility and adaptability in the context of building software products [3]. Despite the many benefits of adopting an agile method, the adoption still presents a lack of user involvement and participation [1], and product assertiveness. Vilkki [15] claims that agile must be combined with other approaches aiming to fill these gaps. Studies as Innodev [4], Converge [16], Nordstrom [7], and Lean UX [6] present models that combine agile with UCD and Lean Startup in order to boost the agile capacity in software development.

© The Author(s) 2020
V. Stray et al. (Eds.): XP 2020, LNBIP 383, pp. 39–55, 2020.
https://doi.org/10.1007/978-3-030-49392-9_3

Using the combined approach requires a set of preconditions, especially when compared to using a single agile method. The studies report the need to define cross-functional teams, and the roles represent each methodology (e.g., software engineers - agile, product designers - UCD, and product managers - lean startup) [6]. Also, the adoption puts emphasis on focusing on identifying the problem to be solved rather than only worrying about identifying the scope [4].

Although the prerequisites mentioned in literature to adopting the combined approach, we still know little about what changes and impacts take place at the software team and that might be influenced by or depend upon the organizational level when facing the adoption. Motivated by the need to discuss the modifications inherent to the adoption process, we conducted a case study with two software teams from a large-scale company. Our research reports from a team perspective the changes related to the teams' mindset, activities, practices, techniques, and rhythm to accommodate the combined approach adoption. Our main contribution is providing an understanding of how the combined use adoption promotes several impacts on the team's software development process. The findings offer inputs to the academia and industry practitioner.

The reminder of this paper is organized as follows: Sect. 2 details the research method. Section 3 reports on the main results. Section 4 discusses the main findings and explores the paper contribution. Section 5 presents previous studies and a comparison with our results. Section 6 concludes the paper with our study limitations and proposals of future work.

## 2   Research Method

We conducted a case study [12] with two teams from a multinational company named ORG (name omitted for confidentiality reasons). Next, we introduce the case setting and the data collection and analysis methods.

### 2.1   Case Setting

We aim to present the changes and impacts perceived by two software teams in an adoption process of a combined approach composed of Agile, UCD, and Lean Startup. Therefore, we briefly explain the case setting, including the company's previous scenario aiming to emphasize and to contextualize the modifications. We also present the product scope each team is responsible for.

*The Company.* ORG has development sites in the USA (headquarters), India, and Brazil. With over 7,000 employees and responsible for about 1,200 internal software products, the IT department started its agile transformation in 2015 and moved to the combined use of Agile, UCD, and Lean Startup principles in late 2017. Before adopting the combined approach, ORG had a well defined roadmap for software product improvements based on an annual budget negotiated among business department and organized into software projects. High-level business features were prioritized and decided upon business personnel to later be transformed into software requirements by IT software project teams. The project deadlines were strict and defined by quarter, i.e., every four months the project teams delivered a set of software features to existing or new software products to the company internal customers.

Associated with the business features definition negotiation, the company had Business Representatives responsible for defining the business needs. Once approved those needs were translated into business features, elected as the starting point for the IT project teams. Mostly, IT Business Analysts transformed these features into software requirements with the help of the Business Representatives and used these to drive software development.

With the introduction of the agile transformation in 2015, project teams used Scrum as the guiding development framework. From this time and on, it become common but not company-wide spread to get more team members (e.g., developers, software architects, testers) engaged into the business feature-to-software requirement translation. Some teams move then to a more product-oriented view while others are still guided by project time slots. The company starts then to discuss how to move from a world-wide roadmap to a product development organization when they realize help was need. This is when they decide to board the agile, UCD and Lean Startup combined journey and hire Pivotal consulting to support such transformation.

Overall, Pivotal brings the Pivotal Labs[1] methodology at core of the transformation. This methodology proposes a 'team rhythm' (or work flow) composed of principles and ceremonies based on the three before-mentioned approaches. It also suggests the adoption of a cross-functional team composed of three leading roles: Product Designer, Product Manager, and Software Engineer. The Pivotal Labs' main goal is to help teams to build software products that deliver meaningful value for users and their businesses. Thus, it offers a framework and initial starting point for any team to discuss the client/user specific needs and define its way towards software development.

The transformation and adoption process is the subject of interest of this research. In order to understand the process, we conducted the study with two software teams that were already half-way to the understanding of how to become product software teams. We present the teams' background next.

*Teams' Context.* We observed *in-loco*, in a lab at the University campus, two teams from the financial area located in Brazil. The lab was intentionally prepared for the teams to work on as part of a PUCRS and ORG research agreement. Both teams develop software product for the company internal use. The teams are composed of 2 Product Managers, 1 Product Designer, and 4 Software Engineers each. Team A is responsible for a software product that calculates the associated cost services offered by the products sold by ORG and displays this information to ORG consumers. The software consolidates information about services offered by the company, such as sale, installation, and equipment configuration, and stores employee data and hours spent on the provided services.

---

[1] https://pivotal.io/Labs.

**Table 1.** Participants' profile

| Team | Role | IT work exp | Company exp |
|------|------|-------------|-------------|
| Team A | Product Manager | 21 | 6 |
| Team A | Product Manager | 16 | 7,5 |
| Team A | Product Designer | 27 | 10 |
| Team A | Software Engineer | 6 | 1 |
| Team A | Software Engineer | 21 | 8 |
| Team A | Software Engineer | 5,5 | 4 |
| Team A | Software Engineer | 20 | 11 |
| Team B | Product Manager | 19 | 0,5 |
| Team B | Product Manager | 23 | 10,5 |
| Team B | Product Designer | 5 | 4 |
| Team B | Software Engineer | 10 | 4 |
| Team B | Software Engineer | 15 | 11 |
| Team B | Software Engineer | 7 | 7 |
| Team B | Software Engineer | 5 | 5 |
| – | BR Transformation Lead | 12 | 7 |

Data are consolidated into a projects by served customer for another product team from the financial area to use this information as input for their product use. Team B is responsible for the software product that gathers information about these services generated by ORG software products and stores them for Team A to use. The team has the goal to automate the calculation average of the equipment and services costs offered by the Brazilian site. Sequentially, the application performs the analysis of these multiple data aiming to provide consolidated information to the accounting area, which uses these data for internal control and reports for the company. Table 1 presents the participants' profile per team.

## 2.2 Data Collection

We observed the two product teams for a 6 months-period and we used multiple data sources to conduct the study. Following, we present each data collection method and its related purpose within our study.

*Questionnaire.* It was used to collect the participants' profile (name, role, main responsibilities, time in years working in IT and at ORG, and whether the person participated of the immersion training in the US.

*Semi-structured Interviews.* They were used first to gather information on the team members perceptions about the combined transformation, the training

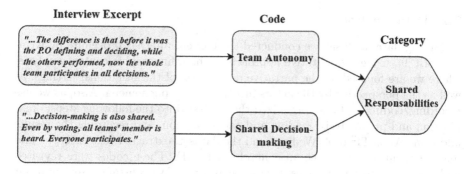

**Fig. 1.** Code analysis example

experience, and benefits and challenges. This interview was extended to the Brazilian Transformation Leader. A second round of interviews were conducted with all team members to gather their perception on team roles changes, interaction among roles, and impact of changes on the work routine. Interviews were also generally used as a means to follow-up and learn more details about diverse aspects unveiled in the observation sessions. All interviews were voice recorded and transcribed for analysis. None lasted more than 30 min as previously agreed with the industry research project sponsor.

*Daily Observations.* These were conducted to observe team ceremonies (e.g., daily standup, retrospective, iteration planning), meetings with stakeholders (user interviews, demos), and work routine. We also conducted shadowing of roles (e.g., product manager, product designer, and software engineer) seeking in-depth knowledge about the responsibilities of each role.

*Focus Group.* We performed six sessions, 3 of them were overall follow-ups and confirmation of data collected through other methods (e.g., to discuss in-depth the Product Designer new role). Moreover, specifically, one session was conducted aiming to consolidate the teams perceptions about the benefits and challenges of the combined approach (reported in [14]). Another session focused on the discussion of the elements of each approach as perceived by the teams (e.g., activities, techniques, and work products). And another session aimed to confirm the mapped elements of each methodology (e.g., naming, meaning, context of use, etc as observed in their daily work routine) into the combined approach representing the team work flow (or team rhythm as called by Pivotal Labs). In this last session we also asked the participants to visually represent this work flow as they saw fit. Each focus group session lasted in average 1.5 h, except the last one that lasted about 3 h (previously arranged with the teams). All sessions were voice recorded and transcribed.

## 2.3   Data Analysis

Regarding data analysis, we conducted the content analysis procedure by Krippendorff [9], using a qualitative approach to the ethnographic content analysis, where we are focused on the narrative description of the situations, settings, as well as the perspective by the actors involved in the phenomena. Also, as we use recording/coding units, we organized the analysis into the following steps: organization and pre-analysis, reading and categorization, and recording the results and using Atlas.TI[2] tool. We first read the dataset, extracted text excerpts, and marked them as codes (see an example in Fig. 1). These codes were revisited and grouped into larger codes, forming categories. We constantly reviewed our coding scheme with the two seniors researchers (the last two authors) aiming to mitigate any limitation or bias in our analysis. The two senior researchers also reviewed the questionnaire and interview scripts and supported the piloting of these instruments for face and content validity with an invited researcher with previous experience working with agile teams in industry.

## 3   Results

The case study results reveal aspects related to the combined approach adoption and usage. For instance, the *product is developed under a new perspective*, using a problem-oriented mindset which included the teams' changes to working attitudes to adapt to this new mindset (Sect. 3.1). We also highlight changes related to *methodological aspects* (Sect. 3.2), such as the addition of UCD activities to promote user involvement and participation. Also, the use of the Build-Measure-Learn loop guided by the underlying concept of experimentation from Lean Startup as a means seek for the proper product solution. Or yet, changes to the current already adopted XP practices to improve quality of code and constant releases. We describe these and other relevant results next.

### 3.1   Product Developing Under a New Perspective

In our previous study [14], we presented the company decision for migrating from agile to the combined approach, including the transformation package of activities to train people. Here, we discuss changes in the teams' day-to-day work, including those that reflect upon or depend on organizational decisions. We start by presenting the change from a project-base structure to a problem-based mindset-oriented way of working.

**Problem-Oriented Mindset.** Teams' members mentioned that one of the most relevant changes experienced during the transition was moving to a problem-oriented perspective to seek for the user needs understanding rather than refining software requirements only:

---

[2] atlasti.com.

*"Before, we usually received a set of predefined requirements. We implemented these requirements and considered our work done. We did not know whether the problem was solved or not. Now, we do participate in and have the opportunity to investigate and understand the problem."*

Team A experience

The participants also considered that the change in mentality was a challenge at first, as this modification directly affects the team's attitudes. The mindset change required that team members start acting as main actors in the development of the product and not just as those who operationalize it. However, it is crucial an ownership attitude from the teams to fit in this new mentality.

**Team Engagement.** The teams' commitment to the entire software development process has increased considerably since the adoption of the problem-oriented mindset. In fact, the teams started to recognize the need to move to an improved way to provide more business-aligned products, changing at the core the manner of understanding the product, during the hands-on training on the new combined approach. This realization led them to understand that achievements were dependent on the team involvement with changes. For instance, they promoted a shared product vision:

*"Everyone needs to understand the product, not just the product designer or the product manager - the software engineer is no longer isolated. The entire team needs to know why the products are working and have an understanding of the product vision. Everyone is always up-to-date."*

Team B experience

**Shared Responsibilities.** With a shared product vision is essential that teams have shared responsibilities. The whole team participates from activities as the problem understanding - where is discussed the product's needs. By establishing a relationship between them and the stakeholders, the team can define a stakeholder map - which allows the teams to be more effective in the next phases of the product development, as well. This change requires a different position from the software engineers since the product designer and product manager already have this participative role with the stakeholders due to the nature of the roles. Now, the software engineers affirm that they need to adapt to a more collaborative attitude in all decisions that involve the product:

*"We have the responsibility to guarantee the environment to the solution developing, make the pipeline implementation using continuous delivery and integration. However, we are now responsible for participating in each decision in the team since the conception of the product, joining the users' interviews, stakeholders meeting, and the other ceremonies."*

Software Engineers from team A and B experience

In the teams' perspective, in terms of methodological aspects, the combined approach adoption depends strongly on the first two elements discussed above.

Having established that, we can describe the aspects related to the teams' way of working on the adoption of UCD and Lean Startup concepts, also the change from the Scrum framework to the XP methodology.

## 3.2   Methodological Aspects

As previously mentioned, we asked the teams to visually illustrate how they perceived the changes related to methodological aspects that guide their work. Figure 2 shows the teams original representations.

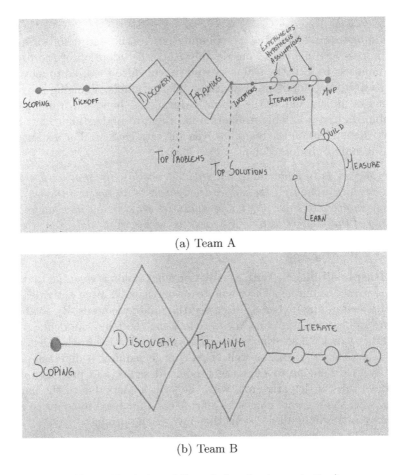

(a) Team A

(b) Team B

**Fig. 2.** Team A and B work flow (or team rhythm)

Following the teams' representation, next, we start exploring the aspects related to UCD as a manner to promote a user involvement in the product development in the teams' perspective.

**UCD to Promote User Involvement and Participation.** Although agile methods encourage the relationship between team and stakeholders, the participants felt that in their context, it seems to be not enough because the product still not address the stakeholders' needs. With the change for the combine approach usage, business people and users reported a set of benefits in terms of user participation in the teams' activities and their daily work, and also the user involvement, since with the introduction of UCD activities, techniques and concepts they seem to be more engaged in the product development.

The participants considered as a significant modification in the UCD context the adoption of the Discovery and Framing framework designed by Design Council[3]. On the two teams' representation (Fig. 2), the framework is in the early stages, aiming to explore the problem and possible solutions to it.

Team members emphasize that the use of discovery and framing framework, it is a consequence of work in a problem-oriented, reaffirming once again the mindset change impacts. Another relevant factor for participants is the need to have the whole team working in the framework stages, as problem exploration, user interviews, user research, and other activities. Team A members consider that team engagement to participate in these activities promotes an approximation with the stakeholders, making them believe in teams' effectiveness:

> *"We gain their (stakeholders) trust when we talk with them and show interest in providing a product that attends and solves their problems."*
>
> Team A experience

Team B participants declare:

> *"Using UCD techniques and also a mindset of being more empathetic with our stakeholders, make them feels indispensable in the development process, and consequently, encouraged to talk and to contribute with us. Our stakeholders see us as problem solvers. We gain their trust when we show interest in providing a product that attends the problems."*
>
> Team B experience

The problem understanding is an outcome of the problem exploration. This outcome allows possible framing solutions to the given problem. The teams reported that the stakeholders' presence is even more necessary at this stage. Team A members affirm that to promotes the stakeholders' engagement is vital to collect stakeholders' feedback all the time and consider it:

> *"We use stakeholder feedback as a tool to refine and redefine problem definition and priority. Being aligned with the stakeholders' needs makes them more confident about our work. We work together with stakeholders, ensure that the developed product is being following the right path."*
>
> Team A experience

---

[3] https://designcouncil.org.uk/news-opinion/what-framework-innovation-design-councils-evolved-double-diamond.

In team B experience, another concept that helps to focus on the problem understanding and provide a more accurate solution to the product is experimentation concept inside the problem discovering:

*"We aggregate value to our products by using experimentation. We explore the problem that business brings to us, and by the end of it, we address their needs in the product."*

Team B experience

Also, addressing the users and business needs in the product, demand a change of mindset to guide the teams. They mentioned that an important value taken for all three methodologies is the BML loop and experiments, which lead us to explore the teams' perspective on the lean startup concepts addition.

**Lean Startup Concepts as a Tool to Be More Assertive.** One of the most powerful concepts derived from Lean Startup in the teams' point of view is the BML loop inclusion. The participants have defined the BML usage as an approach, and the reason for that is that loop is applied all the time:

*"We use BML all the time in any part of our process. For example, a user interview. If we are defining the interview script, we are building the script. We measure the script value by observing after the interview, if we collected the right data or not (e.g., the stakeholders answer the question, but we do not formulate the question for the answer that we aimed.) - and this process allows us to learn from our fails to create a more assertive script to be more accurate in the next one. BML is applicable to any product development activity."*

Team A experience

However, BML usage is not so relevant if used alone. The richness of the loop is combined with experimentation, as teams' members reported:

*"All foundation of the BML brings the experimentation concept in the core of it. We work with a problem-oriented mindset because the experimentation allows it. In the beginning, we have a simple problem view, and this leads us to start making assumptions from that, execute the experiments using prototypes or any technique. The results give us a condition to measure it and to refute or accept our assumptions. At the end of it, we learn from the results and restart the loop, refining our vision."*

Team A and B experience

Team A also experienced an unusual usage of experimentation in a non-software solution. They mentioned that this shows the relevance of the concept usage for the teams, stakeholders, and to the company itself:

*"Our users were claiming a solution to the performance issue in the system. Before we run directly to the code, imagining that the problem in the software solution, we decide to analyze the problem. The stakeholders*

*reported that the use of some spreadsheets contained a significant amount of data, and it was getting a poor performance taking about three days to calculate and return the results. So, we assume that maybe the problem was not in the application, but in the host machines. We decided to run the same application in a more powerful machine, and we have found out that our assumption was right - the problem was in the machine's performance. This experience shows us the relevance of experimentation - and more than that, it shows that sometimes the problem solution could not be a software solution, which for us is a huge breakthrough."*

Team A experience

Besides, the participants perspective, experimentation gives them room to fail up; however, fail and fix quickly:

*"Product development is uncertain and very susceptible to failure. Nevertheless, what matters is the speed at which we will react to those. The experimentation as a core of the BML gives us room to fail but also allows us to fail and fix quickly. We do not need to wait until the end of the iteration to discover that we do not understand the stakeholder needs."*

Team A and B experience

Related to the pivot/persevere usage, the concept follow the same idea of one of the agile principles, in terms of adaptability for team B members. They affirmed that pivot/persevere reinforce the relevance of refining the product and problem strategy, being adaptable to change or persevere:

*"Experiments give us conditions to understand if we are in a smart strategy for our product or not. Also, the stakeholders' relationship with us is an essential factor to persevere in the strategy or start to look another direction, pivoting. Sometimes, the strategy defined in the long-term can not be valid anymore. That is the reason why BML, experimentation, and pivot/persevere perform better together; one depends on the other."*

Team B experience

Notwithstanding, the addition of UCD and Lean Startup has been the main change. In terms of code development, the teams reported a need to align the changes in a possible technological manner. To attend this modification, participants reported the use of XP instead of Scrum as an agile method. Now, we explore how the insertion of XP affected the process, from the teams' perspective.

**XP to Boost Code Quality.** The XP methodology choice as an agile method came with the Pivotal Labs approach proposal. However, team A members recognize that even that the change was top-down from Scrum framework to XP was a great fit. They cited that the use of XP practices (e.g., pair programming, TDD, and unit test) boost the development and increase the code quality:

*"The use of pair programming increases our product development process. We can benefit from using it in many ways: from accelerating the learning process of a new engineer, to promote improvements in the code quality."*

Team B experience

Continuous Integration (CI)/Continuous Delivery (CD) pipeline was considered as a practice that promotes a problem-oriented mindset in the context of software development, as team B participants mentioned:

*"CI/CD pipeline was crucial to address the changes. It promotes faster feedback and help us to validate stories on the production environment. CI/CD inclusion encourages software engineers to feel more proficient."*

Team B experience

The participants also reported significant modifications in terms of the team rhythm. They have changed a set of ceremonies during the daily and the iteration work and also its nomenclature aiming to attend to XP methodology rhythm:

*"We tried to be more aligned, and the ceremonies are useful for that. We continued doing the standup meeting, retrospective, and planning. However, we now have an office standup to be more connected to other teams - also, the ceremony nomenclature change from sprint to iteration. In the planning sessions, we choose if we must have more than one session, for example, a pre-iteration meeting. Finally, we have weekly sessions with all stakeholders to strengthen our relationship with them further."*

Team A and B experience

Once again, BML shows its relevance, as well as experiment concepts in teams' perspectives. The teams reported that the use of these concepts impact the manner they deal with the iteration directly. It is a common-sense between them, the relevance of developing the product, thinking more systematically and investigating the real problem, defining assumptions, executing the experiments, collecting data, and verifying whether the assumptions were accepted or refuted.

Concluding the teams report, the participants attributes the adoption success in terms of mentality, engagement, and modifications related to methodological aspects with UCD and Lean Startup, to a organically approach application:

*"Even though our drawing represents a sequential or continued vision of the methodologies combination, our daily use is adapted. If we are during the iterations and perceived that the problem is not well defined, we are ok to come back to the discovery and framing framework and start again. Alternatively, if we defined some assumptions and discovered that the product/problem vision is not aligned, we can redefine these assumptions. This is secret of the adoption, apply the approach organically."*

Team A experience

## 4   Discussion

Schön et al. [13] mentioned the barriers of access the stakeholders as a challenge in their study. In the reported study, mitigate this barrier was considered as one of the crucial changes that derive the way that the company works now; it is working as a problem-oriented perspective. The teams changed their mindset to map the user and business problems over only refine pre-defined requirements - solving the difficulty of decrease the creativity to the process of solution-finding.

Teams' attitude required an adaption to attend the problem-oriented mindset change. All roles became more engaged in activities as product/problem scoping, user interviews, or stakeholder meetings. Nyfjord and Kajko-Mattsson [10] mentioned in their study that the entire team engagement in these activities often was executed by business people and the teams (especially software engineers) only receive the artifact produced from these activities. Once again, these problems are decreased by changing for the problem-oriented mindset.

Reinforcing the development-oriented by user/business problem perspective, there is an extensive effort on the discovery of the right problem and framing the possible solutions to the right solution. The double diamond structure that the teams applied follows the UCD activities defined at ISO 9241-210 [8]. Schön et al. [13] also defines that this is one of the critical aspects under the integration of UCD and Agile, separate product discovery and product solution. Define the discovery and framing usage brings benefits associated with the added value of the product. Alahyari et al. [2] mentioned that one of the factors that can impact the perceived value on the products is the customer relationship, which is highly explored during the discovery and framing since the UCD activities and techniques usage promotes an approximation between team and stakeholders.

Incorporated to the discovery and framing and also in the iteration, the teams make use of the build-measure-learn loop, aiming to produce a better product. The perceived benefits and the reason for the teams choose to use build-measure-learn derived by experimentation was very similar to those reported by Yaman et al. [17], which reduce the development effort, deeper customer insights, and use experimentation as a guide on development decisions. The teams also reported that the use of a build-measure-learn application was a considerable modification since they work only with agile methodologies before, and they feel that agile does not help them to know what product should be developed. Edison, Wang, and Abrahamsson [5] affirm the same, agile prescribes how to develop, but it is not so accurate to answer and to investigate the products' needs.

Another finding on the combined approach adoption is the use of the pivot and persevere concept original from lean startup [11]. Pivot decision could occur at any moment (e.g., problem/solution definition, scope definition), as well as remain in the same strategy, persevering. This is relevant because inputs to the teams and does not allow the teams to work on products that will not add value to the customers and business people, reducing the waste of the process [11].

The change impacts, related to the insertion of XP practices, were lower since the teams were already familiar with agile methods. However, the change for an XP over scrum framework affects their way of work. The inclusion of the build-measure-learn loop and also the XP practices as pair programming, TDD, and continuous delivery bring perceived benefits to the teams and stakeholders.

As reported, the manner of how the combined approach is adopted is essential. It is possible to notice that even that concepts from UCD and Lean Startup are essential in their new way of work, the core of the approach remains in agile value, which is a response to change over following a plan [3], which means use the approach adaptively. Pivot/persevere concepts explore in the core of it, the change of the team rhythm adopting XP ceremonies, which was claimed to promote the engagement and involvement among the team members and stakeholders. From a team's perspective, these modifications ensure adoption success.

## 5   Related Work

Combine UCD and Lean Startup with Agile software development have been a hot topic in the context of software development [4,16]. In this section, we aim to compare our findings in light of the literature findings of the subject.

Lean UX [6] philosophy is grounded on Agile software development, Design Thinking (DT), and Lean Startup methodologies. This philosophy has focused on the design process incorporated into the development of a product that had defined principles based on the concepts of the three methodologies (e.g., cross-functional teams from DT, permission to fail from Lean Startup, and getting out of the deliverable business from agile). Although the principles are related to the combined approach presented in this study, the fact of Lean UX's focus on the design process illustrates the difference from our case study, which explores the combined approach adoption in the software development context. Nordstrom [7], Converge [16], and InnoDev [4] models also proposes a combined approach of Agile software development, Design Thinking (DT), and Lean Startup. However, the models are focused on software product development. In Nordstrom and converge (which was inspired by Nordstrom), starts applying DT, right after Lean Startup concepts BML, experiments, and pivot and persevere, in the end, the sprints are guided by BML concept also. InnoDev model, on the other hand, starts with an initial phase of scoping, which uses elements from DT, and follows the same flow used by the other two models above.

Similarities could be observed from the literature studies, and our case reported. The double diamond usage and the concepts as BML and experimentation are present Nordstrom Model. Also, the models propose through a set of techniques derived from DT and Lean Startup, the problem-oriented mindset.

However, compared to our study, the literature findings have aimed to propose models for the combined approach. Our studies does not proposes a model. We aim to reports by agile teams' perspective from a multinational company, how UCD, Lean Startup, and Agile are adopted and used in their daily work. Nordstrom and Converge models were evaluated in startups, and even though InnoDev was designed for small to large companies, it was not evaluated empirically. Also, this difference implies that these studies do not have the whole context of persuading users and business people to believe in the adoption.

Another difference compared to our case study and literature findings is the use of UCD over DT. Moreover, also, BML usage is applied from the middle to the end of the presented models. In our study, the teams reported the use of BML during the entire process, followed by experiments. Finally, the models propose the use of the Scrum framework just using some XP practices - in our case study, the teams fully adopted XP practices, techniques, and rhythm (ceremonies).

The comparison between our case study and literature findings gives an understanding of the need for a detailed characterization of the combined approach by teams' perspective, which were the most affected in the adoption. This richness of detail was observed in none of the studies. Also, reinforce the relevance to recognize how this kind of transformation takes place in a large-scale setup.

## 6 Conclusion, Limitations, and Future Work

We reported through a case study the perspective of two teams about the combined approach adoption composed of UCD, Lean Startup, and Agile Software Development. The detailed characterization provided in this study reveals that the adoption is comprised of a set of elements as a new problem-oriented mindset, team engagement, and these two above provides methodological aspects changes.

Also, it is relevant to affirm that UCD and Lean Startup in software development were a significant finding from the study results. UCD contributes by promoting user involvement and Lean Startup with BML usage as an approach, having experimentation in the core. An important conclusion, this combination has the concern of stays adaptable and its usage in a more organic way are characteristics of agile methods that remain at the core of the combined approach.

For the academy audience, our study contributes to essential details about the elements and essence that surrounds this approach. The industry practitioners will take advantage of the described study used by a multinational company and how this approach fits in the software development process setting.

Inherent to any empirical study, this study has limitations. Construct validity regards whether the scenario of study is representative of the real world while external validity is concerned with generalization. We observed two teams in a real setting, which offers them a new setup that aims to promote collaboration. Also, the teams are composed of members playing distinct roles and with different experiences. Moreover, we used interchangeably and overtime multiple data sources aiming to triangulate our findings, which were reviewed continuously by senior researchers. Therefore, although we cannot claim that our results apply to distinct scenarios, these strategies helped reduce limitations.

As future work, we suggest, the replication of the study in other companies with the same configuration, aiming to compare the findings; also, another valuable work could be compare teams who adopt the combined approach and those that use another approach (e.g., Scrum, Kanban), aiming to discover the strengths and weakness of the approach compared to other agile methods.

**Acknowledgements.** We thank the study participants and acknowledge that this research is sponsored by Dell Brazil using incentives of the Brazilian Informatics Law (Law no 8.2.48, year 1991).

## References

1. Abelein, U., Sharp, H., Paech, B.: Does involving users in software development really influence system success? IEEE Softw. **30**, 17–23 (2013)

2. Alahyari, H., Svensson, R.B., Gorschek, T.: A study of value in agile software development organizations. J. Syst. Softw. **125**, 271–288 (2017)
3. Beck, K., et al.: Manifesto for agile software development (2001). https://www.agilemanifesto.org/
4. Dobrigkeit, F., de Paula, D.: The best of three worlds-the creation of INNODEV, a software development approach that integrates design thinking, SCRUM and lean startup. In: Proceedings of the 21st International Conference on Engineering Design, pp. 319–328. Design Society (2017)
5. Edison, H., Wang, X., Abrahamsson, P.: Lean startup: why large software companies should care. In: Proceedings of the International Conference on Agile Software Development, pp. 1–7. ACM (2015)
6. Gothelf, J.: Lean UX: Applying Lean Principles to Improve User Experience. O'Reilly, Sebastopol (2013)
7. Grossman-Kahn, B., Rosensweig, R.: Skip the silver bullet: driving innovation through small bets and diverse practices. In: Leading Through Design, pp. 815–830 (2012)
8. ISO: 9241-210: Ergonomics of human system interaction-Part 210: HCD for interactive systems (2010). https://www.iso.org/standard/52075.html
9. Krippendorff, K.: Content Analysis: An Introduction to Its Methodology. Sage, Thousand Oaks (2018)
10. Nyfjord, J., Kajko-Mattsson, M.: Degree of agility in pre-implementation process phases. In: Wang, Q., Pfahl, D., Raffo, D.M. (eds.) ICSP 2008. LNCS, vol. 5007, pp. 234–245. Springer, Heidelberg (2008). https://doi.org/10.1007/978-3-540-79588-9_21
11. Ries, E.: The Lean Startup: How Today's Entrepreneurs Use Continuous Innovation to Create Radically Successful Businesses. Crown Business, New York (2011)
12. Runeson, P., Höst, M.: Guidelines for conducting and reporting case study research in software engineering. Empirical Softw. Eng. **14**, 131 (2009). https://doi.org/10.1007/s10664-008-9102-8
13. Schön, E.-M., Winter, D., Escalona, M.J., Thomaschewski, J.: Key challenges in agile requirements engineering. In: Baumeister, H., Lichter, H., Riebisch, M. (eds.) XP 2017. LNBIP, vol. 283, pp. 37–51. Springer, Cham (2017). https://doi.org/10.1007/978-3-319-57633-6_3
14. Signoretti, I., et al.: Boosting agile by using user-centered design and lean startup: a case study of the adoption of the combined approach in software development. In: Proceedings of the International Symposium on Empirical Software Engineering and Measurement, pp. 1–6. IEEE (2019)
15. Vilkki, K.: When agile is not enough. In: Abrahamsson, P., Oza, N. (eds.) LESS 2010. LNBIP, vol. 65, pp. 44–47. Springer, Heidelberg (2010). https://doi.org/10.1007/978-3-642-16416-3_6
16. Ximenes, B.H., Alves, I.N., Araújo, C.C.: Software project management combining agile, lean startup and design thinking. In: Marcus, A. (ed.) DUXU 2015. LNCS, vol. 9186, pp. 356–367. Springer, Cham (2015). https://doi.org/10.1007/978-3-319-20886-2_34
17. Yaman, S., et al.: Introducing continuous experimentation in large software-intensive product and service organisations. J. Syst. Softw. **133**, 195–211 (2017)

# Agile Software Development Practices and Success in Outsourced Projects: The Moderating Role of Requirements Risk

Oliver Krancher[(✉)]

IT University of Copenhagen, Rued Langgaards Vej 7, 2300 Copenhagen, Denmark
olik@itu.dk

**Abstract.** Although agile practices are gaining in popularity, there is little evidence showing how particular agile practices, in particular those involving the client, affect the success of outsourced software projects. Data from a matched survey of sponsors and developers in 60 outsourced information systems projects indicate negative effects of continuous analysis and positive effects of joint decision making and continuous integration on project success. Moreover, interaction analyses show that some positive effects are enhanced and negative effects dampened when requirements risk is high. These findings caution against continuous analysis in outsourced projects while they support joint decision making and continuous integration. The findings also empirically substantiate the largely untested assertion that agile practices help cope with changing requirements.

**Keywords:** Agile software development · Agile practices · Requirements risk · Project success · Continuous integration · Continuous analysis · Joint decision making · Agile requirements engineering

## 1 Introduction

Information systems (IS) projects have a notorious reputation for running over time and budget while not fully satisfying user needs [1]. Many organizations are therefore turning to agile methods, hoping to increase software quality, reduce costs, shorten time-to-market, and better handle changing priorities by using agile methods [2]. Teams using agile methods typically tailor their use of agile methods [2], i.e., they select the practices to be used in a particular project from the practices advocated in methods such as Scrum [3] and XP [4]. A key question for these teams is which practices are most likely to lead to a successful project given the characteristics of the project at hand.

Over the past two decades, empirical research on agile software development has accumulated knowledge that provides valuable guidance to these teams [5, 6]. Some research has found positive associations between the use of agile methods in general (rather than of particular practices) and project success [7, 8], indicating that the general use of agile methods can enhance project success. Other studies have examined the effects of particular agile practices on project success and found positive effects of

© The Author(s) 2020
V. Stray et al. (Eds.): XP 2020, LNBIP 383, pp. 56–72, 2020.
https://doi.org/10.1007/978-3-030-49392-9_4

pair programming [9, 10] and continuous integration [11] and negative effects of daily stand-ups [10].

Notwithstanding these insights, evidence of the links between agile practices and project success remains limited in three major ways. First, in contrast to practices that involve engineers only (e.g. pair programming, continuous integration) [12], less is known about the impact of *practices that involve engineers and business people*, such as joint decision making and continuous analysis. While qualitative research has explored such practices, quantitative evidence of their effect on project success is scarce [13]. Such evidence could help practitioners navigate the tradeoff between the benefits (e.g. enhanced feedback and communication) and drawbacks (high search costs, opportunistic threats) associated with these practices. Second, few studies have examined the effects of particular agile practices in the context of *outsourced IS projects*, i.e., in settings where client organizations delegate development work to external vendors. This is problematic because not all agile practices may work equally well across firm boundaries [14, 15]. For instance, frequent requirements revision and reprioritization can entail high contract adaption costs and opportunistic behavior in outsourced projects. Third, there is surprisingly little evidence of the context factors under which particular agile practices are effective. In particular, we lack evidence of the potential moderating role of *requirements risk* (i.e., the degree to which requirements are uncertain and frequently changing) [1] in the relationship between agile practices and project success despite the frequent claim that agile methods help cope with changing requirements.

This paper theorizes and empirically examines how three agile practices affect the success of outsourced software projects and how these associations are contingent on requirements risk. The three agile practices in the focus of the paper are continuous integration (compiling, building, deploying, and testing code several times a day), continuous analysis (continuously triggering and incorporating new information about requirements), and joint decision making (client and vendor making important decisions jointly). Drawing on a perspective of software development as knowledge integration, it is argued that practices for knowledge integration within the vendor (continuous integration) come primarily with benefits whereas practices for client-vendor knowledge integration (continuous analysis, joint decision making) come with both benefits and costs. As such the overall effects of client-vendor practices will depend on the need for knowledge integration, which is primarily rooted in difficulties to articulate requirements up-front (i.e., requirement risk). Hypotheses derived from these ideas are tested using data collected through a matched survey of 60 client sponsors and 60 vendor engineers. The results emphasize the benefits from within-vendor practices, draw a more differentiated picture of the effects of client-vendor practices, and largely support the often asserted but rarely tested moderating role of requirements risk.

## 2   Theory Background

### 2.1   Software Development as Knowledge Integration

This paper explains the impact of agile practices on the success of outsourced projects by drawing on the perspective of software development as knowledge integration. A knowledge integration perspective holds that project team members possess and acquire heterogeneous knowledge and that a key challenge lies in fusing this heterogeneous knowledge into usable software [16, 17]. Software development teams typically comprise business people possessing business knowledge (e.g. ideas about requirements for the software) and engineers possessing technical knowledge (e.g. programming languages, design patterns) and knowledge about existing software systems [17–19].

From a knowledge integration perspective, a key challenge lies in the *interdependencies between these knowledge areas*. For instance, business people often realize their requirements (business knowledge) only after they have seen a first version of the software [16, 20]. But engineers can build a first version (i.e., apply their technical knowledge) only after business people articulate a first version of requirements (business knowledge). These interdependencies challenge the assumption of independence of requirements (business knowledge) from design options (technical knowledge) and from the functionality of existing software systems (software knowledge), an assumption inherent to plan-based software development [16, 17]. Interdependencies exist not only between the business and technical spheres but also within spheres. For instances, interdependencies within the technical sphere manifest because engineers need to know about design decisions and code changes made by other engineers to ensure alignment with own code contributions. The strength of these interdependencies is, to large extent, driven by *requirements risk* (i.e., the degree to which requirements are uncertain and frequently changing) [1]. The fuzzier the ideas about requirements are, the more efforts will be needed to arrive at a shared understanding of how a useful software for the given purpose should look like and the more efforts will be needed to coordinate development actions in the face of changing requirements.

Although knowledge integration issues and requirements risk arise in a variety of projects, *outsourced projects* face the peculiar challenge of integrating the client's business knowledge and the vendor's technical knowledge *across firm boundaries* [17, 18]. The rich literatures on IS outsourcing and on theories of the firm point to two key challenges that arise from this boundary [21–23]. First, individuals from different organizations often lack shared knowledge and shared assumptions about effective problem-solving processes, which makes coordination more difficult [21, 22]. Second, different organizations may work towards different goals. In particular, fuzzy requirements may invite opportunistic behavior by the vendor because it is difficult to legally enforce contracts when requirements are unclear at the outset [22, 23].

### 2.2   Agile Practices for Within-Vendor and Client-Vendor Knowledge Integration

Agile methods help address knowledge-related interdependencies by establishing feedback processes and team-based organizing structures [20]. Three agile practices may be particularly suitable to this end: continuous integration, continuous analysis, and joint decision making. While continuous integration addresses within-vendor knowledge integration, continuous analysis and joint decision making address knowledge integration between client and vendor.

**Within-Vendor Knowledge Integration.** A key agile practice for within-vendor knowledge integration is *continuous integration*, i.e., the practice of engineers compiling, building, and testing code many times a day, typically by relying on tools for automating build and deployment processes [11, 24]. Continuous integration promotes knowledge integration within the technical sphere (i.e., between engineers) because it provides engineers with immediate feedback about how their code contributions work together with other engineers' contributions [20]. An attractive feature of continuous integration in outsourcing is that it enables rapid feedback without involving the client, allowing the use of the practice even in projects in which clients do not fully embrace agile methods. Although there is evidence linking continuous integration to higher quality and productivity in open-source development [11], there is little research examining whether these benefits also hold in outsourcing.

**Client-Vendor Knowledge Integration.** A key agile practice for client-vendor knowledge integration is *continuous analysis*, i.e., continuously triggering and incorporating new information about requirements. The notion of triggering information about requirements alludes to the fact that business people often lack clarity about their requirements at the outset of projects and trigger this information through activities such as testing early versions of the software. They incorporate this information by revising or reprioritizing requirements for the next iteration. In Scrum, continuous analysis manifests through the revision and reprioritization of the product backlog during sprint planning and through the test of the software in the sprint review [3]. Continuous analysis is in line with the agile manifesto principles to "[w]elcome changing requirements, even late in development" and to "[d]eliver working software frequently" [25]. It encompasses concepts such as iterative requirements engineering [26], dynamic prioritization [27], agile requirements prioritization [13, 15], and iterative requirements [13]. Continuous analysis enables client-vendor knowledge integration because it establishes a feedback loop between requirements that result from the business knowledge primarily held by the client and the working version of the software that results from the technical knowledge primarily held by the vendor [17]. Although this feedback loop may be particularly valuable for addressing the lack of shared understanding in outsourcing, continuous analysis may also entail contract adaption costs and opportunistic threats in outsourcing, as I will argue later. Given this trade-off, an important unresolved challenge for practitioners is to decide on the amount of analysis that is made up-front versus continuously throughout a project [28].

A second key practice for client-vendor knowledge integration is *joint decision making* [29], defined as the extent to which important decisions are jointly made by client and vendor. In Scrum, joint decision making manifests in decision making by a team that comprises not only engineers but also the product owner as a business representative [3]. Joint decision making is related to the agile manifesto principle that "[b]usiness people and developers must work together daily throughout the project" [25]. Although daily interaction with business people may not always be possible in outsourced software projects, it is possible to frequently interact in order to make important decisions jointly, which is akin to a team-based organizing mode [14]. Joint decision making promotes knowledge integration between client and vendor because it urges each party to communicate and to incorporate the other party's perspective when making important decisions. While joint decision making may thus help address the frequent lack of shared knowledge in outsourcing, it may also entail lower benefits of specialization and opportunistic threats, as I will argue later. An important unresolved issue is thus under which circumstances projects should leverage joint decision making versus an approach where clients make business decisions and vendors technical decisions [28].

## 3  Hypotheses

Drawing on the knowledge integration perspective outlined above, this section develops hypotheses about how the three practices and their interaction with requirements risk affects project success. In line with prior studies on IS project success [30, 31], the focus lies on two dimensions of success: effectiveness and efficiency. Effectiveness (also termed product performance) refers to the degree to which the developed software meets the client's requirements whereas efficiency (also termed process performance) refers to the extent to which a project is completed within time and budget [31].

### 3.1  Continuous Integration

Continuous integration is likely to enhance success by enabling rapid feedback within the vendor's development team and efficiency gains due to automation. By frequently compiling, deploying, and testing software, vendor engineers receive rapid feedback on their code contributions, allowing the early discovery of integration problems (within-vendor knowledge integration). Identifying defects early has positive impact on the quality of the delivered software (i.e., effectiveness) because it will make it easier for developers to fix defects before go-live. Continuous integration will also have positive impact on efficiency because problems are identified more easily when only small code contributions are added at a time and because the automation infrastructure behind continuous integration shortens work and wait times [32]. In outsourcing continuous integration appears particularly suitable because it allows leveraging feedback processes irrespective of the degree to which clients are willing to adopt agile practices.

While continuous integration is likely to have a positive main effect on project success, this effect will be more pronounced under high requirements risk. When requirements are uncertain and frequently changing, this has downstream effects by making the engineers' work more uncertain, increasing thus the need for knowledge integration. Continuous integration will help address this increased need by providing engineers with rapid feedback on their code contributions. These arguments suggest:

*H1a: Higher amounts of continuous integration are positively associated with success (i.e., effectiveness and efficiency).*
*H1b: The association between continuous integration and success depends on requirements risk such that the association is stronger when requirements risk is high.*

### 3.2  Continuous Analysis

Unlike continuous integration, continuous analysis presents projects with a trade-off between the benefits and the costs that arise from the practice. Continuous analysis enables client-vendor knowledge integration by allowing clients to learn about requirements and their relative importance when looking at new versions of the software and discussing requirements with the vendor [13, 26]. In line with these ideas, a case study reported increased client satisfaction due to continuous analysis [33].

Notwithstanding these benefits, continuous analysis practices are also associated with two caveats. First, continuous analysis may involve a long and costly search process where business people realize their true requirements only after developers have spent high efforts on developing functionality that ends up discarded. In outsourced projects, these search processes can also entail high efforts for adapting contracts [14]. Second, frequently revising requirements introduces opportunistic threats in outsourced projects [23]. Vendors may opportunistically leverage the fuzziness of initial specifications to ask for generous compensation of work that was not originally anticipated.

Given these benefits and drawbacks, it is difficult to predict the net effect. However, it is likely that the benefits and drawbacks are salient to a different degree depending on requirements risk. Under high requirements risk, it may not be feasible to accurately identify requirements during a detailed up-front analysis [16]. Continuous analysis will then often be the only feasible alternative. Conversely, when requirements risk is low, articulating requirements up-front is feasible and disciplined up-front analysis may be more efficient that continuous analysis. This leads to the following hypothesis:

*H2: The association between continuous analysis and success depends on requirements risk such that the association is more positive when requirements risk is high than when requirements risk is low.*

### 3.3  Joint Decision Making

Like continuous analysis, joint decision making presents projects with a trade-off between benefits and drawbacks of the practice. If client and vendor make key decisions jointly, this entails high amounts of communication, which allows the different stakeholders to integrate their knowledge and may lead to higher project success [34, 35]. Indeed, studies of agile software development point to the importance of close customer collaboration [36] and of reconciling the perspectives of all participants [37].

Notwithstanding these benefits, joint decision making comes at the costs of sacrificing economies of specialization and of opportunistic threats. Economies of specialization may be sacrificed because, as indicated by the knowledge integration literature, it can be difficult and effortful to transfer knowledge from one domain to another [17, 38]. From this perspective, joint decision making can involve high communication efforts and the risk that the voice of the person most knowledgeable in a domain is overruled by others. A potentially more efficient alternative can be to leave business decisions to the client and technical decisions to the vendor. Joint decision making may also entail opportunistic threats because vendors may, for example, falsely attribute a problem in the software to a joint client-vendor decision rather than to their own omissions.

Like in the case of continuous analysis, the net effect of these benefits and drawbacks is unclear. It is likely, though, that the relative size of these benefits and drawbacks depends on requirements risk. When requirements risk is low, the need for knowledge integration is low. It is then feasible for the client to make business decisions and for the vendor to make design decisions based on the client's business decisions [17]. With each party making decisions in the area in which the party is most knowledgeable, this approach will ensure efficiency and accountability [14, 17]. Conversely, when requirements risk is high, this separation of decisions rights may not be feasible because clients will make poor decisions about requirements at the outset, and design decisions based on poor requirements are unlikely to yield a satisfactory software. I therefore anticipate:

*H3: The association between joint decision making and success depends on requirements risk such that the association is more positive when requirements risk is high than when requirements risk is low.*

## 4    Methods

### 4.1    Data Collection

I tested the hypotheses through a matched survey involving client sponsors reporting on project success and vendor engineers reporting on agile practices and further variables. A matched survey addresses concerns of common-method bias [39] and allows gathering data from the informants most knowledgeable about each construct (i.e., sponsors reporting about success, engineers reporting about agile practices). The sampling frame were outsourced IS projects that were completed within the last 12 months. Students and I contacted client organizations from Switzerland and Denmark. Once they agreed to participate, they identified a list of suitable projects along with contact information of the sponsor, the project manager (not used for this study), and a developer from the vendor. We then invited sponsor, project manager, and developer to respond to an online questionnaire that was specifically designed for their role (sponsor, project manager, developer). We obtained responses from 100 sponsors and 92 engineers. Responses matched for 65 projects. From these 65 projects, I removed 5 due to missing data or due to unengaged responses, yielding a final sample size of 60. Table 1 shows sample characteristics. 49 responses (82%) were from the public sector. The sample did not include offshore projects. All projects except for 2 were single-sourcing.

**Table 1.** Sample characteristics

| Project size | # Projects | Country | # | Sector | # | Type | # |
|---|---|---|---|---|---|---|---|
| $0–$100 K | 12 | Switzerland | 40 | Public | 49 | Development | 38 |
| $100 K–$1 M | 33 | Denmark | 20 | Private | 11 | Enhancement | 22 |
| $ > 1 M | 15 | | | | | | |

### 4.2    Instrument Development, Validation, and Estimation

Table 2 shows the final instrument. I relied on existing scales with the exception of the continuous analysis construct for which I developed new items. In line with the definition of continuous analysis as the continuous triggering and incorporating of information about requirements, the items asked about triggering (CA4-5) and incorporating (CA1-3) information, measuring the frequency of these activities in order to capture to what extent they were performed continuously. Following established positivist survey design procedures [40], we performed a pretest with 6 practitioners using an item rating task and a pilot test comprising 43 responses. I used SmartPLS (v3.2.8) to assess the validity of the final instrument. To establish convergent validity, I verified that average variance extracted (AVE) was greater than .50 for all latent constructs (lowest AVE value: .56) [41]. Moreover, all factor loadings were at least .6, with their average exceeding .7 for all constructs [42]. To establish discriminant validity, I verified that construct correlations were below AVE square roots [41]. Discriminant validity was also supported by the HTMT Ratio Test [43]. Reliability was supported by Cronbach alpha values above .7 (see Table 2).

I used OLS regression to estimate the models. OLS regression has higher power for detecting interaction effects than alternative strategies such as PLS or AMOS [44]. The regression models included several control variables. *Task interdependence* reflects the degree to which development team members affect each other in their work [45]. *Knowledge specificity*, a construct from outsourcing research, reflects the degree to which engineers need knowledge specific to client in order to perform their work [46]. Both high task independence and high knowledge specificity might invite the use of agile methods and may correlate negatively with success. It is therefore important to control for these variables. I also controlled for project size, country (Switzerland vs. Denmark), and sector (public vs. private), for similar reasons. As established in social science research, I relied on hierarchical regression, where I first estimated a model with main effects and then added interaction effects. Given the relatively small sample size of 60 (which is largely due to the matched survey design), I considered significant effects at the $p < .1$ level in the analysis. I verified that the assumptions behind OLS regression were met. Variance inflation factors were below 10 (highest value: 2.67), indicating no concern with multicollinearity. Residual plots were in line with the pattern of a normal distribution. Scatter plots showed no departure from linear effects.

**Table 2.** Survey items

| Construct | Items | Source |
|---|---|---|
| Effectiveness ($\alpha = .89$) | The software ...<br>[Effect1] ... meets the functional requirements[a,]<br>[Effect2] ... meets end user requirements[a]<br>[Effect3] ... fulfils technical requirements[a]<br>[Effect4] ... is reliable[a]<br>[Effect5] ... meets expectations with respect to ease of use[a] | [47, 48] |

(*continued*)

**Table 2.** (*continued*)

| Construct | Items | Source |
|---|---|---|
| Efficiency ($\alpha = .90$) | [Effic1] All services were provided on time[a]<br>[Effic2] The services in this project were provided exceptionally quickly[a]<br>[Effic3] We ([client]) incurred large unplanned efforts for coordinating and monitoring [vendor] (reverse-coded)[a]<br>[Effic4] We ([client]) incurred large unplanned efforts for guiding [vendor] (rev.)[a] | [46, 47, 49] |
| Continuous integration ($\alpha = .82$) | [CI1] Members of the development team integrate code changes several times a day[a]<br>[CI2] The development team has a process that generates a build of the software several times a day[a]<br>[CI3] The developer team is automatically notified of any issues related to the automated compiling, deployment or testing of code[a]<br>[CI4] In this project, we create the build (i.e., an executable version of the software such as by including configuration files and an installer) in a fully automated way (e.g. by using a script or code)[a]<br>[CI5] How often does the development team deploy code during development phases to environments to which [client] has no access?[b] | [2] |
| Continuous analysis ($\alpha = .83$) | How often do you perform the following actions:<br>[CA1] … Adjust requirements[b]<br>[CA2] … Evaluate the priorities of requirements[b]<br>[CA3] … Set the delivery scope for a particular period[b]<br>[CA4] … Have software tested by employees of [client][b]<br>[CA5] How often does the development team deploy code during development phases to environments to which [client] has access?[b] | Newly developed |

*(continued)*

**Table 2.** (*continued*)

| Construct | Items | Source |
|---|---|---|
| Joint decision making ($\alpha = .76$) | In this project, [client] and [vendor] ...<br>[JDM1] ... set goals together[a]<br>[JDM2] ... developed task strategies together[a]<br>[JDM3] ... diagnosed problems together[a]<br>[JDM4] ... evaluated deliverables together[a] | [29] |
| Requirements risk ($\alpha = .81$) | This project was characterized by ...<br>[RR1] ... continually changing scope and system requirements<br>[RR2] ... unclear requirements<br>[RR3] ... conflicting requirements<br>[RR4] ... requirements not adequately identified | [1] |

[a] 5 point Likert scale (completely disagree, rather disagree, neutral, rather agree, fully agree)
[b] 7 point scale (less than once a month, once a month, several times a month but not every week, about once a week, several times a week but not every day, about once a day, more often than once a day)

## 5 Results

Table 3 shows the regression results. High $R^2$ values ranging from .37 to .50 support the explanatory power of the models. H1a predicted a positive relationship between continuous integration and project success. As the results show, continuous integration had no significant association with effectiveness ($\beta = .18$, $p > .1$, Model 1a) but a significant positive association with efficiency ($\beta = .23$, $p < .1$, Model 1b). H1a is thus supported for efficiency but not for effectiveness. H1b predicted a positive interaction of this relationship with requirements risk. I found a significant positive interaction effect for effectiveness ($\beta = .20$, $p < .1$, Model 2a) and an insignificant interaction effect for efficiency ($\beta = .02$, $p > .1$). H1b is thus supported for effectiveness but not for efficiency.

Even though no main effects of continuous analysis were hypothesized, there was a significant negative effect of continuous analysis ($\beta = -.31$, $p < .05$) on effectiveness. H2 predicted a positive interactive effect of continuous analysis and requirements risk on success. The results show such a positive interaction effect for effectiveness ($\beta = .31$, $p > .05$) but not for efficiency. H2 is thus supported for effectiveness.

Although not hypothesized, joint decisions had a significant main effect on efficiency ($\beta = .24$, $p < .1$). H3 predicted a positive interactive effect of joint decision making and requirements risk on success. Such a significant positive effect was found for efficiency ($\beta = .24$, $p < .1$) but not for effectiveness ($\beta = .17$, $p > .1$).

**Table 3.** Regression results

| Predictor | Model 1a: Effectiveness, main effects | Model 2a: Effectiveness, main and interaction effects | Model 1b: Efficiency, main effects | Model 2b: Efficiency, main and interaction effects |
|---|---|---|---|---|
| Intercept | −.06 (.28) | .02 (.26) | −.13 (.27) | −.10 (.26) |
| Task interdependence | −.15 (.13) | −.18 (.12) | −.11 (.13) | −.11 (.12) |
| Knowledge specificity | **−.24$^\dagger$ (.14)** | −.20 (.13) | **−.29* (.13)** | −.24 (.13) |
| Project size | .25 (.20) | .03 (.20) | .27 (.20) | .07 (.20) |
| Public sector | −.28 (.40) | −.29 (.37) | −.42 (.39) | −.45 (.37) |
| Switzerland | .43 (.38) | .44 (.35) | **.72$^\dagger$ (.37)** | **.83* (.36)** |
| Requirements risk | −.02 (.13) | .00 (.13) | .04 (.13) | .01 (.13) |
| Continuous integration | .18 (.13) | .18 (.12) | **.23$^\dagger$ (.13)** | **.23$^\dagger$ (.12)** |
| Continuous analysis | **−.31* (.12)** | **−.31** (.11)** | −.17 (.12) | −.17 (.12) |
| Joint decision making | .17 (.13) | .13 (.12) | **.24$^\dagger$ (.13)** | .20 (.12) |
| Continuous integration × requirements risk | – | **.20$^\dagger$ (.11)** | – | .02 (.11) |
| Continuous analysis × requirements risk | – | **.31* (.13)** | – | .19 (.13) |
| Joint decision making × requirements risk | – | .15 (.12) | – | **.27* (.12)** |
| R$^2$ | .37 | .50 | .41 | .50 |
| Adj. R$^2$ | .26 | .38 | .30 | .37 |
| F | **3.26** (9, 50)** | **3.97*** (12, 47)** | **3.83** (9, 50)** | **3.84 (12, 47)*** |

($^\dagger$ p < .1, * p < .05, ** p < .01, *** p < .001, n = 60, standard errors in parentheses, significant numbers in bold, all variables standardized except for binary variables)

## 6 Discussion

This research was motivated by a lack of studies that examined how particular agile practices affect the success of outsourced projects and how these effects depend on requirements risk. I found a positive main effect of *continuous integration* on efficiency and a positive interactive effect of continuous integration and requirements risk on effectiveness. The left-hand side of Fig. 1 illustrates this interaction effect. As the plot shows, continuous integration contributes strongly to effectiveness when requirements risk is high (i.e., one standard deviation above the sample mean, see the steep slope of the dashed line) while continuous integration hardly contributes to effectiveness when requirements risk is low (i.e., one standard deviation below the sample mean, see the relatively flat solid line). By and large, these findings echo the expectation that teams hardly face a trade-off when deciding for or against continuous integration practices. It appears that the rapid feedback and automation efficiencies associated with continuous integration make it easier for teams to deliver software on time and in budget. Moreover, when requirements are uncertain and frequently changing, continuous integration helps teams to develop software of high quality despite a volatile environment, as indicated by the positive interaction effect on effectiveness. These findings echo Vasilescu and colleagues' [11] observation that continuous integration led to higher quality and productivity in open-source software development while the findings extend the boundary conditions of this effect to outsourced projects.

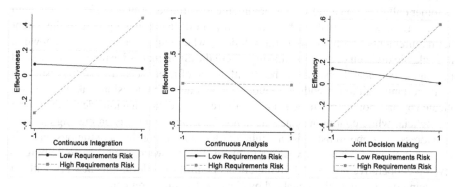

**Fig. 1.** Interaction plots

I found no significant effect of *continuous analysis* on efficiency and a significant negative effect on effectiveness, which is dampened under high requirements risk. The interaction plot in the center of Fig. 1 illustrates this interaction. As the plot shows, continuous analysis has a strong negative relationship with effectiveness under low requirements risk (see the negative slope of the solid line) and hardly any effect on effectiveness under high requirements risk. These results indicate that, in outsourced projects, the drawbacks from continuous analysis dominate over its benefits, in particular in projects with low or moderate requirements risk. It seems that continuously revising and reprioritizing requirements based on the insights gained from testing the software is jeopardizing the quality of the software, unless in settings where requirements are highly uncertain. Possibly, continuous analysis results in search processes where engineers spend high efforts addressing requirements that turn out not to be needed, giving thus engineers too little time to develop the features that are needed. It might also be that vendors opportunistically shirk efforts when continuous analysis has eroded the accountability required for contractual governance. While these findings resonate with the classic finding that scope creep jeopardizes project success [31], they suggest that the positive effects of incorporating ongoing customer learning found in other settings [13, 20, 33] need not necessarily transfer to outsourced projects, where the interface between engineers and business people is complicated by firm boundaries. It may also be that the negative results on continuous analysis reflect the fact that 82% of the projects were from the public sector, an environment where public tendering procedures can make it difficult to deviate from initial specifications [50].

I found no significant effect of *joint decision making* on effectiveness but a significant positive effect on efficiency, which is even stronger when requirements risk is high. The interaction plot on the right-hand side of Fig. 1 illustrates this interaction. While joint decision making hardly has an effect on efficiency when requirements risk is low, it has a strong positive effect when requirements risk is high. This suggests that clients and vendors should make important decisions jointly in those projects where at least moderate amounts of uncertainty is surrounding software requirements. Under these circumstances, joint decision making may help ensure that both economic and technical concerns are taken into account when problems or modified requirements call for new decisions to be made. These findings are in line with the benefits from tight customer collaboration and frequent communication found elsewhere [35–37] although my findings also show that the benefits from joint decision making fade to the extent that requirements become more certain. Indeed, when requirements are well known, a more classic division of decision making where the client makes business decisions and the vendor technical decisions can be slightly more efficient according to the results.

Importantly, although both continuous analysis and joint decision making are complicated by firm boundaries in outsourcing, the results indicate that joint decision making is beneficial while continuous analysis is not. Possibly joint decision making can better address the opportunistic threats inherent to outsourcing than continuous analysis because it allows clients and vendors to blend their knowledge while also helping to develop cooperative norms and giving clients control over development work without sacrificing the accountability enabled by clear up-front requirements.

### 6.1 Contributions

This study makes three key contributions. First, it contributes to the discourse on agile practices in *outsourced projects*. While existing work on outsourcing has provided case study evidence [15] and developed arguments centered on geographic dispersion [14], this paper extends existing work by providing quantitative evidence of the effects of practices on success and by incorporating arguments of the theory-of-the-firm literature, which focuses on opportunistic threats and knowledge barriers due to firm boundaries. The findings reported here echo Batra's [14] expectation that continuous integration (or delivering working software frequently) is effective in outsourcing while continuous analysis (or welcoming changing requirements) can be problematic. These findings are also consistent with our expectation that continuous feedback processes within the vendor team (i.e., continuous integration) are less problematic than continuous feedback processes that involve client and vendor (i.e., continuous analysis). Extending Batra's expectation that joint decision making (or business people and developers working together daily) is difficult to enact, the results show that joint decision making can contribute to project efficiency, making this a prime strategy for client-vendor knowledge integration under the opportunistic threats associated with outsourcing. Taken together, a key practical recommendation for outsourced projects is to engage in a detailed up-front analysis akin to plan-based software development (i.e., low use of the continuous analysis practice) involving both client and vendor, while leveraging continuous feedback during development through continuous integration practices.

Second, the paper contributes to the discourse on agile practices that involve engineers and business people. While research on continuous requirements engineering has produced important insights into *how* teams can best enact continuous analysis and joint decision making [13, 15, 26], the study at hand contributes evidence of the effects of these practices on project success, and thus implications for *whether* teams should rely on these practices in a given project. Indeed, important unresolved challenges for practitioners are to decide on the amount of analysis that is made up-front versus continuously throughout a project and on the extent parties from all business and technical domains should be involved in decision making [28]. These questions are gaining importance as agile practices are increasingly used in enterprise-level projects where organizations blend agile and plan-based practices to balance the needs for control and flexibility [28, 51]. Although the findings obtained here on outsourced projects need not generalize to other settings, they point to the potential caveats of business-facing practices, in particular continuous analysis. Moreover, this paper shows a research design that allows empirically evaluating business-facing agile practices in other settings.

Third, this study provides some empirical justification for the largely untested assertion that agile methods help cope with changing requirements. The results demonstrate that all three agile practices have more positive effects (either on effectiveness or on efficiency) when requirements risk was high. This is important evidence for teams wishing to select the practices most likely to increase the success of a project at hand.

## 6.2 Strengths and Limitations

The study presented here has strengths and limitations. A strength is the matched survey design to avoid common-method bias, which is otherwise often difficult to rule out in survey research. A drawback of this approach was the low sample size, which implied relatively low power. Another strength of the paper is the relatively high variance explained ($R^2$ values) due to the use of control variables (e.g. knowledge specificity) that have high explanatory power and that have rarely been used IS project research. Yet, despite the use of powerful control variables, the correlational research design does not allow ruling out endogeneity due to self-selection of agile methods. Future research could rely on econometric techniques to allow stronger causal inference. Another limitation is the sample, which is characterized by a high percentage of projects from the public sector. Future research could examine whether the findings hold in sample with more projects from the private sector. Finally, this study examined the moderating role of requirements risk but not of other potentially relevant factors such as geographic distance, project size and type, the client's agile culture, and the sourcing design (e.g. multi-sourcing [52], plural sourcing). This remains future research.

# References

1. Keil, M., Rai, A., Liu, S.: How user risk and requirements risk moderate the effects of formal and informal control on the process performance of IT projects. Eur. J. Inf. Syst. **22**, 650–672 (2013)
2. Tripp, J.F., Riemenschneider, C., Thatcher, J.B.: Job satisfaction in agile development teams: agile development as work redesign. J. Assoc. Inf. Syst. **17**, 267 (2016)
3. Schwaber, K.: Agile Project Management with Scrum. Microsoft Press, Redmond (2004)
4. Beck, K.: Embracing change with extreme programming. Computer **32**, 70–77 (1999)
5. Dingsøyr, T., Nerur, S., Balijepally, V., Moe, N.B.: A decade of agile methodologies: towards explaining agile software development. J. Syst. Softw. **85**, 1213–1221 (2012)
6. Fitzgerald, B., Stol, K.-J.: Continuous software engineering: a roadmap and agenda. J. Syst. Softw. **123**, 176–189 (2017)
7. Maruping, L.M., Venkatesh, V., Agarwal, R.: A control theory perspective on agile methodology use and changing user requirements. Inf. Syst. Res. **20**, 377–399 (2009)
8. Serrador, P., Pinto, J.K.: Does agile work?—A quantitative analysis of agile project success. Int. J. Proj. Manag. **33**, 1040–1051 (2015)
9. Kude, T., Mithas, S., Schmidt, C.T., Heinzl, A.: How pair programming influences team performance: the role of backup behavior, shared mental models, and task novelty. Inf. Syst. Res. **30**, 1145–1163 (2019)
10. Recker, J., Holten, R., Hummel, M., Rosenkranz, C.: How agile practices impact customer responsiveness and development success: a field study. Proj. Manag. J. **48**, 99–121 (2017)
11. Vasilescu, B., Yu, Y., Wang, H., Devanbu, P., Filkov, V.: Quality and productivity outcomes relating to continuous integration in GitHub. Presented at the Proceedings of the 2015 10th Joint Meeting on Foundations of Software Engineering (2015)
12. Tripp, J.F., Armstrong, D.J.: Agile methodologies: organizational adoption motives, tailoring, and performance. J. Comput. Inf. Syst. **58**, 170–179 (2018)
13. Inayat, I., Salim, S.S., Marczak, S., Daneva, M., Shamshirband, S.: A systematic literature review on agile requirements engineering practices and challenges. Comput. Hum. Behav. **51**, 915–929 (2015)
14. Batra, D.: Modified agile practices for outsourced software projects. Commun. ACM **52**, 143–148 (2009)
15. Daneva, M., et al.: Agile requirements prioritization in large-scale outsourced system projects: an empirical study. J. Syst. Softw. **86**, 1333–1353 (2013)
16. Walz, D.B., Elam, J.J., Curtis, B.: Inside a software design team: knowledge acquisition, sharing, and integration. Commun. ACM **36**, 63–77 (1993)
17. Tiwana, A.: Beyond the black-box: knowledge overlaps in software outsourcing. IEEE Softw. **21**, 51–58 (2004)
18. Krancher, O., Dibbern, J.: Knowledge in software-maintenance outsourcing projects: beyond integration of business and technical knowledge. Presented at the 48th Hawaii International Conference on System Sciences (2015)
19. Krancher, O., Dibbern, J.: Learning software-maintenance tasks in offshoring projects: a cognitive-load perspective. In: Proceedings of the 33rd International Conference on Information Systems, pp. 1–18 (2012)
20. Krancher, O., Luther, P., Jost, M.: Key affordances of platform-as-a-service: self-organization and continuous feedback. J. Manag. Inf. Syst. **35**, 776–812 (2018)
21. Kogut, B., Zander, U.: What firms do? Coordination, identity, and learning. Organ. Sci. **7**, 502–518 (1996)
22. Dibbern, J., Winkler, J., Heinzl, A.: Explaining variations in client extra costs between software projects offshored to India. MIS Q. **32**, 333–366 (2008)

23. Williamson, O.E.: The economics of organization: the transaction cost approach. Am. J. Sociol. **87**, 548–577 (1981)
24. Humble, J., Farley, D.: Continuous Delivery: Reliable Software Releases through Build, Test, and Deployment Automation. Pearson Education, Boston (2010)
25. Fowler, M., Highsmith, J.: The agile manifesto. Softw. Dev. **9**, 28–35 (2001)
26. Cao, L., Ramesh, B.: Agile requirements engineering practices: an empirical study. IEEE Softw. **25**, 60–67 (2008)
27. Highsmith, J., Cockburn, A.: Agile software development: the business of innovation. Computer **34**, 120–127 (2001)
28. Cobb, C.G.: The Project Manager's Guide to Mastering Agile: Principles and Practices for an Adaptive Approach. Wiley, Hoboken (2015)
29. Lin, T., Hsu, J.S., Cheng, K., Wu, S.: Understanding the role of behavioural integration in ISD teams: an extension of transactive memory systems concept. Inf. Syst. J. **22**, 211–234 (2012)
30. Gopal, A., Gosain, S.: The role of organizational controls and boundary spanning in software development outsourcing: implications for project performance. Inf. Syst. Res. **21**, 1–23 (2010)
31. Wallace, L., Keil, M., Rai, A.: How software project risk affects project performance: an investigation of the dimensions of risk and an exploratory model. Decis. Sci. **35**, 289–321 (2004)
32. Krancher, O., Luther, P.: Software development in the cloud: exploring the affordances of platform-as-a-service. Presented at the 36rd International Conference on Information Systems (2015)
33. Dagnino, A., Smiley, K., Srikanth, H., Antón, A.I., Williams, L.A.: Experiences in applying agile software development practices in new product development. Presented at the IASTED Conference on Software Engineering and Applications (2004)
34. Espinosa, J.A., Nan, N., Carmel, E.: Temporal distance, communication patterns, and task performance in teams. J. Manag. Inf. Syst. **32**, 151–191 (2015)
35. Krancher, O., Dibbern, J., Meyer, P.: How social media-enabled communication awareness enhances project team performance. J. Assoc. Inf. Syst. **19**, 813–856 (2018)
36. Strode, D.E., Huff, S.L., Hope, B., Link, S.: Coordination in co-located agile software development projects. J. Syst. Softw. **85**, 1222–1238 (2012)
37. Drury, M., Conboy, K., Power, K.: Obstacles to decision making in agile software development teams. J. Syst. Softw. **85**, 1239–1254 (2012)
38. Grant, R.M.: Toward a knowledge-based theory of the firm. Strategy Manag. J. **17**, 109–122 (1996)
39. Podsakoff, P.M., MacKenzie, S.B., Lee, J.-Y., Podsakoff, N.P.: Common method biases in behavioral research: a critical review of the literature and recommended remedies. J. Appl. Psychol. **88**, 879–903 (2003)
40. MacKenzie, S.B., Podsakoff, P.M., Podsakoff, N.P.: Construct measurement and validation procedures in MIS and behavioral research: integrating new and existing techniques. MIS Q. **35**, 293–334 (2011)
41. Fornell, C., Larcker, D.F.: Evaluating structural equation models with unobservable variables and measurement error. J. Mark. Res. **18**, 39–50 (1981)
42. Straub, D., Boudreau, M.-C., Gefen, D.: Validation guidelines for IS positivist research. Commun. Assoc. Inf. Syst. **13**, 63 (2004)
43. Henseler, J., Ringle, C.M., Sarstedt, M.: A new criterion for assessing discriminant validity in variance-based structural equation modeling. J. Acad. Mark. Sci. **43**, 115–135 (2015)
44. Goodhue, D., Lewis, W., Thompson, R.: Research note-statistical power in analyzing interaction effects: questioning the advantage of PLS with product indicators. Inf. Syst. Res. **18**, 211–227 (2007)

45. Langfred, C.W.: Autonomy and performance in teams: The multilevel moderating effect of task interdependence. J. Manag. **31**, 513–529 (2005)
46. Dibbern, J., Chin, W.W., Kude, T.: The sourcing of software services: knowledge specificity and the role of trust. ACM SIGMIS Database **47**, 36–57 (2016)
47. Lee, G., Xia, W.: Toward agile: an integrated analysis of quantitative and qualitative field data on software development agility. MIS Q. **34**, 87–114 (2010)
48. Liu, S.: Effects of control on the performance of information systems projects: the moderating role of complexity risk. J. Oper. Manag. **36**, 46–62 (2015)
49. Krancher, O., Kotlarsky, J., Oshri, I., Dibbern, J.: How formal governance affects multisourcing success: a multi-level perspective. Presented at the Thirty Ninth International Conference on Information System (2018)
50. Stürmer, M., Krancher, O., Myrach, T.: When the exception becomes the norm: direct awards to IT vendors by the swiss public sector. Presented at the 10th International Conference on Theory and Practice of Electronic Governance (2017)
51. Dingsøyr, T., Falessi, D., Power, K.: Agile development at scale: the next frontier. IEEE Softw. **36**, 30–38 (2019)
52. Oshri, I., Dibbern, J., Kotlarsky, J., Krancher, O.: An information processing view on joint vendor performance in multi-sourcing: the role of the guardian. J. Manag. Inf. Syst. **36**, 1248–1283 (2019)

# On the Use of Design Thinking: A Survey of the Brazilian Agile Software Development Community

Matheus Prestes[1], Rafael Parizi[1,3](✉), Sabrina Marczak[1], and Tayana Conte[2]

[1] MunDDoS Research Group – School of Technology, Pontifícia Universidade do Rio Grande do Sul (PUCRS), Porto Alegre, Brazil
matheus.plautz@edu.pucrs.br, rafael.parizi@edu.pucrs.br,
sabrina.marczak@pucrs.br
[2] Instituto de Computação, Universidade Federal do Amazonas (UFAM), Manaus, Brazil
tayana@icomp.ufam.edu.br
[3] Instituto Federal de Educação, Ciência e Tecnologia Farroupilha (IFFAR), São Borja, Brazil

**Abstract.** Design Thinking (DT) has been chosen as an approach to support problem-solving by many software development companies. However, there are divergences between the professionals of these companies concerning which techniques are performed, which steps are followed, and the way to implement this approach, as it proposes itself, to be divergent to generate numerous alternatives and, also, convergent, to find a solution. For this reason, aiming to characterize how the software companies have been implemented DT, this paper presents the results of a survey answered by 127 professionals from the Brazilian software industry. The results report a variety of scenarios in which DT has been applied: more than ten different models (sets of steps) are followed by the professionals; more than 50 techniques have been used, mainly, for meeting the needs in the process, according to the context of use and based on previous experiences. We also present 29 computational tools that, according to the respondents, assist the execution of DT, in addition to the integration with agile methods, allowing them to generate ideas and solutions, to explore and understand the problem.

**Keywords:** Agile · Design Thinking · Industry professionals · Survey

## 1 Introduction

Design Thinking (DT) seeks to solve problems through design principles, exploring possible user needs and validating solution proposals through prototypes. It is used in software development to foster creativity and innovation in the generation of new features and products, as well as DT has been chosen as an approach to problem-solving by many software development companies [1,2].

V. Stray et al. (Eds.): XP 2020, LNBIP 383, pp. 73–86, 2020.
https://doi.org/10.1007/978-3-030-49392-9_5

By bringing the user needs to the center, DT also improves team communication and facilitates knowledge domain acquisition, which are well-known issues in software development [3]. Given its interactive and dynamic nature, DT is considered an easy-in integration and a way to boost agile development [4]. While the focus of DT is on the creation of various prototypes identify the better solution, Agile methods are concerned with uncertainties and risks at the beginning of the development process, seeking to develop software incrementally, delivering the product as soon as possible [5]. Using DT integrated with Agile methods fosters a better alignment of the expectations of both customers and developers. Also, this integration helps to gather the needs of customers in the early stages of software development, ensuring the usability of the software [6].

DT have a flexible structure according to the company's business logic [7]. Therefore, it is important to understand if there is a script to be followed when DT is applied to software development contexts like process model to be followed, techniques to support the model steps, tools, artifacts, and roles involved.

Literature contains gaps about how industry professionals have made use of DT in software development. Thus, we executed a survey to identify which models and techniques and tools the professionals are using, reasons for choosing DT, usage scenarios, and the benefits and difficulties of applying DT.

The main contributions of this papers are (i) discuss about the use of DT into software project, summarizing which techniques are most used, what models, phases, and steps are performed to understand the user's necessities and to create innovative software, and; (ii) know the integration of DT in agile methods by professionals in the Brazilian software development industry.

This paper is structured as follows: Sect. 2 shows earlier studies about Design Thinking and agile software development; Sect. 3 presents the methodology we conducted to achieve our goals, describing in details how we had performed the survey; Sect. 4 exposes the outcomes after the survey application and the results' discussion. Finally, in Sect. 5 we conclude our research showing future actions to gathering new and relevant results.

## 2    Earlier Studies on Agile and Design Thinking

DT is used to create innovative projects for human-centered design [8]. As a property of DT, we have a multidisciplinary strategy, with techniques and practices that can be applied to many types of project, as well as focused on satisfying the expectations of users of the product/service developed based on its structure [9]. Brown (2008) [8] also reports that DT fits the use of designers empathy to address what is technologically suitable and feasible when proposing a solution.

Considering the integration between Agile and DT, there is a vast literature in the field of Software Engineering, since DT allows the search for a solution oriented to meet the user's needs, while agile methods are strongly collaborative, focused on characteristics such as speed, simplicity, continuous and fast deliveries, frequent feedback collection and quick reaction to changes [10–17].

Rhinow and Meinel [18] present an empirical study to evaluate the integration of DT in large corporations with frameworks such as Lean and Scrum, consulting the expectations of project managers through 50 interviews. The results pointed that DT fosters teamwork associating value with deliveries and the continuous improvement of the process, aligned with the philosophy of Lean. In relation to development projects, managers realize that DT encourages the inclusion of visual representation of the need (prototype), the definition of a business model and a complete definition of the activities necessary to produce the appropriate solution (user story map).

Nedeltcheva and Shoikova [19] presented a study about DT combined with Scrum claiming that DT helps to understand what needs to be done, while Scrum gives autonomy to decide how to do it. They also argue that DT and Scrum are similar because both are iterative, requiring adopters to develop sufficient insights to recognize initial successes and failures through constant evaluation and adaptation. The study present a set of advantages of the integration of both methodologies, such as help to create products or services which meet the current user needs, and that organizations can reduce risks from the development achieving better results for their efforts.

Prasad et al. [16] attempted to answer how to apply DT practices to improve customer expectations in Agile process. They conducted 15 interviews with industry professionals from organizations in Sri-Lanka, resulting in a set of best practices, which were classified into five areas, such as (a) customer's real need identification; (b) transforming customer's real needs into pilot solutions, (c) visualizing the pilot solution for customer feedback; (d) idea generation for the pilot solution, and; (e) brainstorming. As a result of the research, they proposed a framework as a way to help organizations enhance customer satisfaction using design thinking practices in agile practices, involving activities that comprise the five major defined areas.

The study of Darrin and Devereux [5] discusses the impacts of the application of Agile and DT principles in systems development processes. Mapping Design Thinking, Agile Manifesto and System Engineering, the authors report that these approaches act to more actively incorporating the users in the whole product and process development, including some practical implications such as a better customer engagement with the team; the requirements releases would result as an iterative process; and the process in an iterative way provides the generation of multiple design and implementation options, supporting the agility and reducing risks and uncertainties.

Pereira and Russo [6] present a literature review to evaluate how DT is integrated with Agile methodologies, selecting 29 studies which report that the integration of these approaches is applied throughout the development cycle, being the Scrum the most commonly Agile method used. Also, the integration between Design Thinking and Agile has shown that the customers are satisfied with the products developed and their needs are fulfilled, as well as there is an improvement of usability, supporting the proper management of challenges or requirements discovering.

Our work reports a study that seeks to characterize how professionals in the software development community, based on Agile methods, use DT in their processes, presenting which techniques, models, phases, and steps are performed. Therefore, our research provides an overview of the use of DT, going beyond the works already presented in the literature.

# 3  Research Setting

Looking for answers to know how industry professionals have used Design Thinking, we developed a survey to seek a more in-depth understanding of the Brazilian software development community. The survey developed in this work is characterized as explanatory [20,21], seeking understanding of the phenomenon through the information collected.

In this section, we start presenting how we carried out the planning and design of the survey, proceeding with it's prior validation, and after we describe details of the execution. In Sect. 4 we show the outcomes gathered with our survey, discussing the findings.

## 3.1  Planning, Design and Prior Validation

We built this survey as a mechanism aimed at deepening the knowledge about the use of DT by the industry. We started to build the questionnaire containing 11 questions as a data collection instrument, using the Qualtrics[1] tool. Table 1 shows the questionnaire structure, where the respondents initially answer questions related to DT, such as DT methods, techniques, and tools (Block 1), and purposes, contexts, benefits and difficulties to using DT (Block 2). Finally, we questioned the professionals about their jobs, in order to draw a profile of the respondents (Block 3). The questions of the survey were created based on data gathered previously through a systematic literature mapping.

Before conducting the survey distribution to the defined target audience, we performed a prior validation process. Following the recommendations given by Kitchenham [22] about empirical research, a pilot test was performed for evaluate the consistency and correctness of our survey.

## 3.2  Execution

Following the survey's planning and design process, we defined the target audience, who should be professionals working with DT in the software development process. We define as a strategy to reach out to such professionals and to electronically distribute the questionnaire, the use of the professional-oriented social network, the *LinkedIn*[2].

In *LinkedIn* we apply filters to find the professionals who serve the target audience, according to the strings: *"design thinking" and "software" and "design thinking"*, filtering by Brazilian nationality.

---

[1] Available in: https://www.qualtrics.com.
[2] Available in: https://www.linkedin.com.

**Table 1.** Questionnaire structure

| # | Question | Type |
|---|---|---|
| **Block 1** | | |
| 1 | There are several process models, which abstract workspaces when using Design Thinking. Do you use any of these models as a reference in your activities? | Closed |
| 2 | Several techniques can be used to support the use of Design Thinking. What techniques do you usually use? | Closed |
| 3 | How do you usually decide which techniques to use? | Closed |
| 4 | On a scale of 0 (No difficulty) to 10 (Extreme difficulty), how difficult do you feel in deciding which techniques to use in a given situation? | Closed |
| 5 | Do you use any software (or computer system, as you prefer to call it) to support the use of Design Thinking techniques? | Closed |
| **Block 2** | | |
| 6 | For what purpose do you use Design Thinking in software development? | Closed |
| 7 | What are the common usage scenarios where you use Design Thinking? | Closed |
| 8 | In your experience of using DT in software development, what would you point out as benefits or positives brought about by adopting the approach? | Open |
| 9 | And what would be the difficulties or the negative points? | Open |
| **Block 3** | | |
| 10 | What is your experience, in years, using Design Thinking? | Closed |
| 11 | What is your current organizational role or function? | Open |

## 4   Results

The survey's period ranged from September 2019 to December 2019. During this time, the survey request was sent to 466 professionals, resulting in 149 participants, of which 127 answered the questionnaire until the end. The response rate was 31,97%. The "n" is variable because not all questions were required, so some may contain fewer answers. As shown in Table 1, we have divided the structure of the questionnaire into 3 blocks. To present the profile of the respondents, we first describe about the background information of them.

### 4.1   The Respondents' Profiles

Respondents were asked about their experience in years of using DT. Table 2 illustrates the professional's experience organized in absolute and percentage values. The largest number of respondents (60 respondents = 47,24%) reported having between 1 and 3 years of experience using DT. Considering those with more than 4 years of experience, we reach to 39 respondents (30,71%).

They were also asked about their position in organization. Most consider themselves a Agile Coach, with a total of 18 answers (14,17%), the second as a

**Table 2.** Years of experience

| Answer | n | (%) |
|---|---|---|
| Less than 1 | 28 | (22,05) |
| 1–3 | 60 | (47,24) |
| 4–7 | 32 | (25,20) |
| More than 7 | 7 | (05,51) |
| Total | 127 | 100% |

**Table 3.** Respondents' position in organization

| Position | n | (%) | Position | n | (%) |
|---|---|---|---|---|---|
| Agile Coach | 18 | (14,17) | Analist | 5 | (3,94) |
| UX/UI Designer | 17 | (13,39) | Engineer | 5 | (3,94) |
| Facilitator | 16 | (12,60) | Developer | 5 | (3,94) |
| Product Owner | 12 | (9,45) | Researcher | 1 | (0,79) |
| Expert | 10 | (7,87) | Other? | 30 | (23,62) |
| Consultant | 8 | (6,30) | Total | 127 | 100% |

UX/UI Designer (17 respondents = 13,39%), and in third place as a Facilitator (16 respondents = 12,60%), as shown in Table 3. Also, 30 respondents (23,62%) pointed out the option "Other". These subset of professionals includes positions such as Product Managers, Development Coordinators, and Process Analysts. This result shows how expressive it is to professionals' positions and the use of DT in software development.

After knowing the profile of the professionals who answered the survey, knowing their level of experience on the subject, and their use of DT in their activities, we did an individual analyze of each question presented in the questionnaire, starting with the questions about DT methods, techniques, and tools.

### 4.2   DT Models, Techniques, and Tools

Respondents were asked about which models they follow in the application of DT. Table 4 shows the results, and in this question, it was possible to choose more than one model, because we consider that more than one model can be used by an organization, even in the same project. The proposed models were extracted from the literature [23].

The four models that were chosen by more than 10% of respondents were: (i) Divergent and Convergent (93 respondents = 72,44%); (ii) Stanford d.school (72 respondents = 56,69%); (iii) Stanford d.School integrated with Hasso Plattner Institute (HPI) (58 respondents = 45,67%), and; (iv) Hasso Plattner Institute (HPI) (47 respondents = 37,01%). On the option "other", were mentioned the Stanford d.School model integrated with Convergence and Divergence; Double Diamond; Massachusetts Institute of Technology (MIT) approach; and a model created by the respondent's own company.

**Table 4.** Models used by the respondent's

| Model | n | (%) | Model | n | (%) |
|---|---|---|---|---|---|
| Divergent Convergent [24] | 93 | (72,44) | Meinel and Leifer [25] | 13 | (10,24) |
| Stanford d.School [26] | 72 | (56,69) | HCAW** [27] | 11 | (8,66) |
| Stanford d.School + HPI [28] | 58 | (45,67) | Diving board [29] | 10 | (7,87) |
| HPI* [30] | 47 | (37,01) | Sandino [31] | 8 | (6,30) |
| Brown [32] | 30 | (23,62) | Other | 6 | (4,72) |
| Nordstrom [33] | 22 | (17,32) | I don't know | 3 | (2,63) |
| IBM Model [34] | 19 | (14,96) | Total | 391 | |

\* Hasso Plattner Institute
\*\* Human Centered Agile Workflow

**Table 5.** 10 most chosen techniques

| Technique | n | (%) |
|---|---|---|
| Brainstorming | 119 | (88,15) |
| Personas | 118 | (87,41) |
| Empathy Maps | 97 | (71,85) |
| Costumer Journey Maps | 94 | (69,63) |
| Business Model Canvas (BMC) | 87 | (64,44) |
| Interview | 84 | (62,22) |
| Storytelling | 84 | (62,22) |
| User story | 83 | (61,48) |
| Observation | 81 | (60,00) |
| Storyboard | 81 | (60,00) |

We also asked what techniques are commonly used during DT application sessions. To do so, we presented 46 techniques that we brought from the literature and even allowed new techniques to be mentioned, if they existed. Table 5 presents the top 10 techniques most chosen by respondents, the three most selected being Brainstorming (119 respondents = 88,15%); Personas (118 respondents = 87,41%), and; Empathy Maps (97 respondents = 71,85%).

All 46 techniques that were made available to respondents in the survey were selected by at least two of them. In addition, 11 new techniques were suggested by the participants. Thus, there are a total of 59 different techniques that provide aid to the application of DT in software development, as well as shows that there is a great variation between the techniques.

In this way, considering this wide range of techniques, we questioned the reasons that lead the professional to choose a particular technique over others (Table 6). The respondents reported that the most determining reason for choosing a particular technique is that it fits their needs (109 respondents = 85,83%); they choose according to the context in which they are working (101 respondents

**Table 6.** Reasons for choosing techniques

| Reason of chosen | n | (%) |
| --- | --- | --- |
| When the technique fits my need | 109 | (85,83) |
| It depends a lot on the context I am going to use | 101 | (79,53) |
| Based on my previous experience | 99 | (77,95) |
| I choose the techniques according to the DT space/step, where each space/step has its own techniques | 82 | (64,57) |
| Recommendation by my company | 24 | (18,90) |
| By referral from a colleague | 22 | (17,32) |
| I already have my catalog of techniques that I always use | 19 | (14,96) |
| I usually need to study the techniques because I never know which one is best for the moment | 13 | (10,24) |
| Another reason? | 3 | (2,36) |

= 79,53%); they choose based on previous experience (99 answers = 77,95%); and the respondents choose the techniques according to DT space/step, where each space/step has its own techniques (82 answers = 64,57%).

Having known the reasons that lead to the choice of techniques, we had questioned how difficult it is to make this choice, to make this decision. We therefore asked what is the difficulty level for the choice, ranging from 0 (slightly difficult) to 10 (extremely difficult). The result obtained for this questions was an average of 4,55 difficulty of choosing the techniques, with a standard deviation of 2,23, which indicates that there is considerable variability in terms of difficulty of choice and it is considered that It is not an easy task to do.

And, to conclude the information on DT models, techniques, and technologies, we encouraged respondents about the computational tools that support the process. Respondents presented a set of 29 different tools that help their work and application of DT techniques for different activities. Table 7 shows the computational tool set. We can conclude that there is no specific software focused on DT and its tasks, since it is a methodology composed of different actions aimed at fostering creativity.

### 4.3 Purposes, Contexts, Benefits and Difficulties to Using DT

Here, our intention was to discover the reasons that led to the choice of adopting DT in the company's processes, in which contexts DT has been applied, the benefits of its use, and what makes application/use of DT a difficult task.

Initially, we questioned about the reasons that lead professionals to use DT. The three most selected answers were (i) to generate ideas and solutions (120 respondents = 94,49%); (ii) to explore and understand the problem (113 respondents = 88,98%), and; (iii) to create innovative ideas, and to reduce uncertainties (both with 89 respondents = 70,08%) (Table 8). This question was multiple

**Table 7.** Tools used by the respondents

| Tools | | |
|---|---|---|
| Marvel app | Build | Illustrator |
| Paint | Canvanizer | Photoshop |
| Evrybo | Google Sheets | SAPBuild |
| Xmind-Stakeholder map | Adobe XD | Smaply |
| Miro | Google presentation | Strategyzer |
| Whimsical | POP | Axure RP |
| Figma | Mindmeister | Touchpoint dashboard |
| Mural | Invision | Creately |
| Real Time | Hotjar | Circle |
| Muraly | Survey Monkey | |
| Total | 29 tools | |

**Table 8.** Purposes to use DT

| Purpose | n | (%) |
|---|---|---|
| To generate ideas and solutions | 120 | (94,49) |
| Explore and understand the problem | 113 | (88,98) |
| To create innovative ideas | 89 | (70,08) |
| To reduce uncertainties | 89 | (70,08) |
| Understand and specify requirements | 84 | (66,14) |
| Improve customer satisfaction | 75 | (59,06) |
| Bring the development team closer to the customer | 72 | (56,69) |
| Easy relationship with agile methods | 57 | (44,88) |
| Win user's empathy | 53 | (41,73) |
| Software Validation | 40 | (31,50) |
| To manage projects | 16 | (12,60) |
| For game development | 5 | (3,94) |
| Other? | 2 | (1,57) |
| Total | 815 | |

choice, i.e. the respondent could choose more than one answer, as DT can be applied for more than one reason (Table 8).

In addition to the purposes listed in the Table 8, DT has also been characterized for assisting agile methods, and as a mechanism for strategic planning, industrial problems, complex problems, adjustments, and process improvements.

We also explored in which scenarios DT is applied on software development. Table 9 shows the professionals understanding that DT is mostly used in multidisciplinary team scenarios (107 respondents = 84,25%); to create innovative

**Table 9.** Scenarios of use of DT

| Scenario | n | (%) |
|---|---|---|
| With multidisciplinary teams | 107 | (84,25) |
| Creation of innovative products/software | 94 | (74,02) |
| Used in partnership with Agile Methods (Lean, Scrum) | 92 | (72,44) |
| Create co-creation among project participants | 79 | (62,20) |
| Innovation as a whole, from the development process to software | 71 | (55,91) |
| Changes and improvements in software development | 51 | (40,16) |
| Within a daily/weekly software development process, accompanied by the entire team (from client to developer) | 39 | (30,71) |
| Other? | 6 | (4,72) |
| Total | 539 | |

products/software (94 respondents = 74,02%), and; used in partnership with Agile methods 92 respondents = 72,44%).

We asked the respondents about the benefits of adopting DT in their projects. They pointed out as a benefit that DT seeks to understand the users in detail and fosters creativity.

Their answers related to benefits for the users were:

- Keep the user at the center of the process without neglecting business needs;
- Greater empathy with the user;
- Focus on customer need;
- High user collaboration;
- Understanding customer pains;
- Closeness of the technical team with the customer;
- Reach endpoint user.

Finally, we asked about the difficulties faced by professionals to apply DT in their software projects. The following quotes were cited:

- Match project to time and scope;
- Adapting people to use methods;
- Detachment of solutions (contributors already come with the solution and not with a real understanding of the problem);
- Transform qualitative data into data valid for the corporate environment;
- In evolution projects with very defined scope (such as migration/ modernization), Design Thinking is not very applicable
- Projects with very defined architecture (with third party technologies or tools) also make it challenging to use DT because in these situations there is little room for innovation;
- Not always does the customer have the time to know the problem in-depth;
- Lack of experience driving the design.

## 4.4   Discussion

Based on the results of the survey, there is a variety to choose DT models to follow, the techniques to be used, the software that supports the activities. Also, it is important to consider that the respondents argued they have difficulties to choose some techniques to apply in DT sessions. This highlights the issue of DT being dynamic, allowing adaptations during the course of its development, considering the profile of the participants, with the needs of the client, and with the context of carrying out the techniques.

Other important point is to consider the integration between DT and Agile methods, since 92 of the respondents answered that in their organizations DT is used integrated with Agile, indicating that approximately 3/4 of the companies represented by the participants integrate both approaches (Table 9).

Regarding the benefits of using DT, we can identify that the user is defined as the center of attention, with the development team being responsible for meeting the needs of this user, showing that the industry understands that DT in software development is an user-centered approach.

In another scenario, DT carries with it difficulties inherent in the integration and collaboration of different professionals in a multidisciplinary way. This issue is clear when we analyze the difficulties in applying DT, such as match the project to time and scope; adapting people to use methods; not always does the customers have the time to know the problem in-depth, or they think they know what is the best solution previously, among others.

## 5   Concluding Remarks and Perspectives

This paper presents a survey to know about the use of DT in software development by industry professionals. As a result, 127 responses from professionals working in the Brazilian software development industry were registered, which allowed us to advance the literature in the field of software engineering.

The survey's answers show the experience of the professionals, their job profiles, how they use the techniques and methods of DT. We also discovered that the most used model is the Divergent Convergent method, as well as a wide range of techniques and computational tools, in addition to those previously presented in the literature. The results indicated too that 3/4 of the companies develop DT integrated with Agile methods, considering like the main proposals to use DT: to generate ideas and solutions; to explore and understand the problem, and; to create innovative ideas.

We presented in this article the main benefits of using DT, according to the participants, including keeping the user at the center of the process without neglecting business needs; greater empathy with the user; focus on customer needs, among others. On the other hand, we listed the difficulties for the application of Design Thinking, being the most important ones, according to the participants: (i) matching project to time and scope; and (ii) preparing people to use it.

Our work presents as limitations that we cannot generalize to the entire universe of software development since we conducted the survey only in the Brazilian scenario, and answers may only represent the respondent's view and not the whole organization of which they are part. Nevertheless, these limitations represent opportunities to replicate this survey in different countries. These replications would allow the community to build a more broad view of DT usage and its integration with agile methods.

Our future work is the creation of a mechanism to collaborate with the decision making in terms of which techniques to select when using DT, as well as deepening the survey in other communities and other countries besides Brazil.

**Acknowledgement.** This study was partially financed by the Coordenação de Aperfeiçoamento de Pessoal de Nível Superior - Brasil (CAPES) - Finance Code 001.

# References

1. Hehn, J., Uebernickel, F.: The use of design thinking for requirements engineering: an ongoing case study in the field of innovative software-intensive systems. In: Proceedings of International Requirements Engineering Conference (RE), pp. 400–405. IEEE (2018)
2. Kolko, J.: Design thinking comes of age (2015)
3. Hiremath, M., Sathiyam, V.: Fast train to DT: a practical guide to coach design thinking in software industry. In: Kotzé, P., Marsden, G., Lindgaard, G., Wesson, J., Winckler, M. (eds.) INTERACT 2013. LNCS, vol. 8119, pp. 780–787. Springer, Heidelberg (2013). https://doi.org/10.1007/978-3-642-40477-1_53
4. Liikkanen, A.L., Kilpiö, H., Svan, L., Hiltunen, M.: Lean UX: the next generation of user-centered agile development? In: Proceedings of the Nordic Conference on Human-Computer Interaction, pp. 1095–1100 (2014)
5. Darrin, M.A.G., Devereux, W.S.: The agile manifesto, design thinking and systems engineering. In: Proceedings of the International Systems Conference, Quebec, Canada, pp. 1–5. IEEE (2017)
6. Pereira, J., Russo, R.: Design thinking integrated in agile software development: a systematic literature review. Procedia Comput. Sci. **138**, 775–782 (2018). Proceedings of the International Conference on Health and Social Care Information Systems and Technologies
7. Brown, T., Katz, B.: Change by design. J. Prod. Innov. Manag. **28**(3), 381–383 (2011)
8. Brown, T.: Definitions of design thinking. Harv. Bus. Rev. **86**(6), 84 (2011)
9. Vianna, M.: Design Thinking: inovação em negócios. MJV Press, Rio de Janeiro (2012)
10. Sohaib, O., Solanki, H., Dhaliwa, N., Hussain, W., Asif, M.: Integrating design thinking into extreme programming. J. Ambient Intell. Humaniz. Comput. **10**(6), 2485–2492 (2018). https://doi.org/10.1007/s12652-018-0932-y
11. Jensen, M.B., Lozano, F., Steinert, M.: The origins of design thinking and the relevance in software innovations. In: Abrahamsson, P., Jedlitschka, A., Nguyen Duc, A., Felderer, M., Amasaki, S., Mikkonen, T. (eds.) PROFES 2016. LNCS, vol. 10027, pp. 675–678. Springer, Cham (2016). https://doi.org/10.1007/978-3-319-49094-6_54

12. Gurusamy, K., Srinivasaraghavan, N., Adikari, S.: An integrated framework for design thinking and agile methods for digital transformation. In: Marcus, A. (ed.) DUXU 2016. LNCS, vol. 9746, pp. 34–42. Springer, Cham (2016). https://doi.org/ 10.1007/978-3-319-40409-7_4
13. Nedeltcheva, G.N., Shoikova, E.: Coupling design thinking, user experience design and agile: towards cooperation framework. In: Proceedings of the International Conference on Big Data and Internet of Thing, pp. 225–229. ACM (2017)
14. Coutinho, E.F., Gomes, G.A.M., José, M.L.A.: Applying design thinking in disciplines of systems development. In: Proceedings of the Euro American Conference on Telematics and Information Systems, pp. 1–8. EATIS (2016)
15. De Souza, R.A.C., de Azevedo Cysneiros Filho, G.A., Batista, G.H.C.: A heuristic approach for supporting innovation in requirements engineering. In: Proceedings of the Iberoamerican Conference on Software Engineering, Lima, Peru, p. 674 (2015)
16. Prasad, W.R., Perera, G., Padmini, K.J., Bandara, H.D.: Adopting design thinking practices to satisfy customer expectations in agile practices: a case from Sri Lankan software development industry. In: Proceedings of the Moratuwa Engineering Research Conference, pp. 471–476. IEEE (2018)
17. Corral, L., Fronza, I.: Design thinking and agile practices for software engineering: an opportunity for innovation. In: Proceedings of the Annual SIG Conference on Information Technology Education. SIGITE 2018, New York, NY, USA. Association for Computing Machinery, pp. 26–31 (2018)
18. Rhinow, H., Meinel, C.: Design thinking: expectations from a management perspective, pp. 239–252. Springer, Cham (2014). https://doi.org/10.1007/978-3-319-01303-9_15
19. Nedeltcheva, G.N., Shoikova, E.: Coupling design thinking, user experience design and agile: towards cooperation framework. In: Proceedings of the International Conference on Big Data and Internet of Thing, BDIOT2017, New York, NY, USA. Association for Computing Machinery, pp. 225–229 (2017)
20. Pfleeger, S.L., Kitchenham, B.A.: Principles of survey research: part 1: turning lemons into lemonade. ACM SIGSOFT Softw. Eng. Notes **26**(6), 16–18 (2001)
21. Kasunic, M.: Designing an effective survey. Technical report, Carnegie-Mellon University Pittsburgh PA Software Engineering Institute (2005)
22. Kitchenham, B.A., et al.: Preliminary guidelines for empirical research in software engineering. IEEE Trans. Softw. Eng. **28**(8), 721–734 (2002)
23. Souza, A., Ferreira, B., Conte, T.: Aplicando design thinking em engenharia de software: um mapeamento sistemático. In: Proceedings of the Iberoamerican Conference on Software Engineering, Buenos Aires, Argentina (2017)
24. Adikari, S., McDonald, C., Campbell, J.: Reframed contexts: design thinking for agile user experience design. In: Marcus, A. (ed.) DUXU 2013. LNCS, vol. 8012, pp. 3–12. Springer, Heidelberg (2013). https://doi.org/10.1007/978-3-642-39229-0_1
25. Keighran, H., Adikari, S.: Developing high-performing teams: a design thinking led approach. In: Marcus, A. (ed.) DUXU 2016. LNCS, vol. 9746, pp. 53–64. Springer, Cham (2016). https://doi.org/10.1007/978-3-319-40409-7_6
26. Mutuku, L.N., Colaco, J.: Increasing Kenyan open data consumption: a design thinking approach. In: Proceedings of the International Conference on Theory and Practice of Electronic Governance, ICEGOV 2012, pp. 18–21. ACM New York (2012)
27. Glomann, L.: Introducing 'human-centered agile workflow' (HCAW) – an agile conception and development process model. In: Ahram, T., Falcão, C. (eds.) AHFE 2017. AISC, vol. 607, pp. 646–655. Springer, Cham (2018). https://doi.org/10. 1007/978-3-319-60492-3_61

28. Carell, A., Lauenroth, K., Platz, D.: Using design thinking for requirements engineering in the context of digitalization and digital transformation: a motivation and an experience report. The Essence of Software Engineering, pp. 107–120. Springer, Cham (2018). https://doi.org/10.1007/978-3-319-73897-0_7

29. Newman, P., Ferrario, M.A., Simm, W., Forshaw, S., Friday, A., Whittle, J.: The role of design thinking and physical prototyping in social software engineering. In: Proceedings of the IEEE International Conference on Software Engineering, vol. 2, pp. 487–496. IEEE/ACM (2015)

30. Berger, A.: Design thinking for search user interface design. In: Proceedings of the European Workshop on Human-Computer Interaction and Information Retrieval, pp. 1–4 (2011)

31. Sandino, D., Matey, L.M., Vélez, G.: Design thinking methodology for the design of interactive real-time applications. In: Marcus, A. (ed.) DUXU 2013. LNCS, vol. 8012, pp. 583–592. Springer, Heidelberg (2013). https://doi.org/10.1007/978-3-642-39229-0_62

32. El-Sharkawy, S., Schmid, K.: A Heuristic approach for supporting product innovation in requirements engineering: a controlled experiment. In: Berry, D., Franch, X. (eds.) REFSQ 2011. LNCS, vol. 6606, pp. 78–93. Springer, Heidelberg (2011). https://doi.org/10.1007/978-3-642-19858-8_10

33. de Paula, D.F.O., Araújo, C.C.: Pet empires: combining design thinking, lean startup and agile to learn from failure and develop a successful game in an undergraduate environment. In: Stephanidis, C. (ed.) HCI 2016. CCIS, vol. 617, pp. 30–34. Springer, Cham (2016). https://doi.org/10.1007/978-3-319-40548-3_5

34. Lucena, P., Braz, A., Chicoria, A., Tizzei, L.: IBM design thinking software development framework. In: Silva da Silva, T., Estácio, B., Kroll, J., Mantovani Fontana, R. (eds.) WBMA 2016. CCIS, vol. 680, pp. 98–109. Springer, Cham (2017). https://doi.org/10.1007/978-3-319-55907-0_9

# Characterising the Quality of Behaviour Driven Development Specifications

Leonard Peter Binamungu$^{(\boxtimes)}$, Suzanne M. Embury,
and Nikolaos Konstantinou

Department of Computer Science, The University of Manchester,
Oxford Road, Manchester M13 9PL, UK
{leonardpeter.binamungu,suzanne.m.embury,
nikolaos.konstantinou}@manchester.ac.uk

**Abstract.** Behaviour Driven Development (BDD) is an agile testing technique that enables software requirements to be specified as example interactions with the system, using structured natural language. While (in theory) being readable by non-technical stakeholders, the examples can also be executed against the code base to identify behaviours that are not yet correctly implemented. Writing good BDD suites, however, is challenging. A typical suite can contain hundreds of individual scenarios, that must correctly specify the system as a whole as well as individually. Despite much discussion amongst practitioners and in the blogosphere, as yet no formal definition of what makes for a high quality BDD suite has been given. To shed light on this, we surveyed BDD practitioners, asking for their opinions on the quality criteria that are important for BDD suites. We proposed, and asked for opinions on, four quality principles, and gave practitioners the option to add more principles of their own. This paper reports on the results of the survey, and presents an approach to defining BDD suite quality.

**Keywords:** Behaviour driven development · Test suite quality · Test suite quality assessment

## 1 Introduction

Behaviour Driven Development (BDD) [14] enables software requirements to be given as a collection of examples (usually referred to as *scenarios*) that use structured natural language to describe how users will interact with the System Under Test (SUT). A typical BDD suite can contain hundreds of individual scenarios [1], organised as several *feature* files. Listing 1 shows a sample scenario from a feature that specifies customer interactions with an ATM.

**Listing 1.** Sample scenario from an ATM feature

```
Given my account is in credit by $100
When I request withdrawal of $20
Then $20 is dispensed
And my balance is $80
```

© The Author(s) 2020
V. Stray et al. (Eds.): XP 2020, LNBIP 383, pp. 87–102, 2020.
https://doi.org/10.1007/978-3-030-49392-9_6

Despite their natural language form, BDD scenarios can be linked to the SUT through *glue code*, allowing them to be executed. This turns the specification into a living document, in which failing scenarios indicate features that are not yet fully or correctly implemented. The following is an example of Java glue code for the second step in the scenario in Listing 1:

```
@When("I request withdrawal of \$(\d+)$")
public void request_withdrawal_of(double amt) {
    account.withdraw(amt, teller);
}
```

The annotation for the method contains a regular expression that is matched against each scenario step as it is executed. When a method is found with a matching annotation, it is executed, with the values extracted from the capture groups passed as the parameter values. Literature has reported both the benefits of using BDD and the challenges that software teams face when using BDD (e.g. [1,13]).

BDD approaches fit well with other agile practices for requirements gathering and documentation, with BDD features mapping naturally to user stories and the individual scenarios mapping (though more loosely) to the conditions of satisfaction sometimes documented on user story cards as the confirmation element of the story. The fact that BDD scenarios are expressed using customer languages means that they can (in theory, at least) be read and understood by non-technical project stakeholders, and compared with their knowledge of the domain. BDD is thus typically characterised as a customer-facing form of testing, that can be undertaken from the earliest stages of the project, once the first user stories have been identified, and that delivers value right through development and (in a regression testing role) the operational lifetime of the software.

Writing a high quality BDD suite is important. BDD suites can quickly grow to include hundreds or even thousands of individual scenarios [1]. The suite must specify the correct behaviour as a whole, as well as through the individual scenarios. For the long term correctness and extensibility of the system, it is important that the BDD suite be written to a high standard. BDD suite quality has been heavily discussed amongst practitioners and in the blogosphere, and is beginning to be considered by the software engineering research community [15–17] but no formal notion of BDD suite quality has been given that can assess individual scenarios and their relation to the rest of the suite.

In this paper, we present the results of a survey of BDD practitioners' views about BDD suite quality. To give structure and precision to the results, we proposed four principles of BDD suite quality, and asked respondents to give their level of agreement with them. We also asked respondents to describe additional quality principles that they thought were important, and that weren't covered by the proposed principles. All the four principles received support, with at least 75% of respondents voting in support of each one, though all of them also received a number of dissenting votes. Respondents also stressed the importance of writing scenarios in way that promotes reuse within BDD, but put most emphasis on readability and clarity of the resulting specification.

This paper makes three contributions:

1. **BDD Suite Quality Principles:** We propose four principles describing features expected of a high quality BDD specification.
2. **Practitioner Support for the BDD Suite Quality Principles:** We report the results of a survey of practitioner support for the BDD suite quality principles.
3. **Other BDD Suite Quality Aspects:** We report about other quality aspects of BDD suites, from which further quality principles can be developed.

The rest of the paper is structured as follows: Sect. 2 surveys related work on test suite quality; Sect. 3 presents the approach we used to obtain quality principles, and the quality principles themselves; Sect. 4 presents practitioners' opinions about the proposed principles; and Sect. 5 concludes the paper and highlights future research directions.

## 2   Related Work

In this section, we first explore how quality is characterised in automated test suites more generally, to see whether these notions of quality can inform the definition of quality for BDD. After that, we review the literature on BDD quality specifically.

**Assessing the quality of tests and requirements:** Tengeri et al. [21] devised a method for test suite improvement based on test coverage proportions. To use the method, an improvement goal is first set (e.g removing duplicate test cases, improving coverage of some parts of code, etc.). Then a granularity of focus is chosen–coarse (e.g. functional level) or fine (e.g. statement level). Various metrics are then computed based on coverage data gathered during test execution, which are then used to inform the process of updating tests and code.

Palomba et al. [18] found that test cohesion and test coupling are important criteria for increasing the quality of automatically generated test cases, and included these criteria in their algorithm for search-based test case generation. Meszaros [12] defines test cohesion and coupling as follows. Test cohesion refers to the simplicity of a test case–a highly cohesive test case should not be involved in the verification of a lot of functionality. Test coupling, on the other hand, measures the extent to which tests overlap with each other. To be easily maintainable, tests should have low cohesion and coupling. Improvement in quality of automatically generated test cases was observed when the two criteria were incorporated into an algorithm for automatic test case generation [7].

Daka et al. [5] used human judgement to develop a model for assessing the readability of unit tests, and then applied this model to generate readable unit tests. Crowdsourcing was used to rate the readability of tests on a five point scale. After that, 24 structural, complexity, and code density unit test features were selected and used to build the model. When compared with the crowdsourced readability results, the model was found to be in agreement by 89%.

Moreover, using the model to augment automatic generation of unit tests, it was found that more readable unit tests were generated, and the speed at which humans could answer questions about maintenance increased by 14% without losing accuracy.

There have been a small number of attempts to assess the quality of natural language tests and requirements through the notion of *smells*. Examples are the work of Hauptmann *et al.* [9] in which a set of smells in manual natural language tests was proposed, along with ways to detect them, and the work of Femmer *et al.* [6] in which nine smells in natural language requirements (and methods for their detection) were proposed.

**Assessing the quality of BDD suites:** Cochran *et al.* proposed a tool to detect smells in BDD suites [4]. Their work is similar to ours in a sense that it is also about the quality of BDD feature suites. However, the tool does not provide a mechanism to assess the quality of a scenario with respect to all other scenarios in a feature suite.

To the best of our knowledge, the work of Oliveira *et al.* [15–17] is the only published work that focuses on quality in BDD specifications. Specifically, Oliveira *et al.* suggested that a good BDD scenario should be *essential, focused, singular, clear, complete, unique, ubiquitous,* and *integrous* [15–17]. However, these attributes define, in general terms, the characteristics expected of a good scenario, but are not precise enough to facilitate the assessment of the quality of one scenario in relation to all other scenarios in a suite.

## 3    BDD Suite Quality Principles

In this section, we first present the process used to produce the principles, and then we describe the four principles in their general form.

### 3.1    Aspects of Quality in BDD Specifications

To understand what constitutes good quality in BDD suites, we first searched the scientific literature for attempts to define quality in BDD specifications. This gave us only the work of Oliveira *et al.* which suggested that good BDD scenarios should be *essential, focused, singular, clear, complete, unique, ubiquitous,* and *integrous* [15–17]. However, these attributes define, in more general terms, the characteristics expected of a good scenario, but are not precise enough to facilitate the assessment of the quality of one scenario in relation to all other scenarios in a suite. Thus, BDD quality facets in the literature have focused on quality at the scenario level, when the present work is interested in quality at the suite level.

To obtain attributes that are suitable for assessing the quality of a scenario relative to all other scenarios across a feature suite, we borrowed ideas from the quality attributes in the work of Oliveira *et al.* [17] and complemented these ideas with other practitioners' opinions on quality in BDD feature suites. To obtain practitioners' opinions on quality in BDD feature suites, we analysed articles from the BDD Addict Newsletter [20], a monthly online newsletter about BDD, which publishes articles about various aspects of BDD from the perspective of BDD practitioners. Articles from 32 issues of the newsletter (from February 2016, when the first issue was released, to December 2018) were analysed for quality facets in BDD suites. We then searched StackOverflow[1] and StackExchange[2] for any additional BDD quality facets that might not have been covered in the BDD Addict Newsletter.

Table 1 summarises the quality facets we obtained from both scientific and grey literature. Some of these quality facets focus on the step level, others focus on the scenario level, and still others focus on the suite level.

**Table 1.** BDD quality aspects from scientific and grey literature

| S/n | Quality Aspect |
|---|---|
| 1 | A good quality scenario should be concise, testable, understandable, unambiguous, complete, and valuable |
| 2 | Reuse of steps across scenarios can improve suite quality |
| 3 | Declarative (high level) steps are preferred to imperative (low level) steps |
| 4 | Business terminology should be consistently used across the specification |
| 5 | Scenarios should focus on the benefit they offer to users, if implemented |
| 6 | Scenarios should use the terminology understood by all project stakeholders |
| 7 | Each scenario should test one thing |
| 8 | Scenario titles should be clear |
| 9 | Scenario descriptions should be focused |
| 10 | Personal pronoun "I" should be avoided in steps |
| 11 | Too obvious and obsolete scenarios should be avoided in the suite |
| 12 | Scenario outlines should be used sparingly |
| 13 | Scenarios should clearly separate Given, When and Then steps |
| 14 | Use past tense for contexts (Given), present tense for events (When), and "should" for outcomes (Then) |

The review of both scientific and grey literature resulted in a useful set of quality notions for general use, but none of them were sufficiently precise to allow, for example, a tool to be created to find violations or propose improvements. We selected 4 of these notions for further analysis, based on their potential to be precisely defined, and created from them four hypothesised principles to be tested against community opinion. These principles are presented in the next four subsections.

---

[1] https://stackoverflow.com/.
[2] https://stackexchange.com/.

## 3.2  Principle of Conservation of Steps

A BDD scenario consists of a sequence of steps, as illustrated in the simple bank-
ing example in Listing 1. The Conservation of Steps principle seeks to maximise
the use of existing step phrases across the suite, and tries to avoid having too
many step phrases that are used only in one or two scenarios. To illustrate this
idea, suppose we need to write a scenario for when the bank customer tries to
withdraw more money than is in their account; this principle suggests we should
reuse the step phrases from the existing scenarios rather than inventing new
ways of phrasing the same idea (e.g. "my account is in credit by $10" rather
than "my account balance is $10").

This principle is based on the rationale that the steps in a BDD suite form a
vocabulary for talking about the functionality of the system. The `Given` and `Then`
steps describe different aspects of the system state, while the `When` steps describe
all the state-changing actions the completed system should be able to take. If
the same functionality can be expressed using a smaller number of steps, that
should reduce the comprehension effort needed to understand the whole suite,
as well as reducing the chance that duplicated or subtly inconsistent scenarios
will be added in future.

## 3.3  Principle of Conservation of Domain Vocabulary

Any organisational process that is supported by software will typically accrue
over its lifetime a set of terms or phrases describing the key ideas in the domain
of the process that are used by the people involved to communicate about and
advance the state of the work. The *Ubiquitous Language* agile practice requires
the software team to use the same terms wherever possible, in the artefacts that
describe and constitute the system [19]. This is also true within BDD suites.
For example, in the scenario in Listing 1, it would be desirable to use the term
"balance" whenever referring to the amount funds remaining in an account,
instead of inventing new phrases which might be synonymous to "balance".

With this in mind, the Principle of Conservation of Domain Vocabulary seeks
to maximise the value of each domain term or phrase that is used in the BDD
suite. Inevitably, in any human endeavour, duplicate terms may be used for the
same concept. But each additional term increases the cognitive load for readers
and writers of scenarios. We therefore consider a suite to be of high quality if it
can express the required semantics clearly with the minimum number of domain
terms and phrases.

## 3.4  Principle of Elimination of Technical Vocabulary

Since BDD scenarios in a suite are meant to be readable by all project stakeholders (including end users), the use of technical terms that, in most cases, only the
development team can understand, is discouraged. For instance, in the "When"
step of the scenario in Listing 1, use of the phrase "I click the button for with-
drawing $20" would reduce the chances of comprehension by some end users, as

well as imposing design choices onto the specification that may be non-optimal in the implemented system. As such, scenarios that use domain terms are generally preferred to scenarios that use technical terms. This principle, therefore, focuses on minimising the use of technical terms in the steps of BDD scenarios across the suite.

## 3.5  Principle of Conservation of Proper Abstraction

One challenging aspect in the creation of a BDD feature suite is to select an appropriate level of abstraction for the scenarios, and in particular for the steps. Higher level steps convey more semantics, so that scenarios can be expressed using fewer steps, and are often closer to the domain concepts that end users are familiar with. But they require more extensive glue code to be written, with more embedded assumptions, so that sometimes the meaning of the suite cannot be understood with precision without reference to the glue code. Lower level steps describe more fine-grained aspects of system state and state change. Scenarios using them will typically be longer, requiring more steps to express the same semantics than when using higher level steps. But lower level steps require smaller simpler glue code to implement them. Feature suites written using very low level steps can be too procedural, resembling traditional testing scripts, rather than end-user focused declarative examples.

In Listing 2 which shows a scenario that belongs to the same feature as that in Listing 1, the "Given" condition (which could be expressed as "my account is in credit by \$10") is broken into two lower level steps on lines 2 and 3. This introduces some inconsistency in the abstraction levels of steps in the two scenarios (the one in Listing 1 and the one in Listing 2), though both scenarios belong to the same feature. Such inconsistency could also manifest in scenarios across different features of the same BDD suite.

**Listing 2.** Scenario for unsuccessful withdrawal due to insufficient funds in the account

```
1        Scenario: Debit account unsuccessful
2        Given I have an account with the bank
3        And my balance is $10
4        When I request withdrawal of $100
5        Then nothing should be dispensed
6        And I should be told that I have insufficient funds
```

Intuitively, therefore, a BDD feature suite in which scenarios are written at a consistent level of abstraction will be easier to understand, extend and maintain. On the contrary, if the feature suite has a mix of scenarios expressed at a low level of abstraction and scenarios expressed at a higher level of abstraction, it can be difficult for a maintenance engineer to decide on the level of abstraction to use in expressing a new scenario. Moreover, there is likely to be duplication of steps and glue code, and the test harness code will also be at inconsistent levels of abstraction, adding to the comprehension and maintenance burden.

## 4   Community Support for the BDD Quality Principles

We used a survey with 9 questions to gather practitioners' opinions on the 4 principles. We wanted to discover whether the principles resonated with practitioners as meaningful facets of BDD suite quality, and to discover whether there were important quality facets we had overlooked.

### 4.1   Survey Design

The survey questions covered respondents' demographics, views on the four principles and opinions on quality aspects not covered by them. The questions on demographics were:

*Q1: Which of the following best describes your job?*
*Q2: What is the size of your organisation?*
*Q3: Which of the following best describes your experience of working with BDD?*
*Q4: What country are you based in?*

To mitigate the potential for bias and allow respondents to react in a natural way, the principles were not formally disclosed in the survey. Instead, we sought respondents' degree of agreement with informal statements of the principles. Thus, the next four questions, Q5 through Q8, are respectively informal statements for Conservation of Steps, Conservation of Domain Vocabulary, Elimination of Technical Vocabulary, and Conservation of Proper Abstraction.

*Q5: When adding new scenarios to a BDD suite, we should strive to reuse existing steps wherever that is possible without compromising readability of the scenario.*
*Q6: When writing the BDD scenarios for a particular domain, we should strive to make use of a minimal set of domain terms in our scenario steps. That is, we prefer to write steps that reuse domain terms already used in other steps, rather than introducing new terms, wherever that is possible without compromising readability of the scenario.*
*Q7: When adding new scenarios to a feature suite, we should prefer to use steps that are expressed using domain terms over steps that are expressed using more technical language, whenever we have a choice.*
*Q8: Within a feature suite, the abstraction levels of steps in one scenario should be largely consistent with the abstraction levels of steps in other scenarios in the suite.*

We then added a question for respondents to mention any other BDD suite quality facets that might not have been captured by the four principles:

*Q9: Please give us any other thoughts on how to keep scenarios and steps of a BDD specification readable, easy to extend, and maintainable.*

Questions 1 to 3 presented respondents with options to choose from, while question 4 was free text. Questions 5–8 asked respondents to indicate their degree of agreement, on a Likert scale, with each of the given statements. An "other" free text option allowed respondents to provide alternative responses or to qualify their degree of agreement. Question 8 was supplemented by 2 example scenarios, clarifying the meaning of "abstraction level". Question 9 allowed free text for respondents to freely describe additional quality aspects.

The survey was pretested on a BDD practitioner. It was deployed using SelectSurvey.NET on our university's servers, and ran for one month from December 2018.

## 4.2   Respondents and Their Demographics

We distributed the survey through a convenience sample using online discussion groups and personal emails. Although this approach to sampling limits the ability to generalise from the findings, convenience sampling is the recommended pragmatic alternative when probabilistic sampling is not possible [8]. The survey was posted to several Google Groups[3] and through an e-mail list of 500+ contributors to BDD projects in GitHub[4], supplemented by our personal industry contacts. Since we requested respondents to share the survey with other interested parties, some respondents might have been recruited through snowballing. Kochhar et al. [10] and Cito et al. [3] used similar methods to recruit survey respondents.

The survey was viewed by 129 people, of whom 56 submitted responses to the questions on BDD suite quality. Hereafter, all discussions of survey results refer to this subset of 56 respondents. We randomly assigned numbers to each respondent and refer to them as R1 to R56. The number of responses to questions on the four principles were: Conservation of Steps (55), Conservation of Domain Vocabulary (54), Elimination of Technical Vocabulary (55), and Conservation of Proper Abstraction (56). Question 9, which asked about quality aspects not covered by the principles, received 31 responses.

The distribution of respondent roles was: Developer (60.7%), Tester (12.5%), Consultant (7.1%), Chief Technology Officer (CTO) (5.4%), Researcher (3.6%), Business Analyst (1.8%), Other (7.1%), and did not say (1.8%). The sizes of respondent organisations were: 1–20 employees (26.8%), 21–99 employees (16.1%), 100–1000 employees (26.8%), more than 1000 employees (21.4%), all sizes (7.1%), did not mention (1.8%). Respondents' experience of working with BDD were: <1 year (7.1%), 1–5 years (28.6%), 6–10 years (51.8%), and >10 years (12.5%). Finally, the geographical distribution of respondents were: Europe (64.3%), North America (21.4%), Asia (5.4%), Zealandia (7.1%), and did not say (1.8%).

---

[3] Cucumber, Behaviour Driven Development, Specflow, Concordion, and Serenity BDD.

[4] The list was harvested through a process described elsewhere [1].

## 4.3  Survey Data Analysis

We first plotted the respondents' levels of agreement for each principle, and summarised other respondents' comments on each principle. Then, we used the thematic analysis guidelines by Braun and Clarke [2] to analyse the free text responses on other ways to keep BDD suites comprehensible, extensible and maintainable. In particular, we conducted *theoretical thematic analysis* [11], in which data analysis is guided by the research question; in our case, the question of interest was how to keep BDD specifications readable, extensible and maintainable.

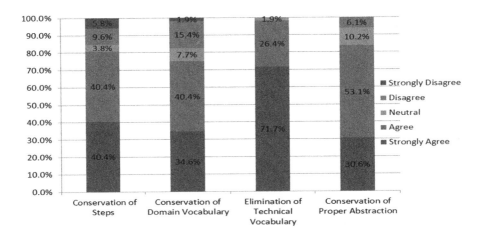

**Fig. 1.** Acceptability of each BDD quality principle by respondents

Data coding began after an initial pass through the responses. We coded everything in the text that related to readability, extensibility and comprehensibility of BDD specifications. We used open coding—we had no predetermined codes. After coding, we grouped related codes together to form the list of initial themes which we iteratively refined to produce the final list. Finally, we categorised the themes as actionable points either for all project stakeholders or for developers/QAs.

## 4.4  Survey Results

Figure 1 shows the respondents' degree of agreement with each principle. Each principle was accepted (strongly agree/agree) by at least 75% of the respondents who answered the question and clearly indicated their degree of agreement. Other comments on the principles were as follows.

– **Conservation of Steps:** steps should also be expressed in general terms; sometimes it can be a good idea to focus on writing clear steps that serve the purpose, and then fix the design later; the main focus should be on the readability, and reuse of steps can affect the readability and maintainability of the specification.

- **Conservation of Domain Vocabulary:** it should be possible to use new domain terms whenever necessary, provided that the specification remains readable to customers.
- **Elimination of Technical Vocabulary:** implementation words can sometimes be used, depending on the product owner and expected readers of the specification; sometimes, it can be challenging to translate domain words used in scenarios into implementation details.
- **Conservation of Proper Abstraction:** the abstraction levels should be determined by capturing correct requirements, and producing scenarios that are readable to customers; lower abstraction levels can be appropriate if scenarios carry data; sometimes, one can use different abstraction levels for Given, When, and Then steps.

Responses to question 9, requesting other opinions on facets of BDD quality, are summarised in Table 2 and Table 3.

### 4.5   Discussion and Threats to Validity

In general, the majority of the respondents supported the principles as acceptable descriptors of facets of BDD suite quality (see "Strongly Agree" and "Agree" responses in Fig. 1). The written comments stressed the importance of reuse within BDD, but put most emphasis on readability and clarity of the resulting specifications. For all the principles, the respondents who stated the reasons for dissenting mainly emphasised that decisions on reuse or use of steps, domain terms, implementation terms and abstraction levels should be determined by the specific contexts.

Moreover, even the other quality facets mentioned by the respondents (Table 2 and Table 3) resonate well with the quality principles we have proposed. For example, themes 3 and 5 in Table 2 respectively resonate with the Principle of Conservation of Domain Vocabulary and the Principle of Elimination of Technical Vocabulary; at the same time, theme 4 in Table 3 proposes keeping an inventory of all steps in a suite, which would be a facilitative environment for the implementation of the Principle of Conservation of Steps.

The threats to the validity of our results are the following:

- We mainly depended on practitioners with online presence, either through GitHub or other online forums where BDD and other agile topics are discussed. Thus, we might have missed some in-house practitioners that are not easily reachable through any of those means. To mitigate the effects of this, we requested those who completed or saw the survey to refer it to others. Also, we sent survey completion requests to some practitioners who were known in person to the authors, and requested them to share the survey to others.

**Table 2.** Other recommended practices for all project stakeholders on how to keep BDD specifications readable, easy to extend, and maintainable

| S/n | Theme | Frequency | Sample Excerpts |
|---|---|---|---|
| 1 | Specification should act as readable business documentation | 11 | - *"The key is to have a multi-layered approach; the gherkin scenarios should focus on being readable as business documentation..."* (R8, Consultant) |
| 2 | Clear description of business goals using examples | 5 | - *"Describe the business goal and the steps on how to achieve them as clearly as you understand at the moment."* (R4, Developer)<br>- *"Focus on clean specifications that are consistent within the bounded context"* (R6, IT Consultant) |
| 3 | Use of common domain concepts and terms across the specification | 5 | - *"...I like the idea of a glossary of terms from the Writing Great Specifications book..."* (R6, IT Consultant)<br>- *"Use the same domain language and terminology as the rest of your organisation/customers/industry"* (R26, Chief Technology Officer)<br>- *"...Have a glossary with important domain concepts, primary term and possible synonyms."* (R44, Principal Software Architect) |
| 4 | Focus on capturing comprehensive requirements for all project stakeholders | 5 | - *"BDD specification should satisfy both business analyst and developer as much as possible."* (R11, Developer)<br>- *"Everything around BDD and Specification by example is around creating a shared understanding. That is the core reason to do examples in the first place; the help us uncover hidden assumptions..."* (R18, BDD Coach) |
| 5 | Specification should be easy to understand based on general domain knowledge | 4 | - *"Test them on other people not involved in the project. Can they understand what they mean? Can they determine the intent of each scenario?..."* (R2, Consultant)<br>- *"Where possible, involve less technical stakeholders and team members in the process of scenario development..."* (R46, Developer) |
| 6 | Share specs with stakeholders for reference and correction, and perform regular maintenance of specs | 4 | - *"I believe the key would be to periodically revisit them and keep updated, if necessary rewrite or reword older ones. I find it very useful to also publish scenarios using ci tools somewhere so business people can read specs and spot inconsistencies"* (R47, Developer)<br>- *"At the very least, have the specs available for reference by the project stakeholders."* (R46, Developer)<br>- *"...Refactoring also applies to BDD scenarios..."* (R44, Principal Software Architect) |

**Table 3.** Other recommended practices for QAs and developers on how to keep BDD specifications readable, easy to extend, and maintainable

| S/n | Theme | Frequency | Sample Excerpts |
|-----|-------|-----------|-----------------|
| 1 | Write reusable and yet focused steps and step definitions | 11 | - "...the gherkin scenarios should focus on being readable as business documentation, and map to reusable steps in the step definitions. It is the DSL code in the step definitions where the real reusability benefits occur" (R8, Consultant)<br>- "It's best to re-use steps either by referring to them directly (Using Given, And...), or creating a new step definition using the underlying API, not calling one step definition from another" (R24, Software Engineer in Test) |
| 2 | Aim for more stateless scenarios | 4 | - "The scenarios should be stateless, in the sense that they should store as few data as possible." (R50, Developer) |
| 3 | Proper use and order of Given, When, and Then steps; and careful choice and use of framework-specific BDD features | 4 | - "Ensure that WHEN's only perform actions and THEM's only assert ( do not modify the SUT state ) and are expressed as such" (R43, Tester)<br>- "...Choose good titles (scenario/feature) 9) Don't send test data from feature file, (but examples of behavior are allowed)10) Less is More 11) Limit one feature per feature file. This makes it easy to find features. 12) Hide data in the automation 13) Steps order must be given/when/then - not other order'" (R25, Test Architect) |
| 4 | Miscellaneous: Keeping an inventory of all steps in a project; clear separation of customer-readable tests from glue code and the underlying API; and leveraging the full capabilities of underlying BDD framework and regular expressions | 3 | - "I'm not aware if this is already possible but it would be helpful to produce a dictionary of all the steps used in a project by extracting them from the feature suites." (R1, Developer)<br>- "The key is to have a multi-layered approach; the gherkin scenarios should focus on being readable as business documentation, and map to reusable steps in the step definitions. It is the DSL code in the step definitions where the real reusability benefits occur" (R8, Consultant)<br>- "Make full use of the underlying BDD framework / regular expressions and craft the step definitions like a powerful text-based API." (R33, Developer) |

- The four quality principles we propose were partly influenced by our choices of what to focus on in order to come up with an initial set of BDD suite quality principles for testing against community opinion (Sect. 3.1). To mitigate the effects of this, our choices of quality aspects to focus on were mainly informed by the quality facets from the state-of-the-art and the state-of-practice (Sect. 3.1). Moreover, all the principles were supported by majority of survey respondents from the BDD practitioner community (Fig. 1).

- Most of the respondents might have been using a particular BDD tool, so that our results could be valid for users of a specific BDD tool only. To cover practitioners using a variety of BDD tools, we followed the objective criteria mentioned in Sect. 4.2 to identify email addresses to which survey completion requests were sent. We also posted the survey in a general BDD forum, in anticipation that respondents from that forum might be using different tools.
- The use of convenience sampling (in our case, depending on self-selecting respondents within the groups we contacted) might limit the ability to generalise from the survey findings. To mitigate the effects of this, we survey 56 respondents from 5 continents across the world (Sect. 4.2), and some of the respondents were contributors to sizeable BDD projects in GitHub (Sect. 4.2). Still, our results may not generalise to all BDD practitioners across the world. For example, our results do not represent BDD practitioners who are not proficient in English.

## 5    Conclusions

BDD is currently used by industry teams to specify software requirements in a customer understandable language [1]. This produces a collection of examples that act as executable tests for checking the behaviour of the SUT against the specifications. However, large volumes of BDD suites can be hard to understand, maintain and extend. Duplication, for example, can be introduced by members joining the teams at different points in time.

We have proposed four principles for assessing the quality of BDD suites. Each principle was supported by at least 75% of the practitioners we surveyed. Practitioners also emphasised the importance of reuse within BDD, but stressed more on readability and clarity of the resulting specifications.

In the future, we will investigate the operationalisation of these principles, so that they can be used to assess the quality of BDD suites. Moreover, we will investigate the possibility of developing and evaluating more principles from other issues reported by practitioners (Table 1, Table 2, and Table 3). For example, we need a principle on "readability" of scenarios in a suite, a property that was rated highly by the survey respondents, and that probably trumps all over other quality principles. Respondents would prefer to keep the scenario that breaks our rules if it is the more readable one. This suggests a future work idea, looking for general metrics of text readability, to see if they can be applied to BDD suites. As well, we will investigate novel ways to help practitioners to manage steps, terms and abstraction levels of specifications. It might also be worthwhile investigating how the quality of BDD feature suites is related to the overall system quality, to inform software quality planning in organisations.

# References

1. Binamungu, L.P., Embury, S.M., Konstantinou, N.: Maintaining behaviour driven development specifications: challenges and opportunities. In: 2018 IEEE 25th International Conference on Software Analysis, Evolution and Reengineering (SANER), pp. 175–184. IEEE (2018)
2. Braun, V., Clarke, V.: Using thematic analysis in psychology. Qualitative Res. Psychol. **3**(2), 77–101 (2006)
3. Cito, J., Leitner, P., Fritz, T., Gall, H.C.: The making of cloud applications: an empirical study on software development for the cloud. In: Proceedings of the 2015 10th Joint Meeting on Foundations of Software Engineering, pp. 393–403. ACM (2015)
4. Cochran, R., Vaughn, C., Anderson, R., Patterson, J.: cuke_sniffer. https://github.com/r-cochran/cuke_sniffer (2012)
5. Daka, E., Campos, J., Fraser, G., Dorn, J., Weimer, W.: Modeling readability to improve unit tests. In: Proceedings of the 2015 10th Joint Meeting on Foundations of Software Engineering, pp. 107–118. ACM (2015)
6. Femmer, H., Fernández, D.M., Wagner, S., Eder, S.: Rapid quality assurance with requirements smells. J. Syst. Softw. **123**, 190–213 (2017)
7. Fraser, G., Arcuri, A.: Whole test suite generation. IEEE Trans. Softw. Eng. **39**(2), 276–291 (2012)
8. Fricker, R.D.: Sampling Methods for Online Surveys. The SAGE Handbook of Online Research Methods (2016)
9. Hauptmann, B., Junker, M., Eder, S., Heinemann, L., Vaas, R., Braun, P.: Hunting for smells in natural language tests. In: Proceedings of the 2013 International Conference on Software Engineering, pp. 1217–1220. IEEE Press (2013)
10. Kochhar, P.S., Xia, X., Lo, D., Li, S.: Practitioners' expectations on automated fault localization. In: Proceedings of the 25th International Symposium on Software Testing and Analysis, pp. 165–176. ACM (2016)
11. Maguire, M., Delahunt, B.: Doing a thematic analysis: a practical, step-by-step guide for learning and teaching scholars. AISHE-J All Ireland J. Teach. Learn. Higher Educ. **9**(3) (2017)
12. Meszaros, G.: xUnit Test Patterns: Refactoring Test Code. Pearson Education, London (2007)
13. Mishra, A.: Introduction to behavior-driven development. iOS Code Testing, pp. 317–327. Apress, Berkeley, CA (2017). https://doi.org/10.1007/978-1-4842-2689-6_10
14. North, D.: Introducing BDD. Better Software Magazine (2006)
15. Oliveira, G., Marczak, S.: On the empirical evaluation of BDD scenarios quality: preliminary findings of an empirical study. In: 2017 IEEE 25th International Requirements Engineering Conference Workshops (REW), pp. 299–302. IEEE (2017)
16. Oliveira, G., Marczak, S.: On the understanding of BDD scenarios quality: preliminary practitioners opinions. In: Kamsties, E., Horkoff, J., Dalpiaz, F. (eds.) Requirements Engineering: Foundation for Software Quality, vol. 10753, pp. 290–296. Springer, Cham (2018). https://doi.org/10.1007/978-3-319-77243-1_18
17. Oliveira, G., Marczak, S., Moralles, C.: How to evaluate BDD scenarios' quality? In: Proceedings of the XXXIII Brazilian Symposium on Software Engineering, pp. 481–490. ACM (2019)

18. Palomba, F., Panichella, A., Zaidman, A., Oliveto, R., De Lucia, A.: Automatic test case generation: what if test code quality matters? In: Proceedings of the 25th International Symposium on Software Testing and Analysis, pp. 130–141. ACM (2016)
19. Shore, J., et al.: The Art of Agile Development: Pragmatic Guide to Agile Software Development. O'Reilly Media Inc., Newton (2007)
20. Specsolutions. BDD addict newsletter (2020). Accessed 2 Feb 2020
21. Tengeri, D., Beszédes, Á., Gergely, T., Vidács, L., Havas, D., Gyimóthy, T.: Beyond code coverage–an approach for test suite assessment and improvement. In: 2015 IEEE Eighth International Conference on Software Testing, Verification and Validation Workshops (ICSTW), pp. 1–7. IEEE (2015)

# "I Don't Understand!": Toward a Model to Evaluate the Role of User Story Quality

Daniel Hallmann[1,2]([✉]) [ID]

[1] University of Bamberg, Bamberg, Germany
`daniel.hallmann@uni-bamberg.de`
[2] University of Applied Sciences Dresden, Dresden, Germany

**Abstract.** User stories are popular for conveying requirements in agile software projects. Despite existing quality criteria, authors make formal mistakes that result in "bad" user story quality. If developers have insufficient experience in balancing quality problems, the creation of a shared mental model is impossible, thus increasing the risk of impacts on the project's success. This article provides a work-in-progress research model to set these variables in relation and establish a systematic method to uncover answers regarding their correlation. Details on the effects support research in agile requirements engineering to gain a better understanding of cognitive processes in the comprehension of user stories. In addition, insights can help to develop design recommendations and AI tools to improve user stories. A first evaluation of the model provides promising insights into the behavior and forms a basis for future research.

**Keywords:** Agile software development · User story quality ·
Developer experience · Shared mental model · Project success

## 1 Introduction

In agile software projects, user stories are widely used to communicate requirements between authors such as a product owner—a business role in Scrum [4]—and developers. The short text documents specify a requirement in the form [title]—As [persona], I want [what] because [why]—[acceptance criteria]—[attachments] [4]. CCC (Card, Conversation, Confirmation) [10], INVEST (Independent, Negotiable, Valuable, Estimable, Small, Testable) [18] and Cohn's Guidelines [4] are quality criteria, but mistakes from authors pervade, which can result in "bad" user stories. These might be incorrect or missing form fields (e.g., [acceptance criteria]) [4]. Additionally, developers with different experience levels work together on projects according to their career and time in a team [2].

Developers attempt to build a mental model [5] of the implementation steps and necessary effort based on problems in user stories during an estimation session, such as planning poker [18]. Without sufficient knowledge to balance inadequate information, it is not surprising that developers become frustrated and respond with *"I don't understand!"*. These individual problems can prevent

V. Stray et al. (Eds.): XP 2020, LNBIP 383, pp. 103–112, 2020.
https://doi.org/10.1007/978-3-030-49392-9_7

the forming of a shared mental model [5] between the author and developers and increase the risk of impacts on project success, such as lengthy discussions or unnecessary work [2].

Empirical work provides analyses of user stories in estimation sessions to identify important factors for reasonable estimates of story sizes [9, 12]. Accordingly, groups generate better results than do single individuals, and sufficient experience is essential for estimating coarse-grained user stories. Within the empirical studies, the focus is on optimizing the estimates made by experts. However, the existing research lacks a cognitive psychological perspective on understanding the content—especially in the case of issues in user story quality—as a further factor for obtaining proper estimates. For example, it is currently unclear how variances in user story quality with varying levels of developer experience affect the understanding or shared mental model [5] between the author and developers. If there is no shared view, the question of the impact on project success arises, a research gap we address in this paper. As a starting point for our research, we therefore ask the following research question:

**RQ:** *What is the relationship between user story quality, developer experience, shared mental model between the author and developers, and project success?*

If we know details of the relationship, we can make statements regarding the effect of user story quality—and their "bad" and "good" variations—on human and project factors. We can close the gaps in agile requirements engineering research, especially in the introduction of user story comprehension as a level for evaluating the correctness of estimates. Subsequently, if we know the "bad" aspects, we can then create "good" aspects in design recommendations, thus helping authors in practice when they write user stories. In addition, it is conceivable to provide an intelligent AI tool support for the creation of user stories.

In this paper, we present a model to systematically create and evaluate the relationship. The structure of the model is based on the cognitive psychological perspective, which allows for the definition of latent constructs and their theoretical relationship. In addition, the paper presents our multi-method approach, which addresses the empirical data collection and evaluation of the model. The latent constructs are not directly measurable, so the methodological section includes a presentation of the measurable indicators. The initial evaluation results of the model subarea for user story quality appear promising. The structure of indicators can represent the structure in our data set, which allows for first steps in determining the correlation to the other constructs. However, the instrument is not currently error free, and the measurements can be inaccurate. The first analysis suggests that the low data size and differences in the indicator variances may cause the weakness. In the subsequent steps of the evaluation, we analyze the causes in greater detail to correct the inaccuracies. For this purpose, we will extend the test with additional user stories from other completed projects.

We subsequently present our model in Sect. 2, which describes the constructs and a priori assumptions of the relationship. Then, Sect. 3 provides details of the methods and indicators with which we organize our collection and analysis of the empirical data. Finally, in Sect. 4 we present our initial results of the preliminary evaluation, conclusions, and upcoming steps.

## 2   Research Model

We selected structural equation modeling [3] as the first approach to answer the research question and systematically determine the strength of the correlations between the research objects. This method is a well-known and widely used in psychology [3], social sciences [11], and information systems [19].

First, we extracted the four latent constructs user story quality, developer experience, shared mental model, and project success from the research question and built connections with hypotheses to form the basic structure. Each construct was then operationalized via four indicators to enable empirical data collection and evaluation. Figure 1 describes our model with constructs, hypotheses, and indicators. The following section presents details for the constructs and hypotheses. Details to the indicators are shown in the method Sect. 3.

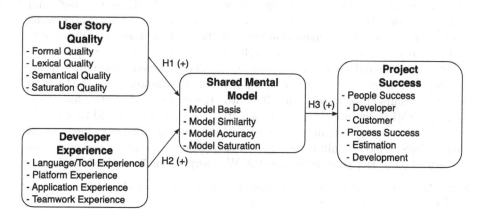

**Fig. 1.** Research model

**User Story Quality.** The quality aspect of a user story is a central construct given its essential role in the problem statement. It represents the goodness and badness of the content and structure, with a focus on pure text features. Sentences, words, and syllables provide the basis for formal and semantical dimensions of quality. The number of filled-in form fields and business domain keywords can help to determine the degree of quality. Our approach reflects the existing quality criteria from CCC, INVEST, and Cohn's Guidelines, especially regarding value generation and testability.

**Shared Mental Model.** This construct describes the knowledge structures of the team members regarding the actual experiences and abilities of the team [5]. This knowledge creates the prerequisite for the coordinated joint processing of a task in a particular situation. Agile methodology focuses on individuals, interactions, and collaboration [1] in addition to a joint understanding of user stories in teams [4]. This orientation on humans and coordinated teamwork helps in accomplishing goals quickly.

A user story should be negotiable [18] to support conversation [10] and make estimation possible [18]. The format and quality criteria of the user story addresses text and in-person interaction. It should support information extraction and communication to form an individual and then team approach [4]. Therefore, a "good" user story with high readability and updates can support individual comprehension and a discussion promoting a shared mental model. Thus, we posit the following:

**H1:** *The more that user story quality increases, the more shared is the mental model of the team members.*

**Developer Experience.** Project insights are significant for development [2], especially in agile projects, with a focus on individuals [1]. Developers should understand technical (e.g., programming languages, tools), business domain (e.g., applications, requirements), and team (e.g., skills, attitudes) properties to make the proper decisions during implementation. Details of existing application components (e.g., sign in, security) are mandatory to determine which must be involved in implementation ideas. If the existing source code cannot be reused, everyone should be aware of technologies to generate a new approach.

Studies of shared mental models [5] reveal that personal properties, such as experience, impact the creation of a proper shared understanding in the team. In addition, results in software teams [2] identify the importance of prior familiarity with application components to obtain a stronger shared team and task mental model. Simultaneously, agile approaches mention the importance of having sufficient technical and domain knowledge in estimation sessions to arrive at a group agreement on a user story estimate [15]. We therefore propose the following:

**H2:** *The more that developer experience increases, the more shared is the mental model of the team members.*

**Project Success.** The portion of the model that concerns project success covers economic aspects, with a focus on time and money [2]. It addresses the enhancements of projects in the light of people and process aspects. Therefore, developer experiences and requirements can positively influence the economic factors of a project. Triggers include sufficient developer experience and the fulfillment of requirements, such as user stories. All these aspects could save resources and must be supported.

Achieving a rapid understanding of a user story between all developers and a shared mental model with the author can support the motivation of developers and quick discussions in an estimation session. In addition, a shared understanding can increase appropriate implementation results later in a feature presentation and the satisfaction of an author and customer. The accepted feature without additional time for bug fixing also enables the direct development of additional software functions, which can have a positive effect on the performance and project schedule. Therefore, we posit the following:

**H3:** *The more shared the mental model of the team members, the more supported is the project success.*

## 3   Method

The methodological process to test the hypothesis and answer the research question begins with an ex-post analysis based on data from completed projects. It is common practice to conduct a preliminary study to gather initial findings, thus allowing for early model optimization [3]. Through exploratory factor analysis [3], we verify the consistency of indicators from subareas of the model. We began with existing user stories to evaluate the specification of user story quality, and our initial results are presented in Sect. 4. In addition, further improvements of indicators and an evaluation of the hypotheses are planned in two consecutive steps. First, we will perform a field study to gather new data from ongoing projects; this step is essential to address the data collection for all indicators, which allows for testing the entire model and our hypothesis. Afterward, we conduct an experiment based on small student teams to obtain data in a controlled situation. The focus here is on the evaluation of corner cases to stress the model and consolidate the parameters and predictions. User story quality is measured via document analysis and shared mental model and project success through observing estimation sessions. Project success is captured through document analysis and observation during the development phase and customer review. Obtaining data for developer experience is planned as a two-step process. Developers first rank their experience in a team meeting, and we then measure experience by observing estimation sessions.

The indicators for measuring the constructs are created based on conference feedback [7], a literature review [8], two expert interview studies, and research group meetings. The focus during creation was on proper content saturation, test quality criteria, linear behavior, and the reuse of project indicators [3]. In addition, a simple structure and fast value collection are aspects of indicator design. The scale of all indicators is positive with low $(-)$ and high $(+)$ values that define the low and high representation of the constructs. Details of each indicator and their specific scale and range are provided in the following section.

**User Story Quality.** *Formal quality* consists of the number of filled-in form fields (e.g., [title]) needed to identify a fulfillment status based on the story format [4]. A story should contain a set of information to maintain the promise for conversation. The scale is ordinal, with values of $0, 1, \ldots, 6$. *Lexical quality* is based on text properties, such as sentences and words, to compute the readability as a number [6]. It addresses the complexity of the lexical structure in which information is encoded that must be decoded by developers. The scale is rational, ranging from 0 to 100. Next, *semantical quality* measures the percentage of business keywords (e.g., VAT) versus the total number of words to indicate the strength of the value focus for the customer [18]. It highlights semantic details that developers must decipher to identify the concepts. The scale is rational, ranging from 0% to 100%. Finally, *saturation quality* focuses on the number of changes in form fields (e.g., [what]) prior to implementation. It covers a saturation status because documents must be refined to increase their benefit as an information source [4]. The scale is rational, ranging from 0 to greater than 20.

**Developer Experience.** *Language and tool experience* addresses the average language (e.g., Java) and tool (e.g., editors) experience in time of the team [2]. Developers must be familiar with feature sets and limitations to design feasible implementation approaches. The scale is rational, ranging from 0 to greater than 6 years. *Platform experience* focuses on the infrastructure (e.g., database) experience necessary to manage components essential for the application to run [2]. The scale is rational, ranging from 0 to greater than 6 years. Next, *application experience* covers knowledge of the application components involved in the estimation process [2]. The team must implement the story content in the existing source code, and therefore, changes must be evaluated to provide a correct estimation. The scale is rational, ranging from 0 to greater than 6 years. Finally, *teamwork experience* covers the time that colleagues have worked in teams to gain thorough collaboration and communication social experience [1]. The scale is rational, ranging from 0 to greater than 6 years.

**Shared Mental Model.** *Model basis* describes the percentage of developers in the estimation session versus the total number of people on the team. A shared model is possible when many developers are part of a user story discussion to acquire similar information. The scale is rational, ranging from 0% to 100%. *Model similarity* represents the percentage of developers versus the total number of people in the session, in which the estimate is equal to the final estimation result. The indicator adapts approaches from a similarity rating [13] to evaluate the team agreement to the story point value at the end of an estimation. The scale is rational, ranging from 0% to 100%. Next, *model accuracy* focuses on the number of form fields mentioned during the process. It measures the model accuracy by providing the story details of the author to the developers. The scale is ordinal, with values of $0, 1, \ldots, 6$. Finally, *model saturation* [15] measures the number of questions asked by developers while discussing a story. Additional questions and answers can be helpful in refining ideas within the team. The scale is rational, ranging from 0 to greater than 20.

**Project Success.** *People success (developer)* is defined to measure the percentage of developers versus the total number of people in the estimation who are indicating happiness (e.g., through utterances) [17]. It addresses developers who can build a mental model [5]. The scale is rational, ranging from 0% to 100%. *People success (customer)* covers the percentage of accepted acceptance criteria versus the total number of criteria in a customer review. It reflects a satisfaction status [14] and includes the quality criteria that stories should be testable. The scale is rational, ranging from 0% to 100%. Next, *process success (estimation)* is the percentage of time that an estimation is lower than the highest duration for a story point value. It corresponds to quick discussions [15] and reflects quality criteria, in which stories should be negotiable. The scale is rational, ranging from 0% to 100%. Finally, *process success (development)* measures the percentage of time that the team spends less on the implementation than the highest amount for that story size. Time is calculated for the initial coding, functional issues and bugs [16]. The scale is rational, with a range from 0% to 100%.

## 4    Preliminary Evaluation and Conclusions

As we worked on this paper, we began with the ex-post analysis and conducted an exploratory factor analysis [3] of the model subarea for user story quality. Our data set consisted of 74 user stories from a completed agile software development project. The project from the German automotive sector was conducted from March 2013 to December 2015 with a Scrum team of eight developers, one product owner, and one Scrum master. We considered only fully developed user stories that progressed equally through all development steps. Thus, the user stories had the same prerequisites of increasing comparability.

Before performing the factor analysis, we reviewed preconditions to begin appropriately and obtain details to further interpret the results. We first prepared our data by eliminating eight outliers to mitigate incorrect results, so our final data set contained 66 user stories. In addition, we evaluated the sample size, which should be between 100 and 200, to obtain more accurate parameters [3]. As our data set is smaller than 100, some limitations may be present in the estimates. An overview of the indicator distributions and correlations is presented in Fig. 2. The results reveal a balanced distribution of semantical quality, a slight left shift distribution of lexical and saturation quality, and a slight right shift distribution of formal quality. Due to the small deviations, we can assume an acceptable normal distribution for all indicators. In addition, we analyze the multicollinearity of the indicators, as high correlations greater than 0.850 can cause problems in estimating parameters [3]. The indicator correlations are low, so we were unable to find multicollinearity.

Next, we tested the overall fit of the indicator specification for user story quality. The analysis resulted in a chi-square ($\chi^2$) statistic of 4.220 with two degrees of freedom. The p-value was 0.121 at a significance level of $p < 0.050$. This result demonstrates a sufficient overall fit of the model, with a p-value higher than the significance level. In detail, our model can represent the structure in our data set, as the theoretical model-implied indicator correlations are similar to the empirical correlations (see Fig. 2).

In addition, we evaluated the indicator loadings and reliabilities to obtain details regarding the internal consistency of our model. Recommendations of the test theory [3] define indicator loadings higher than 0.300, reliabilities higher than 0.600, and overall reliability with Cronbach's alpha between 0.800 and 0.900 to be a good fit. Table 1 displays our findings. Semantical quality achieves the best fit, with high loading and reliability. Lexical quality has a medium fit with a moderate loading and low reliability, and both formal quality and saturation

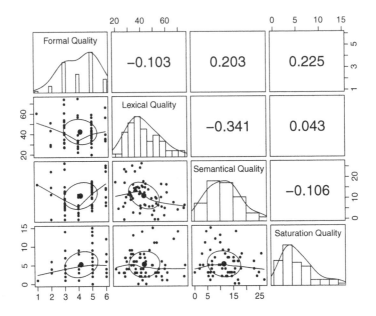

**Fig. 2.** Distributions and correlations of indicators

quality have a low fit, as they fall below the loading and reliability index. The low agreement with the internal consistency is also confirmed by the global test, as the indicators measure user story quality with a correctness of 0.350, or 35%.

**Table 1.** Descriptive statistics and loadings of indicators

| Indicator | Mean | Std. Dev.[a] | Ind. Loading[b] | Alpha $(\alpha)$[c] | Comp. Alpha $(\alpha)$[d] |
|---|---|---|---|---|---|
| Formal quality | 4.167 | 1.223 | 0.203 | 0.041 | 0.350 |
| Lexical quality | 42.280 | 12.345 | −0.342 | 0.117 | |
| Semantical quality | 11.347 | 6.397 | 0.997 | 0.995 | |
| Saturation quality | 5.258 | 3.479 | −0.106 | 0.011 | |

[a] Standard Deviation, [b] Indicator Loading, [c] Cronbach's Alpha, [d] Composite Cronbach's Alpha.

In summary, the overall fit suggests that our approach is promising in measuring user story quality with the formal, lexical, semantical, and saturation dimensions. Our indicators subsequently allow for a first evaluation of user story quality in interaction with other constructs (see Fig. 1). However, our instrument is not error free, as indicated by the different loadings and low reliabilities. The first cause for the weakness may be the low sample size and differences in the indicator variances. We will first verify these causes and then enhance the loadings and reliabilities to achieve better evaluation of user story quality in the further ex-post analysis steps. These optimizations helps obtaining details regarding the relationship between quality and human, and project factors, which assists agile requirements engineering research. Deeper insights also have benefits in practice. The identification of "good" criteria aids to prepare design recommendations and AI tools that support authors to write "good" stories.

**Acknowledgments.** Thanks to Dr. Schmid, Dr. Lüttgen, Dr. v. d. Weth, unknown reviewers, colleagues, friends, and my family for their great support.

# References

1. Beck, K., et al.: The agile manifesto (2001). http://www.agilemanifesto.org. Accessed 13 July 2017
2. Boehm, B., Clark, B., Horowitz, E., Westland, C., Madachy, R., Selby, R.: Cost models for future software life cycle processes: COCOMO 2.0. Ann. Softw. Eng. **1**(1), 57–94 (1995). https://doi.org/10.1007/BF02249046
3. Bühner, M.: Einführung in die Test- und Fragebogenkonstruktion. Pearson, München [u.a.] (2011)
4. Cohn, M.: User Stories Applied: For Agile Software Development. Addison-Wesley Professional, Reading (2004)
5. Converse, S., Cannon-Bowers, J. A., Salas, E.: Shared Mental Models in Expert Team Decision Making. Individ. and Gr. Decis. Mak.: Curr. Issues. 221–246 (1993)
6. Flesch, R.: A new readability Yardstick. J. Appl. Psychol. **32**(3), 221 (1948)
7. Hallmann, D., Schmid, U., Weth, von der, R.: Gemeinsame mentale Modelle in der agilen Softwareentwicklung: Ein Ansatz zur Erstellung von Gestaltungsempfehlungen für gute" erfahrungsspezifische User Stories. In: Informatik 2016. LNI, vol. P-259, pp. 1969–1974. GI (2016)
8. Hallmann, D.: The COCOMO-models in the light of the agile software development. Technical report no. 104/2018, Bamberger Beiträge zur Wirtschaftsinformatik und Angewandten Informatik, University of Bamberg (2018). https://doi.org/10.20378/irbo-53211
9. Haugen, N.C.: An empirical study of using planning poker for user story estimation. In: AGILE 2006, pp. 9–34. IEEE (2006). https://doi.org/10.1109/AGILE.2006.16
10. Jeffries, R.: Essential XP: Card, Conversation, Confirmation. https://ronjeffries.com/xprog/articles/expcardconversationconfirmation/. Accessed 7 Mar 2019
11. Kline, R.B.: Principles and Practice of Structural Equation Modeling. Guilford Publications, New York (2015)
12. Mahnic, V., Hovelja, T.: On using planning poker for estimating user stories. J. Syst. Softw. **85**(9), 2086–2095 (2012). https://doi.org/10.1016/j.jss.2012.04.005
13. Mohammed, S., Klimoski, R., Rentsch, J.R.: The measurement of team mental models: we have no shared schema. Organ. Res. Methods. **3**(2), 123–165 (2000). https://doi.org/10.1177/109442810032001
14. Motogna, M.: Customer satisfaction in IT professional services research. In: Vaduva, S., Fotea, I.S., Thomas, A.R. (eds.) Development, Growth and Finance of Organizations from an Eastern European Context, pp. 75–99. Springer, Cham (2017). https://doi.org/10.1007/978-3-319-54454-0_5
15. Raith, F., Richter, I., Lindermeier, R., Klinker, G.: Identification of inaccurate effort estimates in agile software development. In: APSEC 2013, pp. 67–72. IEEE (2013). https://doi.org/10.1109/APSEC.2013.114

16. Ramasubbu, N., Balan, R. K.: Overcoming the challenges in cost estimation for distributed software projects. In: ICSE 2012, pp. 91–101. IEEE (2012). https://doi.org/10.1109/ICSE.2012.6227203
17. Rodrigo, M. T., Baker, R. S.: Coarse-grained detection of student frustration in an introductory programming course. In: ICER 2009, pp. 75–79. ACM (2009). https://doi.org/10.1145/1584322.1584332
18. Wake, B.: INVEST in Good Stories, and SMART Tasks. http://xp123.com/articles/invest-in-good-stories-and-smart-tasks/. Accessed 30 Nov 2012
19. Zelazny, L. M., Belanger, F., Tegarden, D.: Toward a model of information system development success: perceptions of information systems development team members. In: ICIS 2012, pp. 1649–1669. AIS (2012)

# Large-Scale Agile

# Large-Scale Agile Transformation: A Case Study of Transforming Business, Development and Operations

Nils Brede Moe[✉] and Marius Mikalsen

SINTEF, Strindvegen 4, 7465 Trondheim, Norway
{nils.b.moe,maius.mikalsen}@sintef.no

**Abstract.** Today, product development organizations are adopting agile methods in units outside the software development unit, such as in sales, market, legal, operations working with the customer. This broader adoption of agile methods has been labeled large-scale agile transformation and is considered a particular type of organizational change, originating in the software development units. So far, there is little research-based advice on conducting such transformations. Aiming to contribute towards providing relevant research advice on large-scale agile transformation, we apply a research-based framework for evaluating organizational agility on a product development program in a maritime service provider organization. We found that doing a large-scale agile transformation involves many significant challenges, such as having a shared understanding of the problem, getting access to users, and getting commitment to change that needs to be done. In order to overcome such challenges, we discuss the need for a holistic and integrated approach to agile transformation involving all the units linked to software development.

**Keywords:** Large-scale agile transformation · Agile methods · Large-scale · Case study

## 1 Introduction

Software development teams are currently working on developing products providing new digitally enabled customer experiences - while simultaneously incubating and accelerating digital innovations - are facing increasingly complex problems to be solved. Part of the complexity is because solving such problems involves relying on several actors outside of the agile software development team [1, 2]. One example is close cooperation with the business development unit needed in order to achieve the potential advantages of a continuous business and development process [3]. Another example is the need for fast feedback from the customer, which in agile software development is realized by the introduction of frequent software releases to the customer or market. Further, a transformation to continuous delivery needs to consider units such as operations (i.e., the customer-facing side of the organization) and sales and marketing [4]. Agile software teams cooperating with other non-agile units represent a challenge [8], as agile software teams work highly iterative in a sense and respond manner. Other units may be more plan

V. Stray et al. (Eds.): XP 2020, LNBIP 383, pp. 115–131, 2020.
https://doi.org/10.1007/978-3-030-49392-9_8

and document-driven. The need for agile software development teams to interact with other units in the organization dynamically and responsively is why companies today aim to scale agile methods beyond software development. We understand such scaling as a large-scale agile transformation in the organization.

As agile methods scale and more units in the organization or entire organizations become agile, it is referred to as organizational agility. Overby et al. [5] define organizational agility as "the ability of firms to sense environmental change and respond appropriately," and show the different combinations of sensing and response capabilities that organizations should have. They argue that a company that is highly effective at sensing environmental change but is slow to act or acts inappropriately cannot be considered agile. Likewise, a firm that responds appropriately will not be agile if it is unable to sense the correct opportunities to follow. In an agile organization, therefore, if operations sense a change in customer behavior, software development must change the digital customer experience must change, and so must sales and marketing must change accordingly. Worley et al. [6] argue that "agility allows an organization to respond in a more timely, effective, and sustained way than its competitors when changing circumstances require it." Having the ability to make timely and effective and sustained change results in sustained high performance. Worley et al. (ibid.) introduce a framework to assess organizational agility based on the literature of organization design and flexible and agile organizations. The framework was validated with studies of performance data from 20 firms and interviews with executives. The framework explains routines, the features of these routines, and describes how agile organizations apply them. In order to grasp large-scale agile transformation, we will apply the framework. We chose that particular framework because it is based on organization studies theory and on findings from empirical studies (the framework is detailed in Table 1 in Sect. 2). However, as of yet, few other researchers have tested the framework. Motivated by the need for understanding how agile software development teams can interact with other units, how to do a large-scale agile transformation, and the need for research on frameworks for a large-scale agile transformation we ask the following research question:

**How is a Large-Scale Agile Transformation Done in Practice?**

In this paper, we examine large-scale agile transformation in the context of software product development. We understand an agile transformation as broadening the use of agile methods in an organization, that is, involving sales, marketing, development, and operations. The remainder of the paper is organized as follows: In Sect. 2, we present relevant literature on large-scale agile transformation and the agile organization framework we use for understanding such transformation. In Sect. 3, we describe our research method in detail. In Sect. 4, we present results from a case study using the framework. We discuss our findings in Sect. 5. Section 6 concludes and presents key findings from the study.

## 2  Background

In this section, we present existing research on large-scale agile transformation, identify a gap in the research, and suggest a framework for understanding such transformations.

## 2.1   The Challenges of Large-Scale Agile Transformation

Accelerating rates of technological change, shifting customer behavior, and changing business models and markets necessitate software development that is customer-centric, iterative, continuous, and experimental [1]. Organizations apply agile methods to these digital transformations in order to allow themselves to create, react to, embrace, and learn from change while enhancing customer value [7]. While agile methods have traditionally been practiced within software development teams, there is now a need for using agile methods for interaction between software teams and other non-development organizational units, such as markets, sales, and operations. In practice, this requires a close and continuous linkage between business units (market, sales, and operations) and software development units. The process of continuously assessing and improving this link is described as BizDev [3].

Dikert et al. [8] report that interaction with non-development units using agile methods is the second most challenging aspect of large-scale agile transformations. Challenges include adjusting to an incremental delivery pace, adjusting to product launch activities, and organizational reward models that do not encourage cross-unit collaboration. Working with agile methods across different units, therefore, involves handling an increasing number of actors, interface towards existing systems, and unexpected interdependencies [9]. For organizations with hierarchical and centralized decision-making structures, agile methods cause friction between management that work in traditional ways and agile units [10, 11].

## 2.2   Transforming Business, Development and Operations

From the above reported practical challenges with a broadening of the agile method towards including business and operation units, there is a need for a theoretical framework that is capable of explaining what is needed to scale agile to the wider organization. To that end, we have chosen to apply a research-based framework for assessing organizational agility [6]. The framework shows that Agile organizations ought to have a set of strategies, structures, and systems that drive them towards higher performance and business agility. Four routines of agility are key:

- Strategizing: How top management teams establish an aspirational purpose, develop a widely shared strategy, and manage the climate and commitment to execution
- Perceiving: The process of broadly, deeply, and continuously monitoring the environment to sense changes and rapidly communicate these perceptions to decision-makers who interpret and formulate appropriate responses.
- Testing: How the organization sets up, runs and learns from experiments.
- Implementing: How the organization maintains its ability and capacity to implement changes, both incremental and discontinuous, as well as its ability to verify the contribution of execution to performance.

The above routines for strategizing, perceiving, testing, and implementing have 14 dimensions, outlined in Table 1 below.

**Table 1.** The conceptual framework for evaluating organizational agility developed by Worley, Williams, and Lawler [6]

| Routine | Feature | Description |
|---|---|---|
| Strategizing | | How top management teams establish an aspirational *purpose*, develop a widely shared *strategy*, and manage the climate and commitment to *execution* |
| | Sense of shared purpose | The purpose or mission (outcomes other than profit or growth) is widely shared. Values embedded in these statements drive behavior on a daily basis |
| | Strategic intent | The current business strategy is relevant in today's market. It clearly distinguishes the firm from other companies and describes the business model (how we make money) but is flexible enough to change on short notice |
| | Change-friendly identity | There is a clear sense that "who we are" and "what inspires us" aligns with the organization's brand and reputation. This long-term strategy explains success and encourages the organization to change |
| Perceiving | | The process of broadly, deeply, and continuously monitoring the environment to *sense* changes and rapidly *communicate* these perceptions to decision makers who *interpret* and formulate appropriate responses |
| | Strong future focus | The organization possesses effective processes for exploring the future deeply |
| | Maximum surface area structure | The organization is structured in such a way that many people maintain direct and continuous contact with different parts of the business environment |
| | Vertical information sharing | Information from the environment gets to decision-makers rapidly, in an unfiltered way. Information flows easily, in both directions, between the bottom and top of the organization |
| | Transparent information | Business, financial, competitor, and organizational information is easily found and widely shared in the organization |
| Testing | | How the organization *sets up, runs, and learns from experiments* |
| | Flexible resource allocation systems | Capable resources (people, money, time, tools) are available and can be readily deployed to experiment with new ideas |

(*continued*)

**Table 1.** (*continued*)

| Routine | Feature | Description |
| --- | --- | --- |
| | Encourages innovation | Thinking of new ideas, new businesses, and new ways of working is encouraged in the organization |
| | Learning capability | Experience with running experiments is captured and applied with each new round so that the company's capabilities are continuously improved |
| Implementing | | How the organization maintains its *ability and capacity to implement changes*, both incremental and discontinuous, as well as its ability to *verify the contribution of execution* to performance |
| | Change capability | There is a pragmatic ability to change collective habits, practices, and perspectives. It is embedded in line operations, not isolated in staff groups |
| | Development orientation | A human resource strategy of building new skills, competencies, and knowledge is clearly articulated |
| | Flexible reward systems | Incentive systems in the organization—both monetary and nonmonetary—reward both effective performance and change |
| | Shared leadership | A philosophy that views everyone in the organization as a source of influence and expertise is carried from the top to the bottom |

Changing existing organizations is challenging. In some cases, it might be easier to create new adaptable organizations rather than to change an existing organization to be adaptable. However, all organizations have some agile features [12]. An alternative to creating a new organization, therefore, is to start an agile transformation in a part of the existing organizations that already have agile features, which software development units typically do have. The focus in the transformations should be on which features to address to increase agility and how to do it. A part of the organization can, for example, be everyone involved in the development of a product from team management, operation, software development, business, sales, legal, and marketing. In terms of how to do it, as different units are drawn together, it is important to allow for divergent views and opinions to be discussed to allow for transformation to occur. In the concept of "groan zone" [13], it is recognized that everyone has their frame of reference.

Moreover, when people misunderstand one another (which is likely when they all represent different units), they become more confused and impatient. Often, people do not want to be in the groan zone, because it is uncomfortable, but a facilitator can help. The facilitator's main objective in the Groan Zone is to help the group develop a shared framework of understanding.

## 3    Research Design and Method

In this paper, we report findings from a company that conducted a large-scale agile transformation in one of their product development areas (as suggested above [12]), transforming sales and marketing, software development and operations at the same time. Their product development area is our unit of study and allows us to study how multiple disciplines from multiple organizational units interact when creating a software-based product. Our study is a holistic case study [14]. According to Yin, case studies are the preferred research strategy when a "question is being asked about a contemporary set of events over which the investigator has little or no control" (ibid, p. 9). we followed the five-step process proposed by Yin: 1) Case study design 2) Preparation for data collection. 3) Collecting evidence: execution of data collection on the studied case. 4) Analysis of collected data and 5) Reporting.

We collected data through observations of the collaboration over time in meetings and workshops, through interviews, by studying documentation and by participating in the planning of the agile transformation. The Company (name suppressed for anonymity) is a multinational provider of services the energy, process, and maritime industries, and was chosen because it participated in a research program on large-scale agile software development. The organization had developed a digital solution for booking ship surveys through a web portal. The process in which the digital solution replaced was manually and very costly. Further, booking surveys were sub-optimized, resulting in ships doing surveys in harbors that were not cost-effective and that did not allow all work to be done at once. The potential cost savings from using the digital solution was estimated to be over 10 million Euro per year. The challenge, as we entered the case, was that not cost savings were not sufficient.

### 3.1    Data Collection and Analysis

Our data collection (Table 2) started in August 2018, when the company needed to rethink the whole product development process in order to reach the estimated earnings of the digital solution. The company recognized that a critical issue was that the missing interaction between software development, sales, marketing, and operations. The missing interaction and the need for improving the product led to a transformation initiative. The researchers participated in all planning meetings of the initiative, lead two of the workshops and had status and synchronization meetings with representatives from the company, and conducted several interviews with key stakeholders. Besides, four large international customers were visited and interviewed. These customer interviews covered the following topics: Describing the customer business process and model, understanding the survey ordering process, reflecting on the usability of the new technology introduced. All activities were documented by taking notes, meeting minutes, and pictures of materials produced in the workshops. Also, we got access to product documentation, contracts, data on user activity on the digital portal, and plans. We ended the data collection in September 2019. The results from the transformation were presented back to the practitioners involved regularly in feedback meetings. More details about the case, the product, and the large-scale agile transformation is found in the results.

**Table 2.** Data sources

| Data | Description |
|---|---|
| Interviews | 11 interviews. 1 business developer (2 times), 1 product manager (3 times), 1 development manager, and 1 portfolio manager. Interview with 4 major international customers |
| Planning meetings, workshops and feedback meetings | 2 workshops where conducted with stakeholders from all units. The results of the workshops were analyzed and presented back to the participants in feedback meetings. Additional data was collected from planning meetings |
| Documents and user behavior statistics | Analyzed user behavior (data gathered from the portal), strategic documents, roadmaps, innovation plans and contract templates |

We used a variety of strategies to analyze the material [15]. First, we described the project and context in a narrative to achieve an understanding of what was going on in the large-scale agile transformation project. Then, we described aspects of the transformation by using a framework for assessing organizational agility [6] and analyzing the different routines proposed by the framework (as introduced in Table 1). Further, we analyzed the data by mapping it to the continuous processes described by Fitzgerald et al. [3] (i.e., continuous planning, development, and operations) to understand which processes were disconnected. We hypothesized that the disconnected processes were a core reason for why the company did not realize the potential of the solution. Then we categorized the data according to the organizational agility framework [6]. In the analysis, we emphasized how the need for change was interpreted by different participants in the transformation.

## 4   Results

We first describe how the need for an agile transformation was detected (diagnosing phase), then we describe the outcome of the main activities in the transformation workshops and the work done after each workshop. Based on the results, we identified an understanding of how elements of a large-scale agile transformation are dealt with in practice.

### 4.1   Diagnosing

The new product was initiated in 2016, and the goal was to create a system for ship owners to book services for their ships through a portal instead of using the previous manual process. Booking through the portal makes it possible to suggest what combination of services to offer, and when the service should be conducted on a specific ship in a specific port. A system based on machine learning could potentially reduce the cost of surveyor traveling, reduce the total number of services needed, the need to offer services in expensive ports, and reduce the time a vessel needs to be in a port. Both the customers and the company could gain significant savings by replacing the manual booking process. The product development of the booking portal, which also included machine learning, went through several phases, from exploration, ideation to implementation. The work started in April 2016 by an analysis of the market, customer needs, and a concept study. A version of the product was tested in June 2017, and the product was launched in October 2017. Figure 1 shows the innovation journey as described by the company. All managers in the company got training in the innovation method. The planned functionality was implemented and launched, but the product did not meet its expectations. While the software development team implemented all the requested functionality, still only 30% of the customers followed the recommendation by the digital booking process.

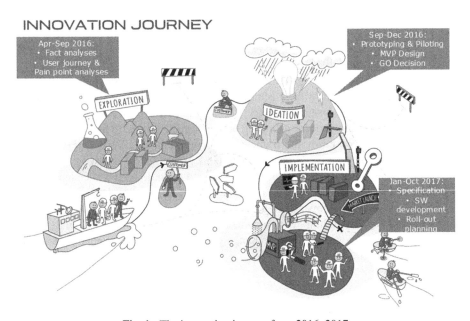

**Fig. 1.** The innovation journey from 2016–2017.

Further, the customers, in general, did not accept the recommendations provided by the planning part of the booking system. Recommendations were related to what services a ship should have, in which port the job should be done in, and when the service should happen. Further, there were many customer complaints regarding invoices. It became clear that there was confusion among some customers regarding the service ordered and the service provided by the company. Because most customers did not use the new booking process and, in general, did not accept the recommendations provided by the system, the cost savings were assessed to be very limited in August 2018.

A diagnosing workshop was initiated involving experts from software development and business and customer insight. The diagnosing workshop concluded that the lack of change in user behavior (such as lack of use) could not be explained by the design of the portal and challenges with the user interface alone. The workshop concluded on the following explanations on why the environed results were not achieved:

- The company lacked important information on how the customers actually conducted the former manual booking process.
- The overall company strategy was not aligned with the product strategy. While the new booking system required the company to offer services in limited ports, the company did not achieve a reduction in the number of ports where they had to offer services. Parts of the company still had wanted services to be provided in these ports, even if it was not cost-effective for the company as a whole.
- Internal processes were not coordinated to help the customer in changing his behaviour (e.g., contracts, support, customer contacts).

A transformation was initiated to make all involved units in the company work together to change how they offered the digital service and then change customer behavior. The maritime sector is an old and traditional sector, which makes changes in business processes in the sector slow. Further, this transformation would enable the company to sense the customer needs better, and then respond to the needs as they change. The agile transformation needed to include the following, different organizational units: software development, legal, market, sales, business, and operations. The software development department had been working in an agile way since 2008 and was experienced in using agile, while the other units were still working in a non-agile way. It was agreed to conduct several workshops involving key stakeholders from all the different units. The question was how to conduct workshops to accelerate a transformation that would enable a large part of the company to sense and respond?

Different stakeholders from very different units in the company would necessarily represent different cultures, practices, and ideas. The workshop then needed to facilitate a period of divergent thinking before they could enter the "groan zone". After a group of diverging ideas brainstormed a list, they found it challenging to discuss the ideas. Everyone had their frame of reference coming from the different units. Moreover, as people misunderstood each other, they become more confused and impatient. The researchers acted as facilitators in the workshops and helped guide the group through the groan zone.

## 4.2 Unfiltered Access to Customer Insight and Aligning Strategies

The first workshop had representatives from key internal stakeholders, such as customer insight, software development, and data analysis (analyzing the customer data), business, sales, and marketing. The highly cross-functional group had the authority to change the future direction of the technical solution and company internal processes. Each stakeholder was responsible for changes in their unit. The focus shifted from: "how do we provide a better user interface to change customer behavior," to "what changes do we need to implement in our organization to be able to change customer behavior." It became evident that to deliver an improved service in fewer ports, the company had to reduce the number of other ports in which the service was delivered. However, then some service stations around the world had to be closed down, and this needed top management support. Such significant changes created internal resistance, as a part of the organization would then need to reduce its service offerings and, as a consequence, would earn less money. Through workshops and meetings, the cross-functional group concluded:

- How certain parts of the sales unit operated where hindering part of the product development organization from meeting directly with the customer, which hindered a more in-depth customer insight. To better understand who uses the new system and those who do not use it, there was a need for direct contact between the software development department and the customers. Several of the previous decisions related to product development were made on wrong assumptions.
- For the company to adjust internally (e.g., stopping offering services in some ports), it was essential that cost and performance are measured on the company level and not per organizational unit. Since costs traditionally were measured per unit, each unit that will reduce their income will resist changes. There was a need to work closely with the world regions that needed to change their offerings of ports. New KPIs (key performance indicators) needed to be set for the whole company, not for individual units.
- Better understand the link between the new business model of the company and how the model is linked to a change in customer behavior. Involving the service planning unit in order to change future contracts was seen as a critical measure.
- Better use of statistics on user behavior in the portal. There is a need to continue analyzing patterns of various customer behavior, and to generate new Power BI Reports.
- Use Machine Learning in a new way to understand better which services to provide in which ports, and which services not to offer.

### 4.3 Testing, Implementing and New Improvement

Based on more unfiltered access to the customer, new parts of the organization got access to new and essential insights. The situation was further improved by organizing meetings with valuable customers and by insight from interviewing these customers. The interview guide was targeted to understand the enablers of barriers to changing customer behavior. As a result, more insights into customer behavior were generated, particularly on the internal business processes that happened before the customer used the portal i.e., the customers' internal planning process. Insight was also gained on what was most valuable when the customer made choices in the portal. Through the insight gained through the interview it was found why the customers did not accept recommendations from the new system. The customer behavior was driven by the need of making sure the ship was always operating, and therefore a familiar port is associated with less risk for the customer. One customer commented: *"The port predictions for container vessels are of no benefit because it does not propose ports I prefer."*

As a result, from the customer interview process, it was concluded that there was a need to understand how the booking system better could support customer preferences, and further insight was needed on how to enable the customer to order services in an unfamiliar port. Knowledge from the workshops and customer activities was fed into the survey planning centers of the company (the planning centers that were spread around the world were engaged in helping customers plan their work). Changes in how the planning centers operated based on new insight is an example of the operational units change the way they deliver the services.

## 4.4 Next Steps

After changing the software and how the company interacted with the customers, it became evident that the changes had helped to result in the company starting to improve earnings on the product and service they provided radically. However, at the same time, it was clear that the agile transformation now also needed to include more unites, and that it would be an ongoing process with no specific end state.

The company started testing new functionality, which started changing customer behavior. Further, from a more in-depth analysis of the interviews, the need to continue pushing the customers to change their behavior by developing new contracts was considered an essential next step. Involving contract responsibilities in this phase was vital, and the second workshop was conducted. However, it became clear that to get the full effect of new features in the system; there was a need to segregate customers into two segments and to identify the service levels for these segments. Creating customer segments also put forward demands for contracts that would support the segments and, at the same time, needed to enable the customer behavior change to continue. The need for what was known as "smart contracts" was agreed upon in the last workshop. However, what a smart contract looked like was not fully understood.

Further, new questions emerged: is the salesforce ready to sell new products and negotiate new contracts for new customer segments? Are the customers ready to be offered different levels of services based on different contracts (the maritime sector is an old and conservative business)? It became evident in the workshop that sales and legal unites needed to be linked closely with the product development, and that future work was needed in this area.

## 4.5 Evaluating of Organizational Agility Using the Agility Framework of Worley

The agility framework defined by Worley et al. guided our agile transformation. The framework includes routines for strategizing, perceiving, testing, and implementing and has 14 dimensions (Table 1). To describe how a large-scale agile transformation is done in practice, we then mapped our findings into the framework (Table 3).

**Table 3.** An evaluation of organizational agility using the agility framework of Worley, et al. [6]

| Routine | Feature | Results/improvements |
|---|---|---|
| Strategizing | Sense of shared purpose | Everyone was aware of the purpose of the program. To make the customer book in the portal and to make smart bookings. However, the units sub-optimized their performance by focusing on their own goals. The need to Involve all units and to align them from the beginning was not understood. It was not until the product was launched and experimented with, and the lack of earnings became clear, that the shared purpose was understood |
| | Strategic intent | The strategic intent of digitalizing and transforming a traditional sector (maritime) was not unique, however, the combination of applying machine learning, domain knowledge, and customer and vessel data were considered a new business strategy in the market. It became clear that the changes in customer behavior and technology also resulted in the need to change business models (such as sales) |
| | Change-friendly identity | The new product aligns with the company brands (removed because of the need for anonymity). There is a strong focus on innovation, and all managers have been through management courses. Pressure on cost due to increased competition leads to a continuous search for innovation through digitalization |
| Perceiving | Strong future focus | The company had a strong focus on digitalizing the maritime industry, and to use the market position and domain insights to do so. Having the willingness to launch such projects and to continue working with the clients on the challenges shows signs that they are working to explore the future by experimenting with new digital solutions and business models |
| | Maximum surface area structure | While it was evident that the part of the organization was missing direct contact with the customer, this changed throughout the transformation initiative. Throughout the change process, the key to success was unfiltered access to customers from the development side and to increase their ability to sense the need of the customer. Easy access to customers was particularly important since the customer did not always know what they wanted |
| | Vertical information sharing | It took a long time for the organization to change – over a year. We did not investigate this issue in particular, but the time it took to change can be considered as an indication that there is room for improved vertical information sharing |
| | Transparent information | The information was not accessible across units in the beginning. However, bringing key stakeholders from different units together in targeted workshops and focusing on collecting and presenting relevant and indicative data helps. The workshop also helped in removing misconceptions (such as reasons for a solution not being used) |

(*continued*)

**Table 3.** (*continued*)

| Routine | Feature | Results/improvements |
|---|---|---|
| Testing | Flexible resource allocation systems | The portal was easy to change, as it did not require much development capacity. However, there was a delay when new requests emerged, as development resources can only be dedicated to fixed periods. They had many other projects to attend. Further, because of people being busy, it took a long time to get all the people from different units to meet |
| | Encourages innovation | The innovation was partly bottom-up, in that suggestions and ideas could come from everyone. However, resistance emerged when new ideas challenge the existing business models and could disrupt the existing operations of the company |
| | Learning capability | They had constant feedback from experiments through MVP that could be launched fast to the customer. Further, there was a willingness to experiment with organizational development. Getting people together across units did not require extra funding |
| Implementing | Change capability | There was a low level of the hierarchy, and easy to get people from different units into the same room to discuss. Throughout the product development habits were changed; however, we did not research to what degree they spread to the next project |
| | Development orientation | We did not investigate the human resource strategy |
| | Flexible reward systems | We found that having a monetary reward system based on individual units as limiting the potential of the digital solution. The sales apparatus that was based in certain regions did not have sufficient incentives to push customers over to the digital solution, as this could limit their potential rewards |
| | Shared leadership | When there was identified a need to work across unites to change the organization and the product, it was not a problem to get access to the needed expertise. Moreover, the expertise had decision making authority, even though senior management needed to be informed |

## 5   Discussion

Large-scale agile transformation is a critical issue in responding to the digital transformations that are ongoing in many sectors [1]. Several barriers to such transformation seen from industry experience have been identified, for example, change resistance [8], and inter-team coordination challenges [16]. While conceptual solutions such as continuous development and BizDev has been suggested [3], there is a lack of research-based advice on how agile transformations are to be performed in practice. Driven by our research question – *How is a large-scale agile transformation done in practice?* - we have reported findings from a case study of a maritime service provider that aimed to transform service bookings digitally. In the following, we answer this research question by discussing our findings in light of a research-based framework on agile organizations [6].

We found how a typical innovation journey was followed, a product was developed and launched, but the economic gains did not meet expectations. Importantly, as a consequence, the company started investigating the reasons why the product did not meet its projected earnings. One critical insight during the diagnosing phase was that it was not the design of the digital solution per se that caused the lack of customer uptake. For the solution to have its envisioned effects, it would require a change in the internal organization to be able to change customer behavior. The company started a change in a product development environment that already had some agile features, i.e., including software development that was already using agile methods, as suggested by [12]. The change process was done in order to improve its capacity for sensing customer behavior and adapting the digital solutions. The software development and business development units needed more unfiltered access to customer behavior. This is in line with [5], who argue that both sensing and adapting is essential for organizational agility.

We analyzed the steps taken by the unit under study in light of a research-based framework on agile organizations [6]. We found how the part of the organization doing a large-scale organizational transformation addressed all four routines in the framework. The first routine, strategizing, involved struggles to get a sense of shared purpose across the organization, changing business model in terms of offering services in fewer ports, and being committed to change. The second routine, perceiving, involved being willing to experiment with new products, being able to change who gets access to customer insight and that bringing stakeholders together across different units is a critical activity in enabling change. The third routine, testing, we found that it was not changing the technical parts of the system that was the most challenging, but rather to being able to experiment with the organization and making the necessary changes. The fourth routine, implementing, we found that monetary rewards systems and involvement of expertise with decision-making authority were vital in making transformation occur. The challenges and steps taken are in line with Dikert et al. [8] findings that show how integrating non-development units can be restricted to reward models that do not encourage cross-unit collaboration.

Our findings indicate that some of the frictions agile methods can cause [7], such as when the new portal started changing the business model of the sales apparatus. Such frictions indicates that large-scale agile transformation needs new decision structures, which means that a company needs to move from a hierarchical decision structure, and isolated decision structures for each department or unit, to a decision structure across the operational and strategic level of individual units.

Finally, we found that an agile transformation is an ongoing process and that the output of an agile transformation is more continuous processes covering several units, many of which are outside software development. A critical insight is that continuous processes require continues learning and continuous experimentation [3]. Our mapping of findings from the case to the agility framework presented in Table 3 signifies the need for continuity.

## 5.1 Limitation and Future Research

The main limitations of our study are the single-case design and the possibility of bias in data collection and analysis. The fact that we used a single-case holistic design makes us more vulnerable to bias and eliminates the possibility of direct replication or the analysis of contrasting situations. Therefore, the general criticisms about single-case studies, such as uniqueness and special access to key informants, may also apply to our study. However, our rationale for choosing the company as our case was that it represents a critical case for explaining the challenges of conducting a large-scale agile transformation in practice. Our mode of generalization is analytical, i.e., we used a previously developed framework as a template with which we compared the empirical results of the case study, which is similar to Yin's [14] concept of Level Two inference.

Another possible limitation is that we based much of our data collection and analysis on semi-structured interviews [17]. The use of multiple data sources made it possible to find evidence for episodes and phenomena from more than one data source; we also observed, talked to, and interviewed the project members over a period of 13 months, which made it possible to study the phenomena from different viewpoints as they emerged and changed.

The results of this study point out several directions for future research. Firstly, our study highlights several challenges that must be met when conducting a large-scale agile transformation. Accordingly, further work should focus on identifying and addressing other problems that may arise when conducting an agile transformation. Secondly, the framework should be used for studying more mature organizations or departments in order to get a better understanding of the main challenges in such transformations. The observed transformation was the first in the company using the framework. When studying the company doing the next transformation on another product, this should be studied since the case then will be more mature, and other issues from using the framework will emerge.

## 6  Conclusion

We have conducted a 13-month study of professionals in a large-scale agile transformation. Our case study of conducting an agile transformation highlights several significant challenges that need to be overcome for a transformation to be successful. This work reports a case study of how a transformation can be done in practice, and also apply a framework for understanding and conducting such an agile transformation. This work is an essential step in its own right since there is much confusion around terms related to agile transformations, similar to early research on the agile transformation of teams [18]. The need for a framework for agile transformation outside of the software development unit is evident when one considers the emergence of phenomena such as Enterprise Agile, Beyond Budgeting, DevOps, Lean Startups, and many other concepts from business agility in general. These are all indicative of the need for a holistic and integrated approach across all the units linked to software development.

**Acknowledgement.** This research is funded by the Digital Class project and the Research council of Norway through grant 309631, and 2.0 which is partly supported by the Research council of Norway through grant 236759.

# References

1. Mikalsen, M., Moe, N.B., Stray, V., Nyrud, H.: Agile digital transformation: a case study of interdependencies (2018)
2. Berntzen, M., Moe, N.B., Stray, V.: The product owner in large-scale agile: an empirical study through the lens of relational coordination theory. In: Kruchten, P., Fraser, S., Coallier, F. (eds.) XP 2019. LNBIP, vol. 355, pp. 121–136. Springer, Cham (2019). https://doi.org/10.1007/978-3-030-19034-7_8
3. Fitzgerald, B., Stol, K.-J.: Continuous software engineering: a roadmap and agenda. J. Syst. Softw. **123**, 176–189 (2017)
4. Neely, S., Stolt, S.: Continuous delivery? Easy! just change everything (well, maybe it is not that easy). In: 2013 Agile Conference, pp. 121–128 (2013)
5. Overby, E., Bharadwaj, A., Sambamurthy, V.: A framework for enterprise agility and the enabling role of digital options. In: Baskerville, R.L., Mathiassen, L., Pries-Heje, J., DeGross, J.I. (eds.) TDIT 2005. IIFIP, vol. 180, pp. 295–312. Springer, Boston, MA (2005). https://doi.org/10.1007/0-387-25590-7_19
6. Worley, C.G., Williams, T.D., Lawler, E.E.: Assessing Organization Agility. Wiley, San Francisco (2014)
7. Conboy, K.: Agility from first principles: reconstructing the concept of agility in information systems development. Inf. Syst. Res. **20**(3), 329–354 (2009)
8. Dikert, K., Paasivaara, M., Lassenius, C.: Challenges and success factors for large-scale agile transformations: a systematic literature review. J. Syst. Softw. **119**, 87–108 (2016)
9. Rolland, K.H., Fitzgerald, B., Dingsøyr, T., Stol, K.-J.: Problematizing agile in the large: alternative assumptions for large-scale agile development. In: International Conference on Information Systems, Dublin, Ireland (2016)
10. Cao, L., Mohan, K., Xu, P., Ramesh, B.: A framework for adapting agile development methodologies. Eur. J. Inf. Syst. **18**(4), 332–343 (2009)
11. Moe, N.B., Aurum, A., Dybå, T.: Challenges of shared decision-making: a multiple case study of agile software development. Inf. Softw. Technol. **54**(8), 853–865 (2012)
12. Worley, C.G., Lawler, E.: Agility and organization design: a diagnostic framework. Org. Dyn. **39**(2), 194–204 (2010)
13. Kaner, S.: Facilitator's Guide to Participatory Decision-Making. Wiley, Hoboken (2014)
14. Yin, R.K.: Case Study Research: Design and Methods. Sage, Thousand Oaks (2009)
15. Langley, A.: Strategies for theorizing from process data. Acad. Manag. Rev. **24**(4), 691–710 (1999)
16. Stray, V., Moe, N.B., Aasheim, A.: Dependency management in large-scale agile: a case study of DevOps teams. In: Proceedings of the 52nd Hawaii International Conference on System Sciences (2019)
17. Diefenbach, T.: Are case studies more than sophisticated storytelling?: Methodological problems of qualitative empirical research mainly based on semi-structured interviews. Qual. Quant. **43**(6), 875–894 (2009)
18. Moe, N.B., Dingsøyr, T., Dybå, T.: A teamwork model for understanding an agile team: a case study of a scrum project. Inf. Softw. Technol. **52**(5), 480–491 (2010)

# Improving Risk Management in a Scaled Agile Environment

Eva-Maria Schön[1]([⊠]) [iD], Dirk Radtke[2], and Christian Jordan[2]

[1] University of Applied Sciences (HAW), Hamburg, Germany
eva-maria.schoen@haw-hamburg.de
[2] OTTO GmbH & Co KG, Hamburg, Germany
{Dirk.Radtke2,Christian.Jordan}@otto.de

**Abstract.** Agile methods are designed for handling uncertainty as well as reducing risks in product development through transparency, inspection, and adaptation. Applying an effective risk management is in the nature of agile methods. However, when multiple agile teams work on the same product, a higher coordination effort is required and more formal practices are applied. The objective of this paper is to study how risk management can be improved in a scaled agile environment. Therefore, we conducted a case study in a large-sized ecommerce company and interviewed several project managers. The results show that there are differences for risk management in terms of two contexts. On the one hand, informal risk management is rated as good enough for one autonomous team. On the other hand, more formal approaches are needed, when several teams work on the same requirement. Furthermore, a tool for the support of risk management in a scaled agile environment is presented. We can conclude that hybrid development approaches consisting of agile practices and traditional practices, are beneficial, when several teams work in parallel.

**Keywords:** Risk management · Agile methods · Agile software development · Scaling agile · E-commerce

## 1 Introduction

Digital Transformation has an impact on the way an organization copes with challenges that arise, such as rapidly changing markets, evolving customer experiences, and disruptive technologies. In this context, many organizations have already recognized that agility is an important asset; they adopt agile methods like *Scrum* [1], *Kanban* [2], or *Extreme Programming* [3] for product development.

Agile methods have an impact on the organizational culture because of the agile values [4]. Those methods are designed to deal with complex, adaptive problems in the domain of emergence. People in agile environments need to probe first, then sense and then respond in order to handle the complexity [5]. Moreover, agile methods provide empirical approaches, which allow organizations to optimize predictability and control risk caused by iterative and incremental approaches [1]. In light of this, applying an effective risk management is in the nature of agile methods but is often implicitly handled.

V. Stray et al. (Eds.): XP 2020, LNBIP 383, pp. 132–141, 2020.
https://doi.org/10.1007/978-3-030-49392-9_9

In larger organizations, several teams often work on one product. For this reason, large-scale agile development becomes more important with the increasing spread of agile process models. When several agile teams work together on a product, there is a tension between the autonomy of a single team and the overall coordination of several teams. This often results in a considerable coordination effort caused by functional or technical dependencies among the teams [6]. Agile practices such as *Daily Standup Meeting, Kanban Board* or *Product Backlog* support the transparent handling of risks for an individual team. If several teams are working on the same requirement, these agile practices reach their limits. This can lead to a reduction in transparency and decisions cannot be taken on the basis of what is known. However, consistent practices and processes across teams and implementation of a common tool are seen as valuable in helping scaling agile methods [7]. Dingsøyr et al. [8] address the topic of large-scale agile development in a special issue. In particular, the special issue covers topics like the application of scaling frameworks, knowledge sharing, product ownership, and decision-making.

In this paper, we aim to address the research question (RQ): *How can the risk management in a scaled agile environment be improved?* Therefore, we conducted a case study in the ecommerce sector. The ecommerce sector is known for its rapid market development. Therefore, vendors need to react flexibly to changes and adapt early to new technologies to provide a unique customer experience.

The paper is structured as follows: Sect. 2 gives a brief overview of related work. Section 3 presents our research method and outlines the study context. Section 4 summarizes the key findings of our study, covering gaps and measures as well as presenting a new tool for risk management. Section 5 discusses the meaning of findings and limitations of this study. Finally, Sect. 6 concludes this work.

## 2   Related Work

There is a difference between *uncertainty* and *risk*. Uncertainty can be perceived as both an opportunity and a threat [9]. On the other hand, a risk is characterized as an event that will have negative impacts when it occurs. In literature, some studies related to risk management in agile product development can be found. Analyzing the related work, we observe some similarities among the works. Authors investigate risk factors in agile environments and propose approaches to mitigate the identified risks.

Shrivastava and Rathod [10] study risk factors that affect the performance of distributed agile product development. In this context, they present a categorization of risks faced by practitioners as well as frequently used methods to reduce the impact of those risks. In 2017, Shrivastava and Rathod [11] propose a risk management framework, that consists of ranked risks for distributed agile development, its causes, and appropriate risk management approaches. Elbanna and Sarker [12] analyzed risk factors related to adopting agile development across multiple sectors like utilities, transportation, or financial services. In addition, they study their causes and consequences and present how different organizations deal with those risks. Tavares et al. [13] propose an extensive list of risk management practices for agile projects based on a literature review and relate them to subcomponents of agile methods, which are ranked by experts in accordance with their importance for risk management. Buganová and Šimíčková [14] investigate the possibilities of the implementation of risk management in traditional and agile approaches to project management. They provide a comprehensive comparison between traditional, and agile and discuss the impact of risk management in the context of transportation companies.

# 3 Research Method

The aim of this study is to investigate how risk management can be improved in a scaled agile environment. To this end, we used a case study in order to investigate this contemporary phenomenon in its context in industry [15].

## 3.1 Study Context and Research Setting

The case study was carried out in 2018 in a large-sized ecommerce company, located in Germany. Today, the company generates more than 90% of its total sales through the online shop otto.de. In the past financial year, 7 million customers ordered online from OTTO. At peak periods, otto.de receives up to 10 new orders a second.

Currently, the team behind otto.de has 320 people working in 20 teams, of which 13 are functional teams that provide functions. Each team is purely vertical, consisting of different professions (Product Manager, Analyst, Usability, Interaction Designer, Quality, DevOps), and works in an interdisciplinary manner. They are fully responsible for the whole development process and operations in the cloud. The rest of the teams provide supporting services.

At the team level, there is complete freedom of choice for the team, as to which methods, practices, or variations are suited best. For some teams, the process is already ongoing for 200+ sprints. All core development teams are working on-site on a shared open plan office ground. The company heavily relies on face-to-face communication and tries out a flexible team assignment model, to support teams with laden backlogs.

Before conducting the study, we learned that there are two different contexts in which risk management must be considered. On the one hand, there is the context of *continuous product development,* in which agile teams implement features for the product in an autonomous manner. In this study, this context refers to the work of an autonomous team. This context is characterized by a decentralized, informal treatment of topics.

On the other hand, there is the context of the *cross-team project,* in which several agile teams work together to implement requirements. This context is characterized by explicit project constraints with regard to scope, timing, and budget. In comparison with the previous context, a more formal procedure for implementation is used.

## 3.2 Data Collection and Analysis

We started with an analysis of the as-is situation (see Fig. 1). Therefore, we gathered qualitative data by means of semi-structured interviews. The interview guidelines asked questions related to the roles and responsibilities of the participants, the as-is situation of risk management, types of risks, how risks are managed, and the measures taken. We closed the interview with an open question, so that participants had the option to express their further thoughts.

In sum, we conducted eight face-to-face interviews with a duration of 45 min each. We had four interviews with Production Leads, who are responsible for the context of *continuous product development*. Production Leads are only responsible for a single team. In addition, we had four interviews with *cross-team project* managers, who are responsible for the context of *cross-team projects*.

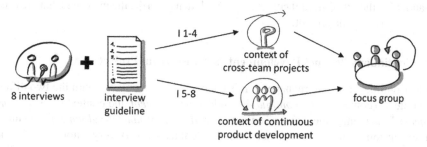

**Fig. 1.** Research approach for analyzing the as-is situation

The interviews were documented in written form and aggregated into a result report. Then, the result report was discussed in a focus group in order to playback the results to the participants and to get feedback on the observations made so far. We discussed the identified problems concerning risk management. The participants then came up with measures that could be taken to remedy them.

## 4   Results

We will first provide an overview of the different scaling levels in order to present how we optimized the risk management in the scaled agile environment under study. For this purpose, we explain which measures have a positive effect on which level. Figure 2 shows the optimized context after the measures have been applied. In particular, it outlines how the handling of risks across the various scaling levels was optimized. The relationships are as follows: a program has one or many *cross-team projects*, whereas a *cross-team*

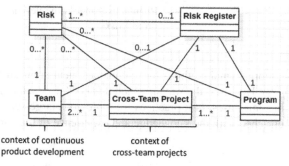

**Fig. 2.** Overview of the improved risk management in a scaled agile environment

*project* involves two or more teams. One team has none or many risks, which might be part of a risk register. In addition, one *cross-team project* can have none or many risks. A risk is documented by means of a template. In terms of the *cross-team project*, the handling of risks is improved by means of a mandatory risk register. The important risks of the *cross-team projects* are summarized into a risk register on the program level.

In the following, we will present our findings. We will outline how risk management is handled in the two different contexts. We will then describe the measures that are used to improve risk management.

### 4.1  Continuous Product Development vs. Cross-Team Project

Table 1 outlines how risk management is conducted in accordance with the two different contexts (context of the *continuous product development* and context of *cross-team project*). Risk management in the context of *continuous product development* is an internal responsibility of the team. Since the individual teams work very autonomously and there is little dependency on other teams, the teams also deal with risks very differently. Nevertheless, there are some similarities. Implicit risk management is carried out through agile practices. In the daily meetings, urgent problems are discussed and, so, transparency about risks within the teams is created.

**Table 1.** Risk management in the context of *continuous product development* and in the context of *cross-team project*

| Context of the *continuous product development* | Context of *cross-team project* |
| --- | --- |
| Informal risk management by agile approach | Formal risk management in the responsibility of dedicated project manager |
| Agile practices like daily standups, review meetings, and retrospectives promote a transparent management of risks | Explicit clarification of risk-related conditions and escalation instances during the project setup |
| Regular exchange among teams on best practices in risk management | Standardized approach for identification, management, and evaluation of risks, based on experience from previous, larger projects |
|  | Regular exchange with relevant stakeholders on project risks |

In comparison, more formal methods for risk management are used for the context of *cross-team projects*. However, the way in which this is done depends strongly on the project manager. In some cases, best practices from previous large-scale projects have been applied and enriched with the knowledge and experience of the particular project manager.

## 4.2  Gaps and Measurements Related to Risk Management

After the results were discussed in the focus group (see Fig. 1), the participants came to the conclusion that informal risk management is sufficient for the context of continuous product development. In this context, therefore, only one workshop was conducted to exchange best practices for risk management in order to sensitize the teams to the topic and strengthen a conscious management of risks.

**Table 2.** Identified gaps in terms of risk management and measures to improve them

| Context | *Continuous product development* | *Cross-team project* |
|---------|-------------------------------|---------------------|
| Responsible for risks | Production lead, triade, team | *Cross-team project* manager, leading team |
| Identified gaps | For this context, informal risk management has been assessed as sufficient. | 1. Clear, coordinated responsibility for risks is often lacking<br>2. Clear, coordinated responsibility for the implementation of measures is often lacking<br>3. Escalation instance for risks is unclear<br>4. Transparency with regard to risks from the perspective of the teams is often not given<br>5. Information flow at the project intersection *continuous product development* requires optimization |
| Measures | Best practices workshop on internal team risks | a) Optimization interface *cross-team project - continuous product development* (improves Gaps 1, 2, 4, 5)<br>b) Optimization tooling for project management, and especially for risk management (improves Gaps 1, 2, 4, 5)<br>c) Optimization project setup and management (improves Gaps 1, 2, 3) |

However, the situation is different for the context of *cross-team project*. Some challenges could be identified (see Table 2), which can be summarized under the topics of responsibilities and transparency. During the focus group, appropriate measures were developed with which the identified challenges can be overcome. These are activities that are often associated with project management (see Table 2).

### 4.3 Interface Cross-Team Project and Continuous Product Development

The optimization of the *interface between cross-team project and continuous product development* was carried out by strengthening the information flow in and out direction of the participating teams during the project duration. In detail, a regular communication of the status of individual risks was introduced, transparency in respect of upcoming project decisions (e.g. on risks), and furthermore, a close involvement of the experts from the participating teams in the technical discussions as well as risk assessment.

Moreover, biweekly program exchange meetings with the management were introduced. These meetings were about management support to exchange information on risks and not about reporting the status.

### 4.4 Tooling for Risk Management

One of the measures to optimize the context *cross-team project* was the development of a suitable tool. The requirements for the tool were prioritized by the voting of the stakeholders (see 3.2). The following important requirements were identified: easy handling; filtering; transparency for all; exportability for a report; no mandatory fields; standardization using a template, whereby the principle *less is more* should be followed.

Then, three possible variants were tested. One based on *Excel* (Microsoft), one based on *Confluence* (Atlassian), and a search for suitable plugins on the market. After the evaluation by the stakeholders, the decision to go in for the Confluence-based solution was taken.

The tool is designed as follows: each project page in Confluence has its own subpage for risks. A button is used to capture new risks using a page template. The template includes the fields: topic, category, risk description, date of creation, date of update, probability of occurrence, impact, overall criticality score, measures, and person in charge. Thus, each risk is saved as an editable page. On a portfolio page there is a total cross-team projects risk register, which is automatically fed from the individual risks of the projects. This overall risk register can also be filtered, sorted and exported. Furthermore, the tool enables the aggregation of individual risks across several scaling levels (see Fig. 2) without the same risk being documented several times.

### 4.5 Project Setup and Management

The *optimization project setup and management* included topics such as the explicit clarification of project responsibilities at the start of a *cross-team project*, clear communication of project responsibilities to stakeholders and ongoing support from program management.

For the project setup, an official kick-off meeting with the participating teams was introduced. In this kick-off meeting, information on the motivation of the project, the project goals, the control variables (e.g. timing, budget), the risk responsibilities, and decision-making groups were clarified.

In addition, project managers were regularly invited to the PMO. Participants in the PMO were the management circle and the organization team of the Level 2 Kanban board. In this meeting, the risk register of a cross-team project was discussed with the aim of identifying and clarifying the need for decisions. The clarification of the need for decisions may lead to a further discussion of a specific risk within the program exchange meeting with the senior management.

## 5  Discussion and Limitations

Our results show that there is a need for action at *cross-team projects*, as we were able to identify some gaps here. The *cross-team project* requires more formal practices because several teams are involved, and it is a challenge to create transparency across team boundaries. The measures taken to improve risk management in the context of *cross-team project* (see Table 2) are often found as best practices in traditional project management. As a result, we can conclude that the pure application of agile methods and practices is not sufficient for a scaled agile environment. This is when hybrid process models come into play. Hybrid process models combine different methods and practices and are made up of natural process evolution, which is mainly driven by experience, learning, and pragmatism [16].

In summary, we achieved a proactive, conscious handling of risks because of the iterative actions in which the employees were actively involved. Moreover, we established a common understanding of risk management among the participants of the study. The main achievements for the company can be summarized as follows: support in operational risk management by means of a common tooling, standardized approach for risk management increases transparency, especially in the context of *cross-team projects* and assistance for the training of new employees.

Nevertheless, this study has some limitations. First, our findings are based on a single case study. So, the results might not be applicable to other cases on account of the specific context. Second, there might be a bias in the data collection procedure caused by missing audio or video recordings. However, we were able to mitigate this bias since we played back the summarized results of the interviews to the interview partners in a focus group. And third, the designed process for risk management could only be kept up by giving relevance to the autonomous teams because they decide whether to use it or not. This relevance could be given by management feedback.

## 6  Conclusion

This paper presents findings from a case study conducted in a scaled agile environment in the ecommerce sector. The aim of our study was to improve the risk management within a company as well as improve the overall organizational design. In light of this, we examined two contexts, on the one hand, the context of *continuous product development* and, on the other, the context of *cross-team project*. We found that implicit risk management is sufficient for the former context, whereas a more formal risk management is required for the latter. To this end, we have worked out measures for the context of *cross-team project*, which address the identified challenges. In particular, the measures aim to improve the interface between *cross-team projects* and *continuous product development*, the tooling for project management, and especially for risk management across several scaling levels, as well as project setup and management.

Currently, we are working on an evaluation concerning the effectiveness of the applied measures. Therefore, we are planning several interviews with the participants of the study.

## References

1. Schwaber, K., Sutherland, J.: The scrum guide (2017). https://doi.org/10.1053/j.jrn.2009.08.012
2. Anderson, D.J.: Kanban - Successful Evolutionary Change for your Technology Business. Blue Hole Press, Sequim (2010)
3. Beck, K.: Extreme Programming Explained: Embrace Change. Addison-Wesley, Boston (2000)
4. Beck, K., et al.: Manifesto for agile software development. http://www.agilemanifesto.org/
5. Snowden, D.J., Boone, M.E.: A leader's framework for decision making. Harv. Bus. Rev. **85**, 68–76 (2007)
6. Schön, E.-M., Winter, D., Escalona, M.J., Thomaschewski, J.: Key challenges in agile requirements engineering. In: Baumeister, H., Lichter, H., Riebisch, M. (eds.) XP 2017. LNBIP, vol. 283, pp. 37–51. Springer, Cham (2017). https://doi.org/10.1007/978-3-319-57633-6_3
7. VersionOne Inc.: 13th annual state of agile report (2019)
8. Dingsoeyr, T., Falessi, D., Power, K.: Agile development at scale: the next frontier. IEEE Softw. **36**, 30–38 (2019). https://doi.org/10.1109/MS.2018.2884884
9. Dönmez, D., Grote, G.: Two sides of the same coin – how agile software development teams approach uncertainty as threats and opportunities. Inf. Softw. Technol. **93**, 94–111 (2018). https://doi.org/10.1016/j.infsof.2017.08.015
10. Shrivastava, S.V., Rathod, U.: Categorization of risk factors for distributed agile projects. Inf. Softw. Technol. **58**, 373–387 (2015). https://doi.org/10.1016/j.infsof.2014.07.007
11. Shrivastava, S.V., Rathod, U.: A risk management framework for distributed agile projects. Inf. Softw. Technol. **85**, 1–15 (2017). https://doi.org/10.1016/j.infsof.2016.12.005
12. Elbanna, A., Sarker, S.: The risks of agile software development: learning from adopters. IEEE Softw. **33**, 72–79 (2016). https://doi.org/10.1109/MS.2015.150
13. Tavares, B.G., Sanches da Silva, C.E., De Souza, A.D.: Practices to improve risk management in agile projects. Int. J. Softw. Eng. Knowl. Eng. **29**, 1–19 (2018). https://doi.org/10.1142/S0218194019500165
14. Buganová, K., Šimíčková, J.: Risk management in traditional and agile project management. Transp. Res. Procedia **40**, 986–993 (2019). https://doi.org/10.1016/j.trpro.2019.07.138
15. Runeson, P., Höst, M.: Guidelines for conducting and reporting case study research in software engineering. Empir. Softw. Eng. **14**, 131–164 (2009). https://doi.org/10.1007/s10664-008-9102-8
16. Kuhrmann, M., et al.: Hybrid software and system development in practice: waterfall, scrum, and beyond. In: Proceedings of the 2017 International Conference on Software and System Process - ICSSP 2017, pp. 30–39. ACM Press, New York (2017). https://doi.org/10.1145/3084100.3084104

# The Business of Agile

# "When in Rome, Do as the Romans Do": Cultural Barriers to Being Agile in Distributed Teams

Darja Šmite[1,2]([✉]), Javier Gonzalez-Huerta[1], and Nils Brede Moe[1,2]

[1] Blekinge Institute of Technology, Karlskrona, Sweden
{darja.smite,javier.gonzalez-huerta,nils.brede.moe}@bth.se
[2] SINTEF ICT, Trondheim, Norway

**Abstract.** With the growing interest of adopting agile methods in offshored process, many companies realized that the use of agile methods and practices in companies located outside the location of early adopters of agile methods may be challenging. India, the main destination of offshoring contracts, have received particular attention, due to the big cultural differences. Critical analysis of related studies suggests that impeding behaviors are mostly rooted in the hierarchical culture of Indian organizations and related management behavior of command-and-control. But what happens in distributed projects with a more empowering onshore management? In this paper, we present the findings from a multiple-case study of DevOps teams with members from a mature agile company located in Sweden and a more hierarchical offshore vendor from India. Based on two focus groups we list culturally different behaviors of offshore engineers that were reported to impede agile ways of working. Furthermore, we report the findings from surveying 36 offshore team members from five DevOps teams regarding their likely behavior in situations reported to be problematic. Our findings confirm a number of previously reported behaviors rooted in cultural differences that impede the adoption of agile ways of working when collaborating with offshore engineers. At the same time, our survey results suggest that among the five surveyed teams there were teams that succeeded with the cultural integration of the offshore team members. Finally, our findings demonstrate the importance of cultural training especially when onboarding new team members.

**Keywords:** Culture · Cultural differences · Agile · Distributed development · Distributed agile teams

## 1 Introduction

The times when software could be designed by a single co-located agile team, are long gone and many agile software development environments have become highly distributed. Software companies often collaborate with engineers from multiple sites of the same company or from sub-contractors. Thus, agile teams might be spread over several time zones and geographic locations, implying that different national and organizational

© The Author(s) 2020
V. Stray et al. (Eds.): XP 2020, LNBIP 383, pp. 145–161, 2020.
https://doi.org/10.1007/978-3-030-49392-9_10

cultures are represented [25]. Such setups increase the complexity of the software development work and challenges emerge [10]. One example of such challenges is when more hierarchical organizations from certain Asian countries (e.g., India or China) collaborate with self-managing teams from the Nordic countries. Self-managing agile teams are those given significant authority and responsibility for many aspects of their work, such as planning, scheduling and assigning tasks to members, and making decisions with economic consequences [19]. An interesting question is what happens when teams are set up with a mix of representatives from a mature agile organization and a more hierarchical organization?

The first challenges emerge when crossing organizational boundaries. Several researchers have emphasized the importance of cultural compatibility or fit between the organizational culture and the software development method in use [6, 11], and that companies are likely to encounter difficulties when having incompatibilities. What makes it challenging to reach compatibility is the fact that even in agile organizations you will find several conflicting sub-cultures [13, 20] e.g. when the culture at the agile team level is seen as a threat because it conflicted with existing and established habits of the management. This means that team is a relevant context to study culture.

The next big challenges emerge when crossing national boundaries. Collaboration with Asian vendors is one big trend in many Western companies. Many of these companies report challenges when introducing agile in projects involving offshore engineers, rooted in the cultural differences [1, 5, 10, 15, 27, 30]. In particular, companies from the main offshore destination, India, have focused on rigid process improvement programs as a means of demonstrating organizational capabilities, and therefore often exhibit heavily plan-based culture with corresponding organizational structures and processes [27]. Whether and how to achieve combability between the national culture and agile development methods when creating virtual teams involving team-members with radically different cultural backgrounds has thus become an important research topic. However, some researchers warn that the major differences in norms and values cannot be harmonized, since they derive from deep-seated differences in cultural background, education, and working life [14]. The need to understand how to succeed with the adoption of agile ways of working in globally distributed teams with members from an Indian vendor, motivated us to explore what are the specific cultural barriers, what resulting behaviors impede agility, and whether these behaviors prevail among offshore engineers working in distributed agile teams. Our empirical study therefore addresses the following research questions:

**RQ1:** What are the cultural barriers impeding agile ways of working in distributed teams with members from a hierarchical culture?
**RQ2:** What can agile teams do to integrate the offshore members?

In this paper, we report our results from an empirical study of a Swedish company working with offshore engineers from an outsourcing vendor in India. The rest of the paper is organized as follows. Section 2 summarizes the links between cultural differences and the behavior of Asian software engineers, as well as the role of cultural differences when introducing agile ways of working in offshore projects. Section 3 introduces our research methodology and the case company. The results of our study are presented in Sect. 4, followed by a discussion in Sect. 5. Section 6 concludes the paper with a summary of the findings and implications for practice and further research.

## 2 Background and Related Work

Culture is related to the way we give logic to the world and begins at birth with gestures, words, tone of voice, noises, colors, smells, and body contact we experience [18]. Our culture is what is familiar, recognizable, habitual, it is "what goes without saying", "what is normal". Yet, culture is a multifaceted concept, and can be attributed to a nation, an organization, a group or even an individual, because it is shaped by one's social environment [9]. Therefore, culture is a sensitive subject and not the depiction of wooden stereotypes [3]. Yet, common characteristics may exist that distinguish one culture from another [3]. In our work, we focus on the impact of the national culture and the organizational culture on the ways of working.

National cultures and cultural differences have been studied in-depth by several social scientists (e.g. [9] and [7] to name a few). These studies resulted in several overlapping cultural characteristics that are common for representatives of a particular nation. National culture may determine preferred leadership styles and decision-making processes, perceptions of authorities, attitude towards time, need for formalization, preferred communication and interaction styles, business etiquette and motivation tools [9]. Similarly to organizational incompatibilities with the method in use [6, 11], incompatibilities in the national backgrounds and the differences in the ways of working can prove problematic [10, 14]. In fact, the larger the degree of difference in organizations and national cultures, the larger the cultural distance between the parties involved [4]. In the following, we first explain what characterizes agile ways of working and what organizational culture is conducive for successful adoption of agile methodology, and then summarize research studies related to the challenges of introducing agile ways of working in Asia, relevant for our empirical study.

### 2.1 Agile Ways of Working and Organizational Culture

Agile ways of working stem from a group of methods united by a common philosophy, values, and principles. It emphasizes teamwork and heavily relies on the ability of a software team to self-manage [8, 19]. The principles of self-management and autonomy, central to agile ways of working, put certain demand on the organizational culture, team composition and behavioural norms [8, 21, 28]. Morgan [23] emphasises the importance of teams' ability to engage in self-learning and drive continuous improvement, and ability to act upon minimum critical specification. van Solingen et al. [26] argue that the prerequisites for improvement and learning are openness and the ability to discuss the underlying problems. Based on two large surveys of agile teams, Williams captures practices essential for teams to be considered agile being related to their ability to satisfy the customer through early, continuous and frequent delivery of valuable, working software; the prerequisite for which is, among others, staffing projects with motivated individuals who are given the needed resources and authority to get their job done [31].

A number of studies investigated the relationship between organizational culture and the use of agile methods [8, 12, 13, 29]. Based on a multi-case study of nine projects Strode et al. [29] found that specific organizational culture factors correlate with effective use of an agile method. Their findings suggest that an organization is more likely to be successful if the organization values feedback and learning; social interaction in the organization is trustful, collaborative, and competent; the project manager acts as a facilitator; the management style is that of leadership and collaboration; the organization values teamwork is flexible and participative and encourages social interaction; the organization enables empowerment of people; the organization is results oriented; leadership in the organization is entrepreneurial, innovative, and risk taking; and the organization is based on loyalty and mutual trust and commitment [29]. Similar findings emerged from studying 58 agile practitioners from 23 organizations in New Zealand and India [8]. Hoda et al. found that the prerequisite for self-organizing agile teams to establish and flourish is senior management support, in terms of providing freedom and establishing an organizational culture of trust. They also suggest that an organization with a strict hierarchical structure is not conducive to self-organizing agile teams, because the hierarchy enforces a lack of openness marked by restricted and indirect lines of communication and feedback, which in turn leads to an environment of fear [8]. Based on a multi-case study, Kautz et al. [13] found that agile development thrives in different organizational cultures, even in hierarchical ones, as long as the 4 core values are present to a significant extent. Furthermore, they argue that while organizational culture has an impact on the way agile development is enacted, in practice it is often the method which is adjusted to the organization. Similarly, Iivari et al. argue that the relationship between an organizational culture and agile ways of working is dynamic and therefore will continuously evolve [12]. This means that time perspective matters and studies on the compatibility between the culture and agile ways of working shall take the dynamic nature of this relationship into account.

Another reason to look at the organizational culture from a time perspective is the staff changes. When adding new people to an already established agile team, it is essential to support the new team members in adapting to the existing teams culture and ways of working, which is especially difficult in virtual setups. In their study of onboarding Portuguese developers into existing Norwegian agile teams [22], Moe et al. conclude that the most important success factor is finding people that matched the culture of the existing teams. Therefore, during an onboarding process, all interviews and visits need to focus on communicating the values and culture and on giving insight into the existing organization's norms.

## 2.2  Agile Adoption in Asian Countries

Since, national culture is said to have significant influence on the organizational culture [9] and organizational culture may impact the use and success of agile ways of working [13, 29], there is interest in understanding the use of agile methods and practices in companies located outside the locations of early adopters of agile methods. In particular, researchers and practitioners have wondered about the abilities of the companies and engineers from the Asian region, the primary recipients of offshoring contracts, to adopt the agile ways of working, which are so distinct to their national culture.

To address these questions, a number of studies sought evidence of successful use of agile methods in offshored projects [10, 25]. Some researchers infer the successful adoption from the large number of practices reported as being followed [2, 32]. However, the validity of these studies as well as the research approach are questionable, because high level of commitment to the use of agile practices can be explained by the readiness to accept the established rules in hierarchical (i.e., high power distance) cultures, as found, for example, in a study of agile adoption in Malaysia [1]. Other research studies tried to improve the understanding of what specifically impedes the adoption of agile ways of working in Asian cultures [1, 5, 8, 14, 15, 30] and how to succeed [8, 25]. In Table 1, we summarize a list of impeding behaviors reported on the managerial and engineering levels in related studies.

**Table 1.** Culturally distinct behaviors impeding agile ways of working.

| Level | Impeding behavior | References |
|---|---|---|
| Management behavior | Command-and-control mindset, reinforced deference to superiors | [1, 5, 8, 10, 14, 30] |
| | Leadership style discouraging team members from exposing problems | [5] |
| | Leadership style discouraging from proposing alternatives to perceived directives from superiors | [5] |
| Engineers' behavior | Willingness to say yes to most requests in deference to superiors, reluctance to warn about non-feasible deadlines | [1, 5, 30] |
| | Reluctance to expose problems | [1, 5, 8] |
| | Lack of commitment to self-learning, reliance on top-down improvements | [1, 30] |
| | Reluctance to engage in constructive disagreements and challenging discussions or voicing criticism | [8, 14, 15] |
| | Reluctance to propose alternatives to perceived directives from superiors | [5, 8] |

The cited studies cover different countries within the Asian region, including India [5, 8, 27, 30], Malaysia and Singapore [1] and Asia Pacific in general [15], and are either based on interviews or own experiences.

A closer look at behaviors of engineers in India and neighboring countries reveals that most if not all impeding behaviors are likely to be caused by the hierarchical culture of the organizations and related management behavior, as suggested in related research [8, 29]. For example, Ayed et al. [1] report that Malaysian and Singapore engineers lacked the freedom to decide about their ways of working and therefore did not see the point in self-learning. But what if the hierarchical culture of command-and-control highlighted in numerous studies as poisonous to the agile ways of working [1, 5, 10, 14, 15, 30] would be replaced with the more empowering onshore management; would the offshore engineers working in mixed onshore-offshore teams be able to adopt the agile ways of working? Or would the less hierarchical Western companies fail to ignite the agile culture in their offshore collaborations? The answers to these questions are of high importance for shaping the understanding of the compatibility of agile ways of working with the use of offshoring.

## 3   Research Methodology

To answer our research questions, we conducted an exploratory case study [24]. We executed our study in real world setting and studied collaboration between two companies (see Sect. 3.1). Our study is a holistic multiple-case study, where the context is the offshore collaboration between a mature agile company from Sweden and a hierarchical consultancy company from India; each case is a distributed agile team (five in our study) and individual behavior of the team members as the unit of analysis [24]. Finally, our data collection and analysis were divided into two steps (see Sect. 3.2).

### 3.1   Empirical Background

The context of our study is a collaboration between an outsourcer/customer company from Sweden working in the telecommunication industry and an outsourcing vendor/a consultancy company from India. For confidentiality reasons we are prohibited to disclose the names of either of the companies. Our investigation targeted five distributed agile teams composed of team members from both the Swedish company and the offshore vendor from India. The selection of the teams was done with the help of the companies and represented all important business areas.

The studied teams were set up as DevOps teams consisting of a few smaller mixed Dev and Ops teams working accordingly in the development stream or the operation stream with supporting roles around. Each smaller team was cross-functional and involved developers, testers, a System lead, a Team lead and a Product owner (see the structure in Fig. 1 and profiles of the studied DevOps in Table 2).

DevOps teams followed agile principles and ways of working with iterative development (Scrum or Kanban, decided by each team individually), daily stand ups, and team retrospectives as the primary rituals. The offshore members of the teams were expected to follow the same agile principles and philosophy as the contracting organization. This is why cultural incompatibility across locations was seen as a threat.

### 3.2   Data Collection and Analysis

A mixed approach was employed to study the impact of cultural differences on the collaboration between the Swedish customer and the Indian outsourcing vendor. Data collection was done in several steps including a quantitative data collection approach when exploring the personally experienced misunderstandings and relevant behaviors impeding collaboration, and a more qualitative approach when checking the occurrence of impeding behaviors in five distributed DevOps teams, as visualized in Fig. 2 and described in the following sub-sections.

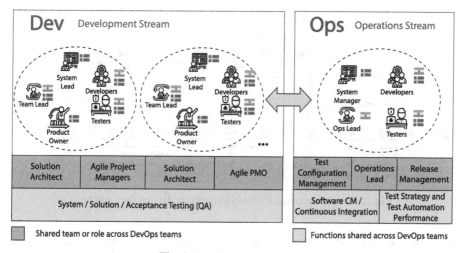

**Fig. 1.** DevOps team structure

**Table 2.** Profile of the studied teams.

| | No of sites | Total no of members | No of participants | Participants | | Offshore member roles |
|---|---|---|---|---|---|---|
| | | | | Onshore | Offshore | |
| DevOps 1 | 2 | 18 | 18 | 11 | 7 | Dev. (3), Test. (2), Architect, Op. lead |
| DevOps 2 | 2 | 22 | 20 | 14 | 6 | Developers (5), Team Lead |
| DevOps 3 | 3 | 28 | 22 | 12 | 10 | Dev. (6), Testers (2), Team leads (2) |
| DevOps 4 | 2 | 44 | 20 | 13 | 7 | Developers (6), Operations Lead |
| DevOps 5 | 2 | 21 | 16 | 10 | 6 | Consultant, Developers (4), Test lead |
| TOTAL | | 133 | 96 | 60 | 36 | |

**Group Interviews to Elicit Misunderstandings.** First, we conducted separate homogeneous group interviews with representatives from Sweden and from India to elicit the main sources of misunderstandings that impede ways of working in the collaboration. Eight representatives participated in the session with the Swedish representatives (N = 8). Two experienced managers participated in the electronically mediated session with the Indian representatives (N = 2). The group interviews were conducted in May 2017,

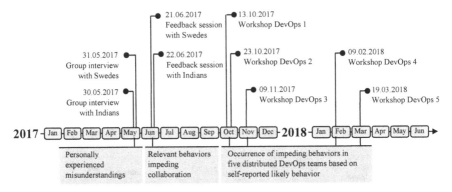

**Fig. 2.** Data collection activities and resulting data on the timeline

ran in English, and moderated by one of the researchers, while another researcher took detailed notes. Both sessions lasted approx. two hours and followed the same agenda – after getting to know each other and presenting the objectives, the participants were given time to connect to a web-based survey service called Mentimeter via mobile phones or computers and report personal experiences related to cultural misunderstandings. The survey form contained just one open question and the participants were encouraged to submit as many items as possible. The submitted items were then brought up one by one and discussed with all participants in the session. The situations in which certain misunderstandings occur were sought and every participant could add their own reflections and bring up new ideas, which were noted down as session notes.

The generated items and the recorded notes were analyzed in iterations. First, we aggregated elicited items in one list of misunderstandings grouped by similarity. This list contained seven larger categories related to cultural differences and their impacts. Then we revisited each category one by one, read through the session notes and formulated items in a particular form: *As a <role and/or site representative> it is confusing for me when <role and/or site representative> <behavior> (when/in <situation>).*

**Typical Impeding Behaviors Prioritized During Feedback Sessions.** The identified 26 different confusing behaviors served as the base for identifying situations, which were reported as sources of misunderstandings. To identify the most relevant impeding behaviors, we discussed our results in feedback sessions with larger groups of onshore and offshore representatives, conducted in June 2017. We discussed the identified problematic situations with expected and unwanted behavioral options in feedback sessions involving homogeneous groups of Swedish participants (N = 12) and Indian participants (N = 4), and refined our results based on the comments received. We also elicited the responses of the Swedish participants regarding the occurrence of the impeding behaviors on a scale: *Happens, Used to Happen, Never Happens*. This was not done in the session with Indian side representatives, because the respondents were too few and included a manager, who could have influenced the results. In this paper, we report a selection of behaviors that are classified as hindrances to the agile ways of working (see Sect. 4.1). These are based on the behaviors reported by both Indian and Swedish participants with the occurrence scores from the Swedish session. The behaviors that are not included in this paper included those related to the estimation precision, attitude towards time (reporting vacations, coming to meetings on time, extending work hours), communication (switching to local language), and a few variations of the behaviors.

**Occurrence of Impeding Behaviors in Surveyed DevOps Teams.** We ran five workshops with DevOps teams (mixing onshore and offshore participants; N = 96) to discuss cultural differences and test the occurrence of impeding behaviors in each team (See the profiles in Table 2). The workshops were held in the fall of 2017 and spring of 2018. During the session we first queried the participants about their likely behavior in the given situations. Then each situation, reported behaviors and reasons for the likely behavior based on cultural studies [9] were discussed. At the end of each workshop, the areas of improvement for the participating team were identified. In this paper, we report and discuss the responses of offshore participants (N = 36) related to the behaviors impeding or enabling agile ways of working.

### 3.3 Limitations and Threats to Validity

In this subsection, we discuss the limitations and issues that might threaten the validity of our results. Given the qualitative nature of our study, in the following we discuss the validity, reliability and generalizability threats following the guidelines by Leung [17].

**Validity** refers to the appropriateness of the method. We designed the empirical study in a two-staged fashion, aiming at improving objectivity when formulating and selecting the situations and impeding behaviors. We also used an anonymized data collection tool and obfuscated the results to ensure anonymity of the respondents, to eliminate the unwillingness to report personal confusions.

**Reliability** in qualitative research refers to the replicability of the results. A margin of variability in results is accepted when dealing with qualitative research [17] or mixed methods, since the subjectivity of the researcher is embedded in the roots of the analysis. The main threat is then related to consistency. To mitigate this threat, we let the participants report their responses in a data collection tool, by being systematic when taking notes and documenting the discussions during the sessions, and by keeping the quotations from the participants as exact as possible. Furthermore, we conducted feedback sessions to validate our interpretation of the impeding behaviors and situations.

Possible threats to the **validity** and **reliability** of our results are related to the reluctance of offshore participants to express their opinion in front of managers or onshore peers, as well as reluctance to talk about compromising issues. To alleviate these threats, we separated the Indian and Swedish participants in the initial group interviews and feedback sessions to be able to talk more openly. In the mixed workshop sessions, we explained the importance of truthful responses and asked onshore team leads to encourage openness. We also used a survey form that allowed participants to provide their responses anonymously, which remained untraceable to individuals even during the discussions. The reported problematic behavior in the survey, confirming comments received from the onshore participants and reflections voiced by more experienced offshore participants (in other words triangulation of the data sources) make us believe that we have elicited as honest and open responses as possible.

Data triangulation is the core principle of case study research [24]. To enhance the **validity** and **reliability** of our results, the individual responses elicited during the group interviews were first discussed in the respective groups and compared across the onshore and offshore groups. We then elicited quantitative data from larger groups of participants (survey responses) to minimize the bias towards selected individuals. The quantitative data elicited through the survey was further triangulated with the qualitative data (notes) from the discussions held during the workshops.

**Generalizability** of the conclusions drawn from our results are of course limited to the studied context. However, our results disprove an existing view that cultural barriers are likely to remain since the major differences in norms and values cannot be harmonized [14]. We believe that it is fair to assume that the gradual changes in behavior that we observed as a result of the gained experience with working in a mixed environment may also happen in similar contexts in other organizations.

# 4    Results

In this section, we first list the culturally distinct behaviors that were reported to cause misunderstandings and impede the agile ways of working in distributed teams. Then we report on the occurrence of the impeding behavior from surveying 36 offshore members from a more hierarchical organization integrated into five DevOps teams.

## 4.1    Behavior Impeding Agile Ways of Working

Based on the interviews, we identified 19 sources of misunderstandings reported by the Swedish participants and 14 sources of misunderstandings reported by the Indian participants. Notably, both sides reported what was confusing in the behavior of their counterparts as well as the own behavior that have led to misunderstandings or confusion. Our further analysis of the situations in which differences in behavior were seen as barriers for collaboration led to an aggregated list of 26 behaviors, which was triangulated with related literature. Of these, 12 behaviors were prioritized as frequently occurring and important to discuss as determined in the feedback sessions. In this paper, we provide an analysis of six of these behaviors that can be classified as impediments to agile ways of working (see Table 3).

The six reported behaviors impeding agile ways of working surface in the daily meetings, task allocation and content discussions, and team retrospectives; and appeared all but one as common sources of misunderstandings between the offshore and onshore members (see the column Happens in Table 3). Evidently, the most typical impediment is willingness to say yes to most requests in deference to superiors and reluctance to warn about non-feasible deadlines. Other impeding behaviors had varying frequency of occurrence. Some respondents indicated that although the impeding behaviors occurred in the past ("Used to happen" in Table 3), social integration of the Indian members led to the assimilation of the established ways of working and put an end to behavioral differences. This is why, in the next step we sought to further understand how common the impeding behaviors are in different teams, and what stimulates cultural integration.

**Table 3.** Behavior impeding agile ways of working and the frequency of occurrence reported by the Swedish representatives (N = 12).

| | Happens | Used to happen | Never happened | Don't know |
|---|---|---|---|---|
| #1 Willingness to say yes to most requests in deference to superiors, reluctancy to warn about non-feasible deadlines | 100% | | | |
| #2 Seeking immediate manager's approval for team tasks in deference to local superiors | 75% | 17% | | 25% |
| #3 Reluctancy to reveal a lack of understanding and ask questions | 58% | 33% | 8% | |
| #4 Reluctancy to expose problems at earliest convenience | 92% | 8% | | |
| #5 Reluctancy to discuss failure | | 8% | 92% | |
| #6 Reluctancy to voice criticism or propose alternatives to perceived directives from superiors | 67% | 8% | | 25% |

## 4.2 Behavior in Five Distributed Teams

Table 4 summarizes our results from surveying offshore members from five distributed DevOps teams regarding their likely behavior in six situations (impeding behaviors are emphasized in red color). Our results suggest that accepting unfeasible tasks in deference to superiors (#1), seeking immediate manager's approval for tasks (#2) and reluctance to confess about lagging behind schedule (#4) are behaviors experienced in all five distributed teams, while confusing behavior in situations #5 and #6 are not that common. It is also evidently from the results that DevOps 1 and DevOps 5 appear quite successful with the cultural integration of their Indian members, while DevOps 2, 3 and 4 are challenged. This is confirmed by a more detailed analysis, which reveals that the most common respondents of impeding behavior are the recently onboarded members. In the following, we further detail our findings from analyzing survey responses and notes capturing the discussions the team members held during the sessions.

**Willingness to Say Yes to Most Requests in Deference to Superiors, reluctance to warn about non-feasible deadlines.** This impeding behavior is one of the most common behaviors among our respondents, with eight members in DevOps 3 reporting to accept unfeasible tasks from superiors. As the technical product owner (TPO) from DevOps 3 reveals: *"We see [this impeding behavior] a lot, it does not just put us in a risk situation, but also other TPOs and stakeholders"*. The offshore member from Team 3 explained that it is difficult for them to say "No" and therefore they are likely to use hinting words as *"I will do my best"*, in the hope that it will be interpreted correctly. Yet, Swedes put no value on what is not said. Thus, team leads suggested that coaching offshore members to be direct and open was important. They explained that for Swedish team members, a "Yes" means "I understand", "I agree", "I accept", "I approve".

**Seeking Immediate Manager's Approval for Team Tasks in Deference to Local Superiors.** This challenge was seen as a fact of life, since Indian team members were a part of the consultancy company and confirmed to local rules and regulations. In fact, many team leaders and product owners established direct communication channels

**Table 4.** Self-reported offshore team member behavior in the given situations. Symbol ☑ determines acceptable behavioral options, while ☒ and the red color determines impeding behavioral options.

| Behavior in different situations | Team 1 (N=7) | Team 2 (N=6) | Team 3 (N=10) | Team 4 (N=7) | Team 5 (N=6) |
|---|---|---|---|---|---|
| **#1: Committing to tasks \| Willingness to say yes to most requests in deference to superiors, reluctancy to warn about non-feasible deadlines** | | | | | |
| ☑ Refuse to commit to non-feasible deadlines | 14% | 0% | 0% | 29% | 17% |
| ☑ Warn about non-feasible deadlines and exchange tasks | 71% | 83% | 20% | 29% | 50% |
| ☒ Accept tasks with non-feasible deadlines | 14% | 17% | 80% | 43% | 33% |
| **#2: Committing to tasks \| Seeking immediate manager's approval for team tasks in deference to local superiors** | | | | | |
| ☑ Start working on the task directly | 71% | 50% | 70% | 14% | 33% |
| ☒ Request an approval from the immediate manager | 14% | 33% | 30% | 86% | 67% |
| ☒ Wait until the task comes from the immediate manager | 14% | 17% | 0% | 0% | 0% |
| **#3: Interaction with product owners and onshore team members \| Reluctancy to reveal a lack of understanding and ask questions** | | | | | |
| ☑ Ask questions directly, when not understanding something | 100% | 50% | 80% | 86% | 100% |
| ☒ Do not reveal non-understanding and seek local peer help | 0% | 50% | 20% | 0% | 0% |
| ☒ Do not reveal non-understanding and act upon assumptions | 0% | 0% | 0% | 14% | 0% |
| **#4: Daily meetings \| Reluctancy to expose problems at earliest convenience** | | | | | |
| ☑ Warn about the problems at the earliest convenience | 86% | 17% | 70% | 43% | 83% |
| ☒ Reluctant to expose problems | 14% | 83% | 30% | 57% | 17% |
| **#5: Team retrospectives \| Reluctancy to discuss failure** | | | | | |
| ☑ Bring up problems and discuss them | 100% | 83% | 90% | 100% | 67% |
| ☒ Wait until others bring up problems and then try to defend | 0% | 0% | 0% | 0% | 33% |
| ☒ Reluctant to bring up problems | 0% | 17% | 10% | 0% | 0% |
| **#6: Team retrospectives \| Reluctancy to voice criticism or propose alternatives to perceived directives from superiors** | | | | | |
| ☑ Voice criticism and propose process changes | N/A | 33% | 40% | 43% | 50% |
| ☑ Voice criticism | | 33% | 0% | 0% | 17% |
| ☑ Propose changes | | 17% | 50% | 57% | 33% |
| ☒ Reluctant to voice criticism or propose process changes | | 17% | 10% | 0% | 0% |

with offshore managers. Therefore, this behavior was not seen as a major impediment. However, the leader of DevOps 2 was recently employed and appeared to be unaware of this difference in behavior, perhaps because a lack of onboarding into the cultural norms of the team. This lack of awareness was seen as problematic since she did not know of the importance of maintaining regular communication with the offshore managers.

**Reluctance to Reveal a Lack of Understanding and Ask Questions.** Few members of DevOps 2 and 3 will hide a lack of understanding when discussing requirements with the product owner, and instead ask peers for help, while one respondent in Team 4 will proceed based on the best assumptions. Members of DevOps 1 discussed that they experienced this challenge especially among the new Indian members joining the team and that exchange visits and personal acquittance between the product owner and the offshore members helps. Interestingly, an offshore member from DevOps 3 said to be surprised by the results and that from his observation, people are still reluctant to ask questions. He explained: *"...when we have discussion between sites, I can see that an offshore person doesn't understand, but doesn't really say that. They might search for an answer in the meantime and then come back with the answer, but probably won't say it in meeting"*. Product owner in DevOps 3 suggested that one way to promote the wanted behavior is to encourage questions; he explained: *"I am used to say if you don't have questions, you don't understand"*. Another useful advice was the "Talk back" approach, which suggests not to ask Yes/No questions, but rather ask to summarize what was said or agreed, or to explain the next steps one would do after the discussion.

**Reluctance to Expose Problems at Earliest Convenience.** Another common challenge in all five teams was the fear of revealing the fact that someone is lagging behind during team daily meetings. As an offshore member of DevOps 1 explained: *"Everyone wants to do their best, they try everything before saying that they are late"*. The reluctance to expose problems was linked to the deference to managers in typically hierarchical organizations and the "Why-management" style (A Why? Question follows when someone reveals a problem, forcing people to engage in uncomfortable explanations and thus making them "lose face"). The meetings were said to differ in Sweden and in India. An offshore member explained: *"They have in mind that the boss is the one who decides their salary"*, while the team leads and managers in Sweden over time were accepted as more accessible and thus raising problems became less frightening. Swedish members emphasized that they prefer engineers to say what they think, and not what they think managers want them to say.

**Reluctance to Discuss Failure.** This challenge was not reported as common in the studied teams, which was motivated by the positive atmosphere of the retrospective meetings with the Swedish team leads. An offshore member of DevOps 1 further explained: *"It depends on who is in the meeting, sometimes we keep silent. It depends who is asking, and who is running the meeting"*. Therefore, keeping local offshore managers outside the retrospectives was seen as an important learning.

**Reluctance to Voice Criticism or Propose Alternatives to Perceived Directives From Superiors.** Similarly, challenging the established ways of working during the retrospectives did not appear as a common challenge. Many offshore members were likely to either challenge the processes or propose improvements.

## 5   Discussion

### 5.1   Cultural Barriers Impeding the Agile Ways of Working

In response to the first research question, we have identified several behaviors rooted in the hierarchical forms of organization as impediments for agile ways of working, which confirm previous research that highlight cultural barriers common to offshore organizations. In particular, we found the reinforcement of deference to superiors [5, 8, 14] to be a common barrier for the studied teams. This in our case led to a willingness to say yes to even unrealistic requests (similarly to [1, 5, 30]), reluctance to expose problems (similarly to [1, 5, 8, 30]) and reluctance to reveal the lack of understanding and ask questions to a superior. At the same time, our findings suggest that the empowering culture and democratic leadership from Sweden encourage the trust and transparency-based behavior among the offshore members. However, the behavioral transformations take time and cannot be taken for granted. In the presence of hierarchical structures and command-and-control leadership locally, cultural integration might take longer, or result in that offshore team members are forced to assimilate different behaviors in parallel. In fact, during one of the workshops an offshore team lead told us that offshore engineers that move between customers might not be rewarded for what is a typical behavior in an agile environment and need to revert to the behaviors typical to hierarchical cultures.

When contrasting our findings with the organizational culture factors that correlate with effective use of an agile method [8, 29], we can say that the culture of the outsourcing vendor did not confirm with the highlighted values and management style. The implication of this is that agile companies might be more likely to succeed with offshoring through establishing their own sites; working with vendors that are already used to agile values and ways of working or recruiting people that matched the culture of the existing teams [22]. In particular, the companies may want to assess the vendors management style, i.e., facilitation-leadership, collaboration-oriented management style and focus on empowerment as crucial factors for adopting agility [29].

### 5.2   Cultural Integration of Offshore Members from a Non-agile Organization

Unlike researchers who suggest that cultural barriers are likely to remain since the major differences in norms and values cannot be harmonized, as they derive from deep-seated differences in cultural background, education, and working life [14], we found that behavior seem to change when engineers are exposed to the culturally distinct environment. Our findings demonstrate that Swedish members succeeded in integrating members of a hierarchical culture and stimulating the changes in their behavior. Our findings are in accordance with Iivari et al. that found that the relationship between an organizational culture and agile ways of working is dynamic [12]. Our experience, however, shows that distributed teams are often left to experiment and adjust their ways of working, since cultural awareness is often gained with experience. This has been noted by Casey [3], who found that the importance of and requirement for cultural training is often not recognized before a lot of time, effort and resources are wasted. We therefore recommend companies and distributed teams to run cross-cultural communication courses to discuss the values that should govern behavior as also suggested in [16]. For team leads and onshore managers struggling to overcome the same cultural barriers as reported in this article, we can recommend the following:

- Establish good communication channels with local offshore managers and agree on an efficient task allocation procedure;
- Schedule more frequent check-ins or updates;
- Create an environment of psychological safety and trust; set an example of taking ownership for failures safely; show how teams can learn from mistakes, reward people for making mistakes if/when they lead to valuable lessons;
- Seek out *one-to-one* conversations; encourage offshore members to be more direct, use "Talk Back" approach to check the understanding;
- Encourage suggestions of better ways of working; do not criticize ideas; complement people for valuable input; set an example of changes that led to action;
- Avoid offshore managers' presence in team retrospectives and meetings where honest and open input and feedback from offshore members is important.

## 6    Conclusions

Distributed collaboration is challenging [10]. In this paper, we explore one specific challenge, i.e., dealing with barriers rooted in the differences in national and organizational cultures. Our results confirm the existing research that organizational and national cultural barriers may impede collaboration in general and adoption of agile ways of working in particular. However, our empirical findings from studying behavior of offshore members from five mixed DevOps teams suggest that behavior does change over time, even when integrating offshore engineers who are used to radically different hierarchical organizational culture into agile ways of working. In other words, Indian developers working in agile projects, learned how to do as their more experienced agile team members from Sweden do. Our study resulted in a list of recommendations for companies willing to discuss cultural differences and foster cultural integration in offshore projects.

**Acknowledgement.** This research is funded by the GoLD project and the Swedish Knowledge Foundation under the KK-Hög grant 2016/0191 and by the A-team project and the Research council of Norway through grant 267704.

## References

1. Ayed, H., Vanderose, B., Habra, N.: Agile cultural challenges in Europe and Asia: insights from practitioners. In: IEEE/ACM 39th International Conference on Software Engineering: Software Engineering in Practice Track (ICSE-SEIP), pp. 153–162 (2017)
2. Baruah, N., Ashima, A.: A survey of the use of agile methodologies in different Indian Small and Medium Scale Enterprises (SMEs). Int. J. Comput. Appl. **47**(20), 38–44 (2012)
3. Carmel, E., Agarwal, R.: Tactical approaches for alleviating distance in global software development. IEEE Softw. **18**(2), 22–29 (2001)

4. Casey, V.: Leveraging or exploiting cultural difference? In: 2009 Fourth IEEE International Conference on Global Software Engineering, pp. 8–17 (2009)
5. Fowler, M.: Using an agile software process with offshore development. https://www.martin fowler.com/articles/agileOffshore.html
6. Gallivan, M., Srite, M.: Information technology and culture: Identifying fragmentary and holistic perspectives of culture. Inf. Organ. **15**(4), 295–338 (2005)
7. Hall, E.: The Silent Language. Doubleday, Garden City (1959)
8. Hoda, R., Noble, J., Marshall, S.: Supporting self-organizing agile teams. In: International Conference on Agile Software Development, Madrid, Spain, pp. 73–87 (2011)
9. Hofstede, G., Hofstede, G.J., Minkov, M.: Cultures and Organizations. McGraw-Hill Education, New York (2010)
10. Holmström, H., Fitzgerald, B., Ågerfalk, P.J., Conchúir, E.Ó.: Agile practices reduce distance in global software development. Inf. Syst. Manag. **23**(3), 7–18 (2006)
11. Iivari, J., Iivari, N.: The relationship between organizational culture and the deployment of agile methods. In: Information and Software Technology, pp. 509–520. Elsevier (2011)
12. Iivari, N.: Culturally compatible usability work: an interpretive case study on the relationship between usability work and its cultural context in software product development organizations. J. Organ. End User Comput. **22**(3), 40–65 (2010)
13. Kautz, K., Pedersen, C.F., Monrad, O.: Cultures of agility - agile software development in practice. In: ACIS 2009 Proceedings - 20th Australasian Conference on Information Systems, pp. 174–184 (2009)
14. Krishna, S., Sahay, S., Walsham, G.: Managing cross-cultural issues in global software outsourcing. In: Hirschheim, R., Heinzl, A., Dibbern, J. (eds.) Information Systems Outsourcing (Second Edition): Enduring Themes. New Perspectives and Global Challenges, pp. 651–658. Springer, Berlin Heidelberg (2006). https://doi.org/10.1007/978-3-540-34877-1_23
15. Lee, S., Yong, H.S.: Distributed agile: project management in a global environment. Empir. Softw. Eng. **15**(2), 204–217 (2010)
16. Lenberg, P., Feldt, R., Wallgren Tengberg, L.G.: Misaligned values in software engineering organizations. J. Softw. Evol. Process. **31**(3), e2148 (2019)
17. Leung, L.: Validity, reliability, and generalizability in qualitative research. J. Fam. Med. Prim. care. **4**(3), 324–327 (2015)
18. Van Maanen, J., Laurent, A.: The flow of culture: some notes on globalization and the multinational corporation*. In: Organization Theory and the Multinational Corporation, pp. 275–312. Palgrave Macmillan UK (1993)
19. Moe, N.B., Dingsøyr, T., Dybå, T.: A teamwork model for understanding an agile team: a case study of a Scrum project. Inf. Softw. Technol. **52**(5), 480–491 (2010)
20. Moe, N.B.: Key challenges of improving agile teamwork. In: Baumeister, H., Weber, B. (eds.) XP 2013. LNBIP, vol. 149, pp. 76–90. Springer, Heidelberg (2013). https://doi.org/10.1007/978-3-642-38314-4_6
21. Moe, N.B., Dahl, B., Stray, V., Karlsen, L.S., Schjødt-Osmo, S.: Team autonomy in large-scale agile. In: Proceedings of the Hawaii International Conference on System Sciences (2019)
22. Moe, N.B., Stray, V., Goplen, M.R.: Studying onboarding in distributed software teams: a case study and guidelines. In: Evaluation and Assessment in Software Engineering, April 15–17, 2020, Trondheim, Norway. ACM, New York (2020)
23. Morgan, G.: Images of Organization. SAGE Publications Ltd., Thousand Oaks (2006)
24. Runeson, P., Host, M., Rainer, A., Regnell, B.: Case Study Research in Software Engineering. Wiley, Hoboken (2012)
25. Šmite, D., Moe, N.B., Ågerfalk, P.J.: Fundamentals of agile distributed software development. In: Šmite, D., Moe, N., Ågerfalk, P. (eds.) Agility Across Time and Space, pp. 3–7. Springer, Heidelberg (2010). https://doi.org/10.1007/978-3-642-12442-6_1

26. van Solingen, R., Berghout, E., Kusters, R., Trienekens, J.: From process improvement to people improvement: Enabling learning in software development. Inf. Softw. Technol. **42**(14), 965–971 (2000)

27. Srinivasan, J., Lundqvist, K.: Agile in India: challenges and lessons learned. In: Proceedings of the India Software Engineering Conference, pp. 125–130. ACM Press (2010)

28. Stray, V., Fægri, T.E., Moe, N.B.: Exploring norms in agile software teams. In: Abrahamsson, P., Jedlitschka, A., Nguyen Duc, A., Felderer, M., Amasaki, S., Mikkonen, T. (eds.) PROFES 2016. LNCS, vol. 10027, pp. 458–467. Springer, Cham (2016). https://doi.org/10.1007/978-3-319-49094-6_31

29. Strode, D.E., Huff, S.L., Tretiakov, A.: The impact of organizational culture on agile method use. In: Proceedings of the Annual Hawaii International Conference on System Sciences, pp. 1–9 (2009)

30. Summers, M.: Insights into an Agile adventure with offshore partners. In: Proceedings - Agile 2008 Conference, pp. 333–338 (2008)

31. Williams, L.: What agile teams think of agile principles. Communications of the ACM. **55**(4), 71–76 (2012)

32. Agile India 2012 survey results final. https://www.slideshare.net/ivaltech/agile-india-2012-survey-results-final. Accessed 11 Feb 2020

# A Quantitative Exploration of the 9-Factor Theory: Distribution of Leadership Roles Between Scrum Master and Agile Team

Simone V. Spiegler[1,2(✉)], Daniel Graziotin[1], Christoph Heinecke[3], and Stefan Wagner[1]

[1] Institute of Software Technology, University of Stuttgart, Stuttgart, Germany
{simone.spiegler,daniel.graziotin,stefan.wagner}@iste.uni-stuttgart.de
[2] Robert Bosch Automotive Steering GmbH, Schwäbisch Gmünd, Germany
[3] Robert Bosch GmbH, Stuttgart, Germany
Christoph.Heinecke@bosch.com

**Abstract.** A number of qualitative studies find that team leadership is one essential success factor for evolving into a mature agile team. One such qualitative study suggests the 9-Factor Theory of Scrum Master roles, which claims that the Scrum Master performs a set of 9 leadership roles which are transferred to the team over time [14].

We aimed at conducting a quantitative exploration that examines the presence and change of the 9-Factor Theory in relation to team maturity. We conducted an online survey with 67 individuals at the conglomerate Robert Bosch GmbH. Descriptive statistics reveal that the Scrum Master and the agile team score differently on the 9 factors and that the Scrum Master role is most often distributed in teams that had been working between 3 and 5 months in an agile manner. Yet, we also find that the leadership roles predominantly remain with one dedicated Scrum Master.

Based on our results we suggest to group the 9-Factor Theory into three clusters: the Scrum Master is rather linked to psychological team factors (1), while the team tends to be linked to rather product-related factors (2). Organizational factors (3) are less often present.

Our practical implications suggest an extension of the Scrum Master description. Furthermore, our study lays groundwork for future quantitative testing of leadership in agile teams.

**Keywords:** Leadership · Scrum Master · Maturity · Agile teams · Quantitative survey

## 1 Introduction

Even though an increasing number of organizations aim at implementing agile teams, how to do so is not yet entirely clear [9,10]. Especially rather bureaucratic companies seem to struggle in their agile transformation [10].

© The Author(s) 2020
V. Stray et al. (Eds.): XP 2020, LNBIP 383, pp. 162–177, 2020.
https://doi.org/10.1007/978-3-030-49392-9_11

Fitting leadership behavior is found to be one key success factor for evolving into an agile team [5]. The agile way of working suggests team leadership in which one dedicated Scrum Master and an agile team share leadership roles [9, 14,15]. Most studies have examined the Scrum Master role applying qualitative methods [1,9,14,15], while there is a lack in studies to explore these roles and to understand how much they change [14].

Studies have found that a Scrum Master influences the ability of a team to work in an agile manner [1,6,9,14,15]. The Scrum Master role not only facilitates the Scrum Method but also protects the team from inappropriate external requests and empowers the team to work self-organized and cross-functional towards a common goal [2]. Different qualitative studies suggest that the Scrum Master role changes while the team matures and that some aspects of it are transferred to team members [9,14,15]. While some studies suggest that the Scrum Master role is entirely transferred to developers in more mature teams [1,15], other studies find that one dedicated Scrum Master plays the role differently in more mature teams [5,9,14]. For example, the Scrum Master is assumed to evolve from command-and-control behavior to a coach [5,9]. Yet, further understanding of the changing Scrum Master role in relation to maturity is needed [5,14]. For example, we still lack in quantitative support for a mature team predominantly playing the Scrum Master activities [14].

The body of knowledge indicates a need to start quantifying such complex constructs. With this paper, we aim to contribute to understanding agile teams by expanding knowledge on the leadership role of the Scrum Master. A former study by Spiegler et al. [14] examined the activities of a Scrum Master by applying Grounded Theory and identified nine leadership roles which, for reasons of brevity, we label the *9-Factor Theory of Scrum Master Roles*. Among their results, the authors found seven of the nine roles to be transferred from a dedicated Scrum Master to the team while it matured over time. The results of a Grounded Theory study are a new theory for future quantitative work [4].

The present study builds on Spiegler et al.'s [14] theory by providing first empirical data on the 9-Factor Theory. Through a quantitative exploration, the present study aims to build groundwork on examining leadership in agile teams quantitatively and shed light on the distribution of leadership roles among the Scrum Master and the agile team with respect to team maturity. It is not our aim to test the process of the role transfer from one Scrum Master to the agile team.

Our research questions, inspired by [14], are therefore:

- Which leadership roles does the Scrum Master play? (RQ1)
- Which leadership roles does the agile team play? (RQ2)
- Are leadership roles distributed between a Scrum Master and the agile team, and if so, is the role more often shared in mature as compared to immature teams? (RQ3).

To answer our research questions we designed an online survey, aimed to quantify the presence of the 9 factors and the maturity of the team. Sixty-seven participants from more than 19 different Scrum teams at the Robert Bosch

GmbH, an international company which is active in the automotive, industrial and consumer industry, took part in the survey. Through descriptive statistics of the collected data, we found that the leadership roles are shared to a varying extent between one dedicated role keeper and the agile team. While the Diciplinizer on Equal Terms (explained in Sect. 3.2) was shared most often, the Method Champion was shared least often.

Moreover, our data support a changing Scrum Master role such that it was shared most often in teams that had been working between 3 to 5 months in the agile manner. Yet, the percentage of teams who did share the roles was only about 20% and no agile team predominantly played the Scrum Master role. We therefore conclude that despite sharing of some of the 9 factors, the role predominantly sticks with one dedicated Scrum Master.

Based on our results, we suggest to group the 9 factors along three different clusters: psychological team factors, organizational factors and product-related factors. While psychological factors were linked most often to the Scrum Master, organizational factors were assigned less often to both parties.

To be able to support organisations in the agile transformation, we provide empirical evidence on leadership in agile teams. We conclude with a suggestion for practitioners on the role description of a Scrum Master which can be implemented in real organizational settings. We suppose our results are valuable input for future quantitative testing of the 9-Factor Theory.

## 2    Related Work

In the following we describe team maturity and the distribution of the Scrum Master role in relation to team maturity, ergo the changing Scrum Master role.

### 2.1    Team Maturity

Team literature research differentiates between static and dynamic teamwork models. While the first refers to teams that are stable and have successfully reached a constant mature stage, the second assumes that a team undergoes different maturity stages. This study refers to dynamic teamwork models since we believe it helps us in explaining the changing Scrum Master role.

An agile team transfers through the different maturity stages until it evolves into a truly agile team [6] and, therefore, developers practice the agile way of working differently over time. Agile teams are linked to the forming-storming-norming-performing model by Tuckman [16], which we now summarize.

The forming phase suggests that team members focus on a leader who sets ground rules for further cooperation [16]. Team members are insecure on how to behave, and they search for opportunities to observe expected behavior. In this stage, agile teams are suggested to be more open towards leadership that is centred on one person [5]. The storming phase often involves role conflicts due to a lack in unity and security [16]. Performance often drops in this stage [7]. The norming phase helps teams to increasingly understand and agree on how to work in an agile way [5] and to build a shared understanding of roles and responsibilities [11]. Team performance increases in this phase [7]. The performing stage describes a high performing team in which the team members play roles flexibly according to the situation [16].

## 2.2   The Changing Scrum Master Role

Several authors assume that the Scrum Master role changes depending on the maturity of the team [1,5,9,14,15]. Moe et al. [9] report on teamwork challenges of a newly implemented Scrum team over a period of nine month. They observe that initially the team leadership role was rather centred on the Product Owner and the Scrum Master. The Scrum Master even started to control team members which diminished team leadership and led to less motivation and trust of the team. While the team matured, the authors observed that team leadership advanced, such that team members started to take on more responsibility.

Even though several studies find similar results [1,5,14,15], researchers do not agree on the extent to which the team plays the Scrum Master role over time. While some authors speculate that only some of the Scrum Master activities are transferred to the team [5,9,14], other authors suggest that the dedicated Scrum Master becomes obsolete in more mature teams [1,15]. While a study by Backländer [1] describes that often developers grow into the Scrum Master role over time, Moe et al. [9] discover that team members rarely take over responsibility. Srivastava and Jain [15] conclude that all team members should be able to take on the Scrum Master role in more mature teams.

Spiegler et al. [14] study suggests a set of 9 leadership roles of which 7 are gradually transferred to the team, while 2 of the roles remain with one dedicated Scrum Master. Their discovered roles are Method Champion, Disciplinizer on Equal Terms, Change Agent, Helicopter, Moderator, Networker, Knowledge Enabler and Protector, which we summarize in Sect. 3.2 but are explained to a greater extent in their paper. We name the nine leadership roles of a Scrum Master the 9-Factor Theory in the present paper.

Since the Spiegler et al. [14] study is a Grounded Theory based theory grounded in empirical qualitative data, the 9 leadership roles of a Scrum Master and how the role distribution unfolds in an immature as compared to a mature team has not yet been quantitatively analyzed.

## 3   Method

This section portrays the participants, the measurement, data collection and analysis of our study.

### 3.1   Company Context and Participants

Our data was collected from the multi-national conglomerate Robert Bosch GmbH with more than 20 different sub-companies producing automotive, electrical and consumer industry goods. Scrum teams have the roles Product Owner, Scrum Master and agile team. Depending on the setting teams may have additional roles like a project manager, business owner, group leader or release train engineer. Yet, there is no company-wide standard.

The Scrum Master is a job title at the Robert Bosch GmbH. The person playing the committed Scrum Master varies among teams. For example, the role keeper can be a developer or a former group leader. Often, the Scrum Master is called 'Agile Master' indicating that the role keeper should rather focus on team dynamics than on the Scrum method. Scrum Masters at the Robert Bosch GmbH are usually not disciplinary supervisors of agile team members, and were probably without authoritative power in our sample.

In total, *67 participants* took part in our study. 46 were from software development projects, 3 from software and hardware development, 4 from software development and IT and the remaining 14 from other topics (e.g. mechanical engineering, purchasing, human resources). 56.7% of the participants had been working more than 11 months with their colleagues.

Our sample contained *37 Scrum Masters* of which 20 had at least 10 months of experience in the Scrum Master role. The remaining *30 participants were team members*. 14 team members stated that they were 9 or more members in their team. We did not measure this item for the Scrum Masters.

Due to confidentiality reasons, providing the team name was optional. 37 participants opted to enter their team name and related to *19 different teams from nine different business divisions* at the Robert Bosch GmbH. Since not all respondents inserted their team name, we could not map responses to teams and were only able to compare individual responses.

### 3.2 Measurement

The research questions guiding this study required a quantitative exploration of Spiegler et al.'s 9-Factor theory [14]. Each of the nine factors describes a leadership role. Besides evaluating the existence of different leadership roles, this study aimed at providing evidence that leadership roles are shared between a Scrum Master and an agile team and that the leadership roles are distributed differently depending on the maturity of an agile team.

We now briefly describe the 9 Factors. A deeper description is offered in the introductory paper [14].

*Factor MC (Method Champion): The role contains organizing meetings, teaching the method, support formulating tasks and setting goals, and discusses how to adapt the method during the retrospective.*

*Factor DE (Disciplinizer on Equal Terms): Supports the team to keep to the rules, ensures that the team focuses on relevant topics and makes sure that team members attend the meetings. Discipline is accomplished via communication on a par.*

*Factor CO (Coach): Observes team members and uncovers which kind of behaviour is missing in a team to improve teamwork, provides feedback, and helps teams to find out what they wish to change and how to do so.*

*Factor CA (Change Agent): Serves as a role model, changes habits, and convinces newly established project teams of the agile way of working.*

*Factor HEL (Helicopter): Possesses the ability to see the bigger picture, to know who possess the right skill for a certain task, to include relevant stakeholders and to structure work.*

*Factor MO (Moderator): Moderates all kind of meetings and builds a bridge between perspectives and domains.*

*Factor NET (Networker): Connects the team with relevant stakeholders from within and outside the organisation.*

*Factor KE (Knowledge Enabler): Realises which kind of knowledge the team needs, supports team members to acquire that knowledge and promotes iterative learning.*

*Factor PRO (Protector): Shelters teams from inappropriate requests from the Product Owner, managers, disciplinary leaders and other departments.*

**Items for Measuring the 9 Factors.** Based on the description of the Scrum Master roles by Spiegler et al. [14], we initially built a set of 67 items. Based on techniques rooted in pool items and item review [12], after two revisions we reduced the initial set to 55 items, each connected to one activity of the nine different roles.

Each factor was covered by 4 to 9 different items. For example, the Disciplinizer on Equal Terms contained the following four items: *Supports team to keep to the rules. Helps team to focus on relevant topics. Makes sure members attend meetings. Communicates on a par.* Yet, items are not grouped in the questionnaires, s.t. participants are blind to the existence of the factors. This helps avoid bias that could artificially form clusters.

**Maturity.** To test maturity, we asked how many months the team had been working in an agile manner. The choice is inspired by Wheelan et al. [17]. They found a significant correlation between the average number of months a team had been working together and the four group development stages [18], in which a mature team was perceived to be meeting 5.2 months or more on average (Stage 3 = 5.2 months on average; Stage 4 = 8.5 months on average). Based on previous results the question *How many months has your team been working in an agile manner?* provided five choices (0–2 months, 3–5 months, 6–8 months, 9–11 months, more than 11 months) (Table 1).

**Table 1.** Maturity

| Months | Team member (N = 29) | Scrum Master (N = 36) |
|---|---|---|
| 0–2 | 0 | 2 |
| 3–5 | 5 | 8 |
| 6–8 | 6 | 3 |
| 9–11 | 4 | 5 |
| More than 11 | 14 | 18 |

**Self-Assessment and External Assessment.** Since teams and formal leaders often rate leadership behavior differently [3], we conducted a self-assessment and an external assessment for evaluation of each item (leadership activity). Therefore, each item contained two Likert items: the self-assessment and the external assessment. More specifically, the Scrum Master conducted a self-assessment of the leadership behavior he or she believed to perform and an external assessment of the leadership activities he or she believed the agile team performed, and the agile team vice verse rated itself and the Scrum Master.

Therefore, the participants answered each item twice (2*55): one to rate the Scrum Master and one to rate the team. The participants rated their perception of leadership activities displayed by the Scrum Master and the agile team using a five-point Likert item with $1 = $ strong disagreement that the activity was done by the respective party, $5 = $ high agreement, and an additional option $= $ Don't know/Not applicable. Questions were randomly ordered.

### 3.3   Data Collection

To assess the 9-Factor Theory we used a web-based survey tool provided by the Robert Bosch GmbH, as part of the agreement to run the study with them.

To invite Scrum practitioners to take part in our survey, we used our personal network within the Robert Bosch GmbH and a internal social business platform provided by the company. An invitation letter contained the link to the online survey and introduced the broader topic of the research and informed that data would be treated anonymously and that participation was voluntarily. Besides treating personal data confidentially on our side, participants had the opportunity to voluntarily insert their team name and their email address to receive their aggregated team results. This personal data was used for the respective team retrospective only and for no scientific or management purpose, which was also emphasized in the invitation letter. Filling out the survey took approximately 15 min. With the exception of the personal data all questions were compulsory. The full questionnaire is available online [13]. Due to confidentiality requirements by the Robert Bosch GmbH, the raw data cannot be provided openly.

### 3.4   Pilot Study

Eight individuals filled out a pilot of the online survey and provided feedback on understanding the content of the items and the convenience to answer the survey.

Some participants had stated to be annoyed when they had to read one item twice on consecutive pages separately for the Scrum Master and the agile team and the company had urged to build a questionnaire that would not take longer than 15 min to be filled out. Rating each item for both parties at the same time and on one page was considered to save time and to be more convenient.

Even though we had used the feedback for modification, drop out rate was 60% after launching the survey officially. Several participants delivered the feedback that reading all the items on one page was inconvenient. Therefore, we modified the questionnaire once again, and put the 55 items on three consecutive pages each containing an equal number of items.

This modification led to a loss of data, which we could not plan for with the tool supplied by the company, in 8 already fully filled-out responses. The modified survey accomplished 121 responses, of which 68 were completed while 53 did not reach the last item. We opted to retain only fully completed questionnaires rather than adding partial data. 16 respondents stopped after they had filled out the first block of items, while 22 respondents dropped out when reaching the first block of items and 15 individuals just opened the link without answering any of the questions. Once again, we received the feedback by participants, that the questionnaire was inconvenient to be read.

Due to the above-mentioned constraints we still kept the questionnaire the way it was designed. Also we cannot say with certainty why so many individuals decided to stop filling out the questionnaire. It may also be that they did not feel comfortable with rating Scrum Master and agile teams separately.

We removed the responses of one individual who rated every item with "agree," likely indicating a lack of motivation to participate in the study. This led to a total sample of 67 (55.37%) respondents.

## 3.5   Analysis

For each of the 9 factors we build a mean value by the related items for the Scrum Master and the agile team separately. To avoid including individuals that had only answered a few items related to one factor, we included responses in the calculation of the mean value when individuals had at least answered $n-1$ items per role. That means, if a factor had 4 items, we only included individuals that had answered at least 3 of the items.

To assess whether leadership roles were shared between the Scrum Master and the agile team we applied a similar approach as Zafft, Adams and Smith's [19] approach to measuring leadership distribution in self-managed teams. Applying a 5-point Likert scale (1 = strongly disagree, 5 = strongly agree), they suggest a leadership behavior to be present when someone scores higher than 4.0 [19]. In our analysis, we considered a factor to be embodied by the Scrum Master or the team if the respective party rated 4.0 or higher. If one participant rated both, Scrum Master and agile team, in one factor higher than 4.0, the respective role was considered to be distributed between both parties within one team.

If at least five of the nine factors were found to be shared within the same team, we considered the Scrum Master role to be shared between the agile team and the dedicated Scrum Master.

## 4   Results

The results are structured as follows: After referring to external and self-assessment, we will answer our three research questions in consecutive order.

*External and Self-Assessment.* The average mean for the nine factors revealed that the Scrum Master tended to rate herself higher than the team rated the respective Scrum Master, while the Scrum Master tended to rate the agile team lower. One exception was the Networker which the Scrum Master rated slightly higher than the team rated itself. Likewise, we found that the team members tended to rate themselves higher than the Scrum Master rated them, while they tended to rate the activities performed by the Scrum Master lower.

## 4.1  Scrum Master

Our first research question is: *Which leadership roles does the Scrum Master play?* (RQ1).

To be able to give evidence on the Scrum Master performing one of the nine leadership roles, the mean value of a factor has to be higher than 4.0 (explained in Sect. 3.5). The mean value for four factors is higher than 4.0, namely Factor MC, DE, CO and MO, and more than two third of the Scrum Masters score high on them. Factor CA, HEL, NET and PRO are linked to about half of the Scrum Masters. Only about one third have a mean value higher than 4.0 regarding Factor KE. More information in Table 2.

**Table 2.** Descriptive statistics for the 9 factors

| Factor | Scrum Master | | | | | Agile team | | | | |
|---|---|---|---|---|---|---|---|---|---|---|
| | N | Mean | Std. deviation | n* | h** | N | Mean | Std. deviation | n* | h** |
| MC | 67 | 4.15 | .56 | 47 | 70.15% | 60 | 3.19 | .67 | 7 | 11.67% |
| DE | 67 | 4.18 | .55 | 49 | 73.13% | 65 | 3.83 | .52 | 32 | 49.23% |
| CO | 66 | 4.09 | .73 | 46 | 69.69% | 64 | 3.58 | .59 | 17 | 26.56% |
| CA | 61 | 3.95 | .65 | 37 | 60.66% | 56 | 3.56 | .52 | 16 | 28.57% |
| HEL | 64 | 3.73 | .68 | 28 | 43.75% | 62 | 3.72 | .54 | 24 | 38.71% |
| MO | 67 | 4.07 | .63 | 49 | 73.13% | 62 | 3.72 | .48 | 22 | 35.48% |
| NET | 65 | 3.70 | .86 | 30 | 46.15% | 62 | 3.44 | .81 | 21 | 33.87% |
| KE | 63 | 3.62 | .76 | 22 | 34.92% | 58 | 3.58 | .66 | 20 | 34.48% |
| PRO | 62 | 3.70 | .88 | 32 | 51.61% | 53 | 3.10 | .84 | 10 | 18.86% |

*n describes the absolute frequency of a factor rating higher than 4.0.
**h describes the relative frequency (n/N per row).
Note: Each column contains summarized results and refers to answers by Scrum Masters and the agile team taken together.

Therefore, we answer RQ1 and find that a majority of the Scrum Masters play the Method Champion, Disciplinizer on Equal Terms, Coach and Moderator, while the Change Agent, Helicopter, Networker and Protector is played by merely about half of the Scrum Masters and the Knowledge Enabler is performed by only about one third.

## 4.2    Agile Team

Our second research question is: *Which leadership roles does the agile team play?* (RQ2).

To be able to give evidence on the team playing one of the nine roles, the mean value of a factor has to be higher than 4.0 (explained in Sect. 3.5). Table 2 illustrates that all mean values of the nine factors related to the agile team are lower than 4.0. Therefore, one could claim that team members tend to not play the leadership roles. Yet, almost 50% of the teams score higher than 4.0 for Factor DE. Between 30% and 40% perform Factor HEL, MO, NET and KE. Factor MC and PRO are rarely aligned to the team.

Based on our results, we answer RQ2 and find that the agile team tends to not play the leadership roles. About half of the teams perform the Disciplinizer on Equal Terms, while only about one third perform the Helicopter, Moderator, Networker and Knowledge Enabler. The Method Champion, Coach and Protector are performed least often by the teams.

## 4.3    Distribution of the 9 Factors Between Scrum Master and Agile Team

The third research question is: *Are leadership roles distributed between a Scrum Master and the agile team, and if so, is the role more often shared in mature as compared to immature teams?*

If a participant scores a factor for both the Scrum Master and the team higher than a mean value of 4.0, the factor is considered to be distributed between the Scrum Master and the agile team. While Factor DE, HEL and MO are distributed in 30% to 40% of the teams, Factors MC, CA, KE and PRO are distributed in 10% to 20% of the teams. Table 3 shows an overview on the distribution for each of the nine factors, starting with the most frequently shared Factor DE to the least frequently shared Factor MC.

**Table 3.** Distribution of the 9 factors

| Factor | Shared | Only Scrum Master | Only team | No one | N | Total % |
|--------|--------|-------------------|-----------|--------|-----|---------|
| DE | 43.30% | 29.90% | 4.50% | 22.40% | 67 | 100.00% |
| MO | 31.30% | 41.80% | 1.50% | 25.40% | 67 | 100.00% |
| HEL | 28.40% | 13.40% | 7.50% | 50.70% | 67 | 100.00% |
| CO | 25.40% | 43.30% | 0.00% | 31.30% | 67 | 100.00% |
| NET | 22.40% | 22.40% | 9.00% | 46.30% | 67 | 100.00% |
| CA | 19.40% | 35.80% | 4.50% | 40.30% | 67 | 100.00% |
| KE | 16.40% | 16.40% | 13.40% | 53.70% | 67 | 100.00% |
| PRO | 14.90% | 32.80% | 0.00% | 52.20% | 67 | 100.00% |
| MC | 10.40% | 59.70% | 0.00% | 29.90% | 67 | 100.00% |

Note: Each column contains summarized results and refers to answers by Scrum Masters and the agile team taken together.

If a respondent scores a mean value higher than 4.0 for at least five of the factors for both, Scrum Master and agile team, the Scrum Master role is considered to be distributed between the agile team and the dedicated Scrum Master. 20.90% of the respondents share the Scrum Master role.

38.5% of the teams that had been working 3–5 months in an agile manner shared the Scrum Master role, 11.11% of the teams rating 6–11 months shared it and 18.8% of the teams rating more than 11 months shared the role. Therefore, teams that had been working for 3–5 months tended to share the role by 20% points more than teams that had been working for 11 months or more, and by 27.39% points more than teams that had been working in an agile way between 6–11 months.

Furthermore, we check if some teams perform the Scrum Master role predominantly, such that the team scored for 5 factors higher than 4.0, while the Scrum Master scored for less than 5 factors higher than 4.0. We did not find such a case in our data.

Based on these results we answer RQ3 and claim that leadership roles can be shared, yet, some roles are shared more often than others. While we find that the Disciplinizer on Equal Terms is most often shared between the team and the Scrum Master, we find that the Method Champion, Coach and Protector are rather centred on one dedicated Scrum Master.

Furthermore, the distribution of the Scrum Master role varies in different maturity stages. We find that teams who share the role had most often been working in an agile way between 3 to 5 months. Therefore, the role was rather shared in immature teams. Furthermore, we did not find a single team in which the Scrum Master role was centred on the agile team.

## 5   Discussion

Our study aimed at exploring the presence of and the change in the 9-Factor Theory [14]. Based on descriptive statistics, we found that the 9 different roles are performed to a varying extent:

While the Scrum Master rates highest in the Method Champion, Disciplinizer on Equal Terms, Coach and Moderator, the agile team scores highest in the Disciplinizer on Equal Terms, Helicopter, Moderator, Knowledge Enabler and Networker. Both, Scrum Master and agile team, tend to perform the Protector less often than the other roles.

Based on this result, we suggest to broaden the 9-Factor Theory by Spiegler et al. [14]. Our results indicate that the 9 factors can be further grouped into three clusters: psychological team factors, product-related factors and organizational factors. We will now elaborate on this idea based on empirical results.

Factor MC, CO and MO rather focus on internal socio-psychological team mechanisms, while Factor CA, NET and PRO involve an external focus towards the organization. Factor DE, HEL and KE are rather product-related and aim at continuous learning and knowledge sharing. The Scrum Master scores higher in roles related to psychological team factors (e.g. Method Champion and Coach).

The team scores higher in product-related factors (e.g. Helicopter and Knowledge Enabler). Roles that bridge the organization with the team were played more often by the agile team regarding the Networker, but less often regarding the Protector (Table 4).

Table 4. 3 proposed clusters of the 9-Factor Theory

| Cluster | Leadership role (Factor) | More important to |
|---------|--------------------------|-------------------|
| Psychological team factors | Method Champion (ME)<br>Coach (CO)<br>Moderator (MO) | Scrum Master |
| Product-related factors | Disciplinizer on Equal Terms (DE)<br>Helicopter (HEL)<br>Knowledge Enabler (KE) | Agile team |
| Organizational factors | Change Agent (CA)<br>Networker (NET)<br>Protector (PRO) | It depends |

Moreover, about half of the teams did not play the Protector, the Change Agent or the Networker which are linked to the organizational factors. In rather bureaucratic organizations, as in our case, it might be more difficult to perform the roles related to bridging the organization and the team. A traditional environment rather focuses on hierarchy as opposed to protect the team from management and on departmentalized structure as opposed to network with each other independent from formal structures [10].

We speculate that if a Scrum Master played the Protector to a larger extent, the agile team would take over the leadership roles more often. The Protector provides hierarchical free space within which team members feel safe to take on the divers roles [14].

Furthermore, 53% of the teams did not perform the Knowledge Enabler and about 51% the Helicopter. A possible explanation for our results would be that either the Scrum Master considers product-related roles to not be part of the job description since the agile team is expected to self-organize their work, or it is more difficult to play the respective roles in a bureaucratic context since that company type is build on experts with specialized skills as opposed to cross-functional knowledge sharing [10]. This may be supported by the teams scoring equally low on this factor.

This study also aimed at exploring the 9-Factor Theory in relation to maturity. The 20% of the teams that did share the Scrum Master role, provided support for the suggestion that the Scrum Master role is distributed differently in different maturity stages. Teams that had been working in the agile manner for 3 to 5 months and more than 11 months shared the role most often.

This finding fits with the maturity model by Tuckman [16]: Teams after 3 to 5 months tend to be in the storming phase, within which teams are not sure about who plays which role within the team. Therefore, both, team and Scrum Master, perform the Scrum Master roles. Teams working in an agile way for more than 11 months could already have reached the performing phase within which roles are played according to the situation and less linked to one dedicated role keeper.

Yet, we did not find any agile team that played the Scrum Master role to a larger extent than the dedicated role keeper. Therefore, our results do not point at the direction that the formal role keeper steps back from the role as suggested by several studies [1,14,15]. This finding also fits with earlier claims that teams in organizational settings rarely develop into high performing teams that take on roles spontaneously [8]. We therefore propose that in most of the teams the dedicated Scrum Master does not become obsolete over time but rather changes the primary role during the different phases of team development.

Another explanation of the results could be that neither Scrum Master nor agile team but someone else took over the role. As described in Sect. 3.1 agile teams and the aligned agile roles vary among different settings at the Robert Bosch GmbH. It might be that some of the nine leadership roles are also played by the Product Owner or disciplinary supervisor. However, those roles were neglected in our study. The last paragraph of the practical implications provide suggestions on how to deal with this in company settings.

## 6   Practical Implications

We found that the leadership roles were rather centred on the Scrum Master. In the following we thus suggest how to develop the Scrum Master description in company settings. Section 5 proposed to group the Scrum Master description into three clusters: psychological team factors, organizational factors and product-related factors.

While some practitioners suggest that the Scrum Master should play product-related roles, others state that interference on a technical level hinders self-organizing teams. We suggest that every team should discuss on its own, to which degree it needs product-related support by a Scrum Master. Yet, a Scrum Master who performs product-related roles builds an understanding of the respective product, thus, can also more easily bridge the agile team with the processes, requirements, tools and standards of a rather bureaucratic surrounding.

For example, the Scrum Master can be a mouthpiece of the team to discuss with the management which processes and requirements of rather traditional project management are still needed despite the team working in an agile way, and which ones are rather unnecessary and hinder the progress of the team. The Scrum Master can argue which tools and processes the team needs to work in a more agile way. Also, taking over product-related roles improves understanding when to protect the team, e.g. from re-prioritization, and when to give in and allow to re-arrange planning due to changes in requirements on organizational level.

Thus, the Scrum Master supports the organization to gradually evolve into a more agile place. Yet, we acknowledge the balancing act of a Scrum Master to support the team in product-related matters and to serve as a coach at the same time. The Scrum Master continuously needs to serve as a coach and support the team to learn how to take on the divers roles.

Agile teams in a traditional industrial conglomerate may not be used to take on leadership activities as a whole team. Yet, if the leadership gap [14] is not filled by the agile team, there is the risk of a leadership vacuum, in which no one takes over leadership roles. This may lead to less performance.

Nevertheless, we found that the Scrum Master and the team tend to play organizational factors to a lesser extent, and encourage managers even further to build an agile friendly surrounding within which the organizational factors can be performed. These factors are necessary to integrate the agile team into the organizational setting, such as having access to relevant stakeholders and information, reducing interfaces and efforts for alignment and building trust between agile teams and traditional structures. Consequently, motivation and progress of agile teams will increase even further. Yet, organizations also need to understand and accept that sometimes teams do not want to take on leadership roles.

Therefore, companies should use our questionnaire to reflect upon the role distribution in their specific industry background and organizational environment relevant to their team. There might be roles beyond the Scrum Master and the agile team that take on the leadership roles. Thus, we suggest to not only focus on leadership sharing among the Scrum Master and the agile team but to broaden the perspective. We propose to use the leadership roles and aligned activities to determine if they are covered by any 'job title' in the setting, which might be the Product Owner or the disciplinary supervisor. After all, the agile way of working is not about establishing a standard regarding which job title plays which leadership role but about making sure that the needs of an agile team are covered in any given situation. Since teams mature and agile settings vary, teams need to find a context-dependent equilibrium of leadership sharing. Therefore, each team has to discuss on its own how to divide leadership activities among each other. Furthermore, since context changes, teams need to discuss regularly upon who takes on which leadership role in a given situation. Practitioners will understand respective leadership needs, learn to balance and evolve them, and thus, improve teamwork.

## 7   Limitations and Future Work

In the following we will suggest future topics for research while referring to limitations of this study.

Objectivity: since we conducted an online survey, we assume a low level of social response bias. Yet, respondents were allowed to insert their email address for receiving their team results. This could lead to a social response bias in such a way that respondents wanted to rate high in the Scrum Master activities.

With 67 participants our sample is limited in size and prevented us to perform a psychometric evaluation of the tool, limiting our confidence in the tool validity. A psychometric evaluation of the tool would not be a familiar step in software engineering studies, so we see this as a missed opportunity rather than a limitation. Future studies should aim for a bigger sample size that allows to perform an exploratory factor analysis, thus quantitatively clustering the factors. As the theorized 9 factors might be difficult to test psychometrically, we suggest future studies to test the three suggested clusters in Sect. 5, thus, allowing for testing agile team behavior along three variables instead of nine.

Since the drop-out rate for this study was quite high, for future studies we suggest, to rate the Scrum Master and the agile team each on separate consecutive pages. Therefore, participants will have to answer six different pages of questions. This will take more time, yet, may lead to a more convenient experience to fill out the questionnaire, and thus, increase the number of responses.

Moreover, even though each business division operates within a different subculture and industry context, still all teams were from the same conglomerate. Even if our study is clearly placed as an exploratory one, we want to highlight that we cannot claim our results to be universally applicable. We suggest a larger sample drawn from different companies with different industry backgrounds to extend our study in the future.

Moreover, almost 50% of the team members stated to be 9 or more persons in their team. We were not able to control for this variable since we had not asked the Scrum Master on their number of team members. Larger groups are found to be less likely to evolve into a mature team [17]. Future testing should take this into account.

Our data points at an evolving Scrum Master role in relation to maturity. However, maturity was rated by the number of months each team had been working in an agile way. We cannot claim with certainty that the time a team has been working in an agile manner is related to maturity stages. Furthermore, we have not conducted a longitudinal study but compared different teams which had been working a varying amount of time in the agile manner.

Future testing should refer to the maturity stage by Wheelan [17] to examine the 9-Factor Theory for a valid measurement of group maturity, investigate time and group development in relation to varied company types and sizes, as well as in a longitudinal study.

# References

1. Bäcklander, G.: Doing complexity leadership theory: how agile coaches at spotify practise enabling leadership. Creativity Innov. Manag. 28(1), 42–60 (2019)
2. Cockburn, A., Highsmith, J.: Agile software development, the people factor. Computer 34(11), 131–133 (2001)
3. Crevani, L., Lindgren, M., Packendorff, J.: Leadership, not leaders: on the study of leadership as practices and interactions. Scand. J. Manag. 26(1), 77–86 (2010)
4. Glaser, B.G., Strauss, A.L.: Discovery of Grounded Theory: Strategies for Qualitative Research. Routledge, London (2017)
5. Gren, L., Goldman, A., Jacobsson, C.: Agile ways of working: a team maturity perspective. J. Softw.: Evol. Process (2019, in press)

6. Gren, L., Torkar, R., Feldt, R.: Group development and group maturity when building agile teams: a qualitative and quantitative investigation at eight large companies. J. Syst. Softw. **124**, 104–119 (2017)
7. Katzenbach, J.R., Smith, D.K.: The Wisdom of Teams: Creating the High-performance Organization. Harvard Business Review Press, Boston (2015)
8. Marks, M.A., Mathieu, J.E., Zaccaro, S.J.: A temporally based framework and taxonomy of team processes. Acad. Manag. Rev. **26**(3), 356–376 (2001)
9. Moe, N.B., Dingsøyr, T., Dybå, T.: A teamwork model for understanding an agile team: a case study of a scrum project. Inf. Softw. Technol. **52**(5), 480–491 (2010)
10. Nerur, S., Mahapatra, R.K., Mangalaraj, G.: Challenges of migrating to agile methodologies. Commun. ACM **48**(5), 72–78 (2005)
11. Neuman, G.A., Wright, J.: Team effectiveness: beyond skills and cognitive ability. J. Appl. Psychol. **84**(3), 376 (1999)
12. Rust, J.: Modern Psychometrics: The Science of Psychological Assessment. Routledge, New York (2009)
13. Spiegler, S.V., Graziotin, D., Heinecke, C., Wagner, S.: A quantitative exploration of the 9-factor theory: distribution of leadership roles between the scrum master and the agile team (2020). https://doi.org/10.5281/zenodo.3634046
14. Spiegler, S.V., Heinecke, C., Wagner, S.: Leadership gap in agile teams: how teams and scrum masters mature. In: Kruchten, P., Fraser, S., Coallier, F. (eds.) XP 2019. LNBIP, vol. 355, pp. 37–52. Springer, Cham (2019). https://doi.org/10.1007/978-3-030-19034-7_3
15. Srivastava, P., Jain, S.: A leadership framework for distributed self-organized scrum teams. Team Perform. Manag.: Int. J. **23**(5/6), 293–314 (2017)
16. Tuckman, B.W.: Developmental sequence in small groups. Psychol. Bull. **63**(6), 384 (1965)
17. Wheelan, S.A., Davidson, B., Tilin, F.: Group development across time: reality or illusion? Small Group Res. **34**(2), 223–245 (2003)
18. Wheelan, S.A., Hochberger, J.M.: Validation studies of the group development questionnaire. Small Group Res. **27**(1), 143–170 (1996)
19. Zafft, C.R., Adams, S.G., Matkin, G.S.: Measuring leadership in self-managed teams using the competing values framework. J. Eng. Educ. **98**(3), 273–282 (2009)

# What an Agile Leader Does: The Group Dynamics Perspective

Lucas Gren[1,2,3]([envelope]) and Magdalena Lindman[3]

[1] Chalmers University of Technology, Gothenburg, Sweden
lucas.gren@cse.gu.se
[2] University of Gothenburg, Gothenburg, Sweden
[3] Volvo Cars, Gothenburg, Sweden
magdalena.lindman@volvocars.com

**Abstract.** When large industrial organizations change to (or start with) an agile approach to operations, managers and some employees are supposed to be "agile leaders" often without being given a clear definition of what that comprises when building agile teams. An inductive thematic analysis was used to investigate what 15 appointed leaders actually do and perceive as challenges regarding group dynamics working with an agile approach. *Team maturity*, *Team design*, and *Culture and mindset* were all categories of challenges related to group dynamics that the practitioners face and manage in their work-life that are not explicitly mentioned in the more process-focused agile transformation frameworks. The results suggest that leader mitigation of these three aspects of group dynamics is essential to the success of an agile transformation.

**Keywords:** Leadership · Agile development processes · Qualitative study

## 1 Introduction

The reported benefits of an agile approach includes increased customer collaboration, better estimation of tasks, and increased quality [1], but also higher job satisfaction [2] as well as overall stakeholder satisfaction and, therefore, project success [3]. All of which have contributed to the popularity of the agile approach to development work. Agile development, compared to the plan-driven/ waterfall, implies more communication and stronger focus on people, which make the social-psychological aspects very important to understand, including leadership and management [4].

The research on leadership was focused solely on the leader as an individual for many decades, often referred to as *great person theory of leadership* [5]. The challenge for leaders was then to be categorized as a leader, but once accepted, the leader could probably act as he saw fit to a larger extent (leadership was also categorized as a male trait). The research on leadership and management then shifted from trying to find the best leader to looking at what the best leaders

V. Stray et al. (Eds.): XP 2020, LNBIP 383, pp. 178–194, 2020.
https://doi.org/10.1007/978-3-030-49392-9_12

actually do, since it turned out not all the behaviors in one accepted leader were towards effectiveness in general [6]. After that, instead of a focus on finding the best leadership style, a more systematic and situational view of leadership has developed [7]. What is the best leadership depends on the context, and, in some theories, on the maturity level of the co-workers, but it also contains a balance between task- and relation-focused behaviors connected to these phases [8]. The leader role has thereby become more demanding and requires adaptability to context in a way that was not highlighted before. Trying to exert leadership from its context, the way researchers and practitioners have done, is probably a mistake. Schein [9] writes that leadership and culture are two sides of the same coin, and Northhouse [10] also emphasizes the importance of context, where he also models leadership as a collective ability of initiative. Dynamic team leadership [7] is not new in psychological science, and also a property of teams that are in the more mature stages of small group/team development [11].

Recent studies in software engineering has shown that the definition of agile teams overlap with what is meant by a mature team in social psychology [12]. We define team maturity in this study as the degree to which a team has navigated through the group development stages according to Tuckman [11]. Teams transitioning towards agile ways of working are often in the middle of two paradigms where the more classical hierarchical management structure is in an organizational change process towards new forms of more dynamic and shared team leadership [13]. Spiegler et al. [14] showed that the leadership function is gradually transferred from the Scrum Master to the team members over time. In more general leadership science, Millikin et al. [15] showed that self-managing teams have higher productivity even in multi-team settings and that the highly cohesive teams perform the best. In the agile space, e.g. servant leadership is advocated as the foundation for leading, but the definition of what that is remains vague [16]. It is, therefore, still unclear what the behavior and challenges are in relation to group/team dynamics when implementing agile teams from the perspective of an appointed leader.

If the goal of leadership in an agile world is for the teams to eventually lead themselves within their mandate and technical expertise, we can also look at psychological theories on how to lead towards self-organization. We define self-organization in this paper as a state where the initiative, responsibility, and drive towards accomplishing team goals are dynamically shared between many team members in the same team. In past psychology research on self-organizing teams, team design has been found to be more important than team coaching when striving for self-organization [17]. In this context, Wageman [17] defines team design as including all the following eleven design features: (1) real team, (2) clear direction, (3) appropriate size, (4) skill diversity, (5) task interdependence, (6) challenging task objectives, (7) core strategy norms, (8) team excellence recognized/rewarded, (9) information for planning available, (10) training/technical consultation available, and (11) material resources available. We define team design in this paper as the eleven features above but want to stress that a role that is less integrated in the team compared to team members, needs to help design the team with regards to these eleven features. In our experience, agile teams are sometimes set up so that the teams themselves are expected do the design work, which is not what Wageman [17] found to work well. She instead highlights the external leader role in enabling teams to self-organize over time.

Furthermore, Wageman [18] describes the different roles of a leader as first having to be a designer, which includes (1) "setting a direction for the performing unit, design a team task and a team reward system," (2) "making sure the team has the basic material resources it needs to do the work," and (3) "establishing the team's authority over and its responsibility for its performance strategies." Only later can an appointed leader be what is refer to as a midwife that should act at natural breaking-points in the team's further development, which comprises "working with the team to establish appropriate performance goals." These goals should be measurable and specify "how a team will take on its work in ways that fulfill its overall direction." Only in the final step should the leader be a coach. Team coaching is only possible with the other two steps fulfilled and only then will the team make good use of the coaching. She continues to state that "because well-designed teams are robust enough to bounce back from inappropriate leader actions, the leader now has the latitude to unlearn old managerial habits and take the time that is needed to learn effective team coaching skills" [18].

We define leadership as a function of initiative or group action [10], and therefore, view all the described behavior as components of leadership. Our research goal is to understand what appointed agile leaders do when building and maintaining agile teams and where that fits into related work on leadership behavior. A qualitative research method allows for a deeper analysis of the complexity of a construct, and allows research participants to speak freely about their reality. Therefore, a qualitative approach is appropriate to study leadership in the context of agile teams. This study aims at investigating how agile leaders at different positions at different industrial development departments interpret the, vaguely defined, concept of agile leadership in relation to group dynamics in their real-world context. The research question is, therefore, **RQ: What are the behaviors and challenges in relation to group/team dynamics when implementing agile teams from the perspective of an appointed leader?**

## 2   Method

This section presents the method we used to analyze the leadership situation in the agile development context.

### 2.1   Procedure

The participants were obtained indirectly through our industry or research contacts. We asked these contacts to suggest fitting participants which we then contacted by email. A heterogeneous sample was achieved by recruiting people from many different companies, both with an overview of the development part of the organizations and people in new agile roles of newly formed teams. All of the people that we contacted participated. We conducted 45 to 90 min open-ended interviews, and thirteen of them were conducted using teleconference. First, a personal introduction of the researcher(s) was done including research background, and what the researcher wanted to find out though the overall research project. The interviewer then asked for permission to record the interview and emphasized the anonymity of the data collection. Two interviews were conducted face-to-face and recorded on a mobile device, but were transcribed in the same way. Thirteen of the interviews were conducted by the first author in English, and two were conducted by the second author but in Swedish. The interviews were transcribed verbatim afterwards and Swedish quotes were translated into English.

*Interview Protocol.* Most of our questions were descriptive in nature, however, some were also contrasting and reflective. The reason why we wanted to be concrete and not ask directly about emotions and interpretations was that we wanted to meet the engineering at their own discourse, i.e. use vocabulary that engineers are used to in their work situation. If the interviewee expressed frustration, emotion or problematized something we asked follow-up questions to prone the person's interpretation and experience around that topic.

The interviews were semi-structured and aimed to answer the research question on what main challenges agile leaders define in connection to group dynamics. We selected participant who saw themselves as leaders in the agile context an did not use any specific role or definition thereof. Examples of questions used to investigate such association were: "What do you think is working/not working with the agile implementation and why?" "Do you see a difference in how high performing teams adopt agile compared to new or less mature teams?" and "How do work processes evolve in agile teams?"

## 2.2 Participants

The participants were practitioners working with an agile approach, according to themselves, on different levels of organizations, ranging from team Scrum Masters to founders or CEOs. The first thirteen participants were involved in software development and the second two were involved in hardware development complementing the sample since agile has spread to other areas than software development. However, the conclusions drawn from the hardware part should be considered with care since generalizations most likely cannot be drawn from only two participants, i.e. we have yet to see saturation in that data.

Table 1 provides a brief guide to the variety of cases that we investigated with information about the interviewees, and their organizational situation. The interviewees worked in companies ranging in size from 35 to 56 000 employees, and represented work cultures in seven different countries. Three of the participants where in an environment that started with an agile approach to work from the beginning. However, since they still described the agile way of working in

**Table 1.** Company information.

| | Interviewees | Method used before agile | Reason for agile |
|---|---|---|---|
| Company A | Agile coach | Waterfall process | More engagement, job satisfaction, and quality |
| Company B | Project manager lead | Waterfall process | Improved business value |
| Company C | Project portfolio management responsible | Ad hoc process | Focus on project priorities instead of personal interest |
| Company D | Project Manager (initiated agile) | Waterfall process | Innovative ways to deliver value |
| Company E | Interviewee 1: Team leader sales and distribution. Interviewee 2: Lead of 25 project managers | Waterfall process | Improve the company |
| Company F | Project manager in project execution | Waterfall process | Had read about agile methods, started a pilot project |
| Company G | Interviewee 1: Scrum Master/Project Manager. Interviewee 2: Scrum Master of two teams. Interviewee 3: Scrum Master | Started as agile teams | Realized that the products needed to be developed faster |
| Company H | Scrum Master/manager in one of the first agile teams | A culture of guessing what users liked | Better and faster feedback and solve organizational problems |
| Company I | A multi-type supporting role | Something very similar to agile methods before they had heard about the concept | Started as an agile company |
| Company J | Founder of an agile company (>10 years experience) | A company built on agile principles and values in a very flat organizational structure | Started as an agile company |
| Company K | Interviewee 1: Scrum Master driving the agile transformation of the team. Interviewee 2: Certified Scrum Master and developer | Waterfall process | Wanted to adapt to the fast development of new technologies |

contrast to their own and their colleagues previous ways of working, we opted to analyze all the transcripts in the same way.

## 2.3  Reflexivity

In accordance with Braun and Clarke [19], we believe that we "cannot free ourselves of our theoretical and epistemological commitments," thus, we acknowledge our previous knowledge of group dynamics as researchers as well as experience from working in various teams and from leadership. We, therefore, acknowledge that we cannot be completely objective when interpreting the challenges stated by the participants. However, we did not have a preexisting coding scheme and tried to let the participants speak freely about their experiences without us intervening. The guidelines by Dahlberg et al. [20] were applied in that a researcher must be prepared that data can present things differently than what was initially thought, i.e. we wanted to be surprised as researchers. The intention was to apply intellectual honesty, and thoroughness in reasoning and in view of condition and consequences. We then also want to avoid favoring one's own person, skewed sampling, omission of negative evidence, one-sided maneuvers and wishful thinking [20]. The second author is an expert engineer without previous knowledge in agile methods but a lot of experience from product development, and could therefore provide an eyes-open-wide approach to the challenges studied. The first author is a researcher on the topic of building self-organizing agile teams and is therefore knowledgeable about the agile approach. However, he sees the agile methods as having a potential of positively transforming many parts of an enterprise, but also sees challenges with how it is sometimes implemented in practice. Therefore, the first author had no preconception about what results would be better or worse in conducting this study.

## 2.4  Analysis

We analyzed the transcripts using the six phases of thematic analysis suggested by Braun and Clarke [19]. The first step was to read the entire transcripts before coding took place. We then consistently focused our analysis on statements regarding challenges of agile leadership in relation to group dynamics in concordance with our research question. The analysis was inductive in nature since we wanted to keep an open mind to emerging themes in the data. The first author began by coding the first thirteen interviews and the second author coded the remaining two. We then cross-checked two transcripts and themes and we discussed and resolved discrepancies. Then, as the third step, different codes were put together into themes and (the fourth step) checked whether we agreed upon which themes fit with the codes. We applied descriptive coding [21] since our research question is in relation to finding separate challenges of group dynamics that the practitioners working with an agile approach need to manage in their daily work. Therefore, connections or hierarchies in the found challenges were not sought for. The fifth step was then to assess the naming of the challenges and, as a final step, connect them to existing literature.

Our epistemological approach leans towards a phenomenological view more than the social constructionist one, since we believe the challenges of group dynamics in relation to leadership roles can be described directly. We believe this partly due to the fact that our interviewees deal with group dynamics in practice every workday, that these concept are less emotional compared to other psychological constructs. They were therefore expected to be able to articulate their challenges as agile leaders accordingly [22].

## 3    Results

The three main leadership challenges found in our data is summarized below. The challenges are shown below together with quotes and a discussion to support the claims.

### 3.1    Team Maturity

When the interviewees compared less and more mature teams, the latter were said to tailor their own agile process based on contextual knowledge. One interviewee saw a strong connection between more mature teams that have met for a longer period of time and how much initiative and responsibility they take for the process and collaboration, implying that their leadership role is easier and more consultative.

> "They reinforce the practices within the teams themselves." [Project manager and initiator of the agile approach]

Another indication that the level of team maturity is highly influencing the appointed leader's leadership style in agile teams, is the fact that more mature teams were said completely adopt the agile practices they find useful, while less mature teams need reinforcement of the practices, otherwise they are reluctant to use them. To enforce the practices is then something the leaders describe that they must do for the team.

> "Those are very visible high performing teams self-directive aspects vs. those needing reinforcement of the practices for them to be there." [Project manager and initiator of the agile approach]

A key seems to be to suggest best practices by the leaders for the team, have a minimum of what is allowed, and then let the teams tailor their process themselves. In such a way, less mature teams will resort to safety by adopting a predefined process but can then redefine their process as the team matures.

> "We really try to get the teams to focus on staying within the framework, but they have latitude and liberty within that framework to, based on their own team style or team makeup." [Project Management Leader]

Another interviewee clearly stated that even the most self-organized teams were different initially. The "agility" simply had to wait for the team to mature, which means that the needed leadership style is different across time.

> "Yeah, these days they don't need me in order to work. These days I am really a facilitator and the team is absolutely able to the normal Scrum process without me. They don't need any guidance any longer so I can easily go on vacations for 2–3 weeks, that's not a problem. /.../ Of course in the beginning I had to stop them in the dailies and say 'Stop discussing solutions,' just the tasks, please, and the three questions bla bla bla. Now it's more or less routine." [Scrum Master]

This indicates that the self-organization of teams emerges over time along with the team maturity from a psychological perspective, which also implies that the leaders must take on the function of leadership initially before that function can be shared. In addition, the built in flexibility of the agile processes is also something teams need maturity in in order to leverage in the intended way. One interviewee stated that more mature teams can easily change their process if asked, which is not something the less mature teams could do in the same way.

> "We are trying to adopt Kanban. But there are other teams here that have only worked with Kanban for a few months. They tried it because they saw some problems we had with Scrum. Some of the teams matured faster (mainly because they didn't break up the teams all the time as we do here) and they changed to Kanban." [Scrum Master]

For teams that are mature, and where the members are dedicated and have set clear roles, the interviewees saw that they could adopt self-organization and team agility without many issues, putting less focus and dependence on them as the designated leader or manager.

> "The team we have is an extraordinary team with a very open mindset and a very innovative team and always open to new things, so they were very open-minded so that was not much to say, and they trusted me." [Project Manager Lead]

To summarize, the first found challenge is that the agile leader needs to take a step back from mature teams and instead facilitate the team's work process in relation to the surrounding ecosystems of the teams. However, in order to implement agility in the less mature or newly formed teams, they also need to provide a lot more direction and guidance in order for such teams to become self-organizing agile teams.

## 3.2   Team Design

The team design process is very much connected to team maturity as described in the previous section. However, the following quotes are in this category because they are a symptom of a lack of team design from an external role, not a symptom of the team being new.

When teams were not given an initial structure, some interviewees were surprised and frustrated when newly formed teams expressed a need for clear and directive leadership.

> "It was the first retrospective that we had, they say that they lack some leadership there and then during the retrospective we were talking like 'no it's not leadership that you need, how about that you decide how you will do things and the new habits that we will create in the next sprint.' What kind of agreements that we have to have for solving that problem, and we're saying that the lack of leadership is the result. That's one thing that appears a lot because we are growing and new teams are being formed."
> [Founder of an agile company]

New team were also described as being open to any work practices and lack the insight into what is useful or needed in their context. This entails that the leader needs to step in and guide the team in making such decision, something that was described frustrating for the leaders since they did not expect that in the agile approach. However, the team must get help in its initial design since no team members can know the context simply because it is new to them.

> "Yeah, for teams that are younger, like formed more recently, they tend to be more open to all the practices, but they don't have the experience to decide which practices that would be the best." [Founder of an agile company]

Also in relation to new teams, one interviewee changed the agile practice of volunteering for task because the team was not ready to take on that responsibility on a team level. This implies that the leader felt the need to step in and be more directive, however, with the expressed frustration that such a leader behavior is not appropriate in the agile context. Teams, though, seem to need help in designing work processes initially.

> "In agile people should volunteer for tasks, but in most cases here we are obliged to... we do task assignment, by me or the person who already worked on this item takes this item. I know that this isn't a good practice in agile, but we do it for our team and for more productivity, but also for responsibility." [Scrum Master]

An interviewee from hardware development also highlighted that, since the company is expanding all the time and therefore consistently gets more team members, it is difficult to design and build self-organizing teams, which is a core part of the agile approach and frustrating for them as leaders.

> "You have to be very involved to be able to get a clear direction from it, and that's hard, especially because our group has grown so much and

we get new people all the time who don't have that direction from the beginning. /.../ The further the team gets, and the more you have worked, the more autonomous the group becomes." [Scrum Master and Software Developer]

We also found support for the distinction between what is an organizational and enforced structure and what is up to the teams themselves, i.e. the right balance in team design. Teams with no provided structure were described as much less effective but it is about providing the right balance of flexibility and control by the people in leadership positions.

"The teams can change as they want [in the process] all the time." [Supporting role]

Traditionally, it seems like most software development processes did not have any team reflection sessions by default. The agile process often adds the retrospective meeting, which is a structure for team reflection, which was described as helpful for the leaders in order to improve the teamwork.

"The developers, I think, also feel that it provides them with a preset structure within which they can communicate with each other; they don't have to set up a meeting to do this. We have our Scrum identify that they need to meet to talk about something, and then they do. So it puts things in place for them and they don't have to think about it." [Project Management Leader]

To summarize, the leaders need to help transitioning teams to design their new agile structure and ways of working. If teams are not ready to tailor their own process, the leaders provide suggestions and best practices, but keep stating that the team should continuously improve their process based on what they learn about their ecosystem. This means that, when the teams are set up, they need an initial predefined team design and then be given the possibility to tweak their processes when the team is ready.

## 3.3 Culture and Mindset

The third and final challenge was that the leadership also needs to be adjusted to the existing more traditional structure and culture of the company. We found that even if members and teams can adopt self-organization, the context might hamper this way of working.

"If the whole company was agile in the end, the teams could be more independent and talk to the business area more themselves, but now I spend a lot of time trying to make decisions on what the teams should do." [Scrum Master]

All the interviewees spoke about the different agile roles changing dynamically based on what is really needed at a point in time. A project manager acts as a Scrum Master, or trying to help people to not fall into old patterns of behavior in relation to the old structure instead of the new agile process.

"After the first project I was able to spend time educating them at the beginning, but had to make almost daily conscious efforts at reminding them, or educating them with when I could see that their though process was tending toward waterfall. So I'll try to point out: 'oh actually, let's think about it this way.' Or, you know, helping them with definitions like what the basic function of the daily Scrum for example and remind them of that. That it's not a status meeting, for example." [Scrum Master and Project Manager]

One participant from the hardware-focused development also highlighted the fact that all individuals do not have the same possibilities, or motivation, to adapt to the new ways of working. The participants from hardware and software development differed in that the hardware-focused interviewees focused on the "old" ways of working as compared to the new agile way, while the software-focused participants reflected more on the team's place in the company as a whole.

"Partially, I believe it's due to... from what I've heard, that [a team member] that is a bit more senior and has had previously bad experience from the agile ways of working in other areas and therefore doesn't think it worked well and actually only sees the negative aspects. [The team member] just does this because everybody else wants to do it, but does not think it will work. And therefore it does not fully work, because you... it's hard. I think it's really hard to have one leg in it, and one outside, you know..." [Scrum Master driving the agile transformation]

From the hardware-focused participants, they described their agile implementation as something that needed to be agile in itself. That means that they had to related their new process to also fit with the old, which was described as challenging.

"We have tried to see the work process as something agile and adaptable too! Now there are more clear toolboxes with how to work in an agile way in the company. When we started that didn't exist, but, I mean that, when you talk about Scrum as an agile method it's not anything more than a toolbox with different practices, and you have to try to pick what suits your organization and your... we started with that mindset that we would have 'what is the smallest part of scrum we can pick?' or 'what is the smallest set of tools we can make use of?' and then, I guess, with time we have realized that, yes, 'we need this' or 'we need do do that one too'. [Scrum Master driving the agile transformation]

To summarize, the participants' leadership style is also adapted to where the company is in its agile journey, not just the internal process structure, as in the previous theme. The leaders act as both more traditional managers and as more agile (i.e. contextually adapted) leaders depending on what is needed at that point in time.

## 4   Discussion

This study found that the main challenges in relation to group dynamics in the agile context is to adapt the leadership to the (1) teams' collaborative maturity, (2) design new teams well, and (3) balance the "old" ways of working with the intended new agile processes and their innate different culture. The first one, called (1) *Team maturity* included that the agile leaders saw a need to step back from mature teams and then be the facilitator with a strong focus on impediments external to the team. However, as agile leaders, the challenge from their perspective was that newly formed, or less mature teams, on the contrary, needed a lot of support in order to grow into agile teams. This was not seen a "agile" by the interviewees and expressed as frustrating.

The second category (2) *Team design* is connected to the first category but focuses on that teams need to be well designed in the agile context and get much more help setting up the agile team than the interviewees initially had thought. Teams do not seem to be able to design themselves when starting their agile journey, but instead need a suggested initial team design. New teams, that are less mature by definition, cannot tailor their own agile process, but need help to get started and can then improve their process based on what they learn about their ecosystem. The third category (3) *Culture and mindset* is about that the needed adaptability of agile teams are also in relation to where the whole company is in its overall agile journey. Agile leaders described that they acted as more traditional managers sometimes, if needed, but also adapted to where in the company teams were more allowed to drive themselves within their predefined mandate.

That team maturity is connected to team agility has been shown in previous studies (e.g. Gren et al. [23]). The third category also confirms previous results on the difficulty with integrating an agile approach to a traditional context (e.g. [13]). The second category, though, on the importance of team design, as conducted by a leader more external to the team, seems to be a novel finding. Even with regards to the other two categories, this study adds to knowledge since it focuses on the appointed agile leaders and what challenges they define in relation to building agile teams. More immature agile teams were said to be more open to all the practices, and that agile leaders need to provide a clear agile work process to the teams for them to get started in a constructive way. While this is not according to the description of an agile and self-organizing team, this is a typical trait of groups in the Forming stage according to group development [11]. Team members are focused on dependency and inclusion when newly formed, and need to build some initial trust before sharing opinions and questioning each other. Giving new teams a structure and directives would therefore help them in their development as compared to trying to get them to self-organize too early. In the results of this study, we clearly see that the agile leaders describe a need for more guidance of newly formed agile teams as well. Not only do teams need more guidance in their internal collaboration, but just like Wageman [17] concluded in her studies on self-organizing teams in general, someone needs to design the teams well also before they are deployed. This aspect seems to be largely ignored in the agile literature. After the team is set up, the role of the leader reassembles the leadership needed in different group development stages, which verifies their importance and clarified the connection between the two concepts. This study has shown that this temporal perspective of needed leadership when creating self-organizing teams is also essential when setting up agile teams, and Wageman's [17] theory fits the result of this study exceptionally well. *If we aim for having only a facilitating and coaching leadership from day one, we hamper the teams' development instead of the opposite.*

The interviewees also described the more mature agile teams as aware of their context, e.g. surrounding teams and overall company strategies, and having the ability to tailor their own process in relation to responding to a change in requirements. This is at the very core of agility [24], and shows that self-organization is a property of collaboratively mature teams. In contrast, one interviewee thought that following the agile process was bad and thus that an agile process was inflexible. Adapting agile methods to a large organization was described as a balance between old and the new work methods, and therefore, there is a large risk of adapting the old organization to the new agile structure and by this not perform an actual agile transformation but a renaming of the existing structure. One example would be to keep a command-and-control approach by the line management instead of providing a structure for teams to grow and eventually self-organize, i.e. letting team members lead when they are ready to take on and share the leadership function more. This challenge was more stressed by our two participants from hardware development. A key to create agile teams, as described by our interviewees, seems to be to suggest good work structures for teams and then let them adjust their process as the development cycle moves along. This is a tricky balance for new agile leaders since new teams need more structure but the appointed leaders then need to take a step back and let the team self-organize when ready. Therefore, a mix of more directive leadership styles in combination with consultative and coaching leadership styles, seems to be what the successful practitioners do in practice. This is not then to be confused with traditional line management control, but instead the application of different types of support for teams guided by the end-goal of the team leading itself.

The guidelines from the agile community have been to be a facilitator of the process only instead of being a more directive leader [25]. The problem with such simplified guidance to new leaders is that such behavior only works in very special cases. With a mature team, and with good organizational support, taking a step back, delegate and be a process facilitator is easy. The problem is that becoming a leader in such a context immediately is pretty rare. There is an awareness in practice that inexperienced teams need more guidance, but this awareness is only in relation to agile practices [26] and not group dynamics over time. Therefore, that explanation model of agility fails to explain why some teams do not become agile over time even if they learn the agile practices. An understanding of group developmental psychology provides that explanation [11], and explains why different leadership styles and team support are needed at the different stages. And maybe even more novel in this current study, teams need to be designed well before they are deployed if they are to self-organize as fast as possible [17]. This motivates the future inclusion of more group dynamics teaching in agile courses both at companies and at universities.

## 5   Threats to Validity

Since leadership is a complex construct, a qualitative method was suggested to provide deeper insights of the reality. However, with fewer participants is becomes more difficult to generalize to a larger population, which should be done with care for our study. The selection of a large variety of interviewees from various organizational settings in the sample, is one major strength of the study, but conclusions from our two participants from hardware development should of course be drawn with even more care and only seen a small additional comparison. The diverse sample with regards to companies provides a broad view of experiences from practitioners working with an agile approach in different stages of its implementation. A high risk in qualitative studies is that our interpretations of what the interviewees said could of course be erroneous and prone to confirmation bias. A way to counter such a threat was to be transparent in the description of our research method, and to be transparent with what quotes we believe supported our claims. In the analysis, we acknowledged our previous knowledge of group dynamics, which many of our participants did not have. Our participants could have a different perception of the constructs under investigation, but as researchers from different areas, one with and one without previous knowledge of agile but both with rigorous experience of leadership, we believe that this combination was advantageous for the analysis. For validation of interpretations and citations, feedback from the interviewees might have improved the quality of the analysis. We recommend that procedure for upcoming studies in the area. We also acknowledge that having a mix of two languages (English and Swedish), and conducting interviews in English with non-native speakers also threatens the validity of this study due to difficulty in obtaining exact translations between languages.

## 6   Conclusion and Future Work

This paper set out to investigate what challenges appointed agile leaders see in relation to group dynamics. Through a qualitative method of interviews and a thematic analysis, we have found that leader adaptability to team maturity, the careful design of new teams, and a continuous balance between traditional and new work principles are all essential to the success of an agile transformation. These findings are an important contribution to both research and practice since it gives an in-depth view of leadership challenges of group dynamics in agile transformations at different scales. In terms of future research, we particularly suggest more use of qualitative research methods both when studying leadership in engineering, but also to apply narrative analysis [27] to large agile transformations, since analyzing the complete transition from a waterfall process to an agile approach has not been done in its entirety. We believe the narrative analysis method is underused in software engineering research and fits well to the study of organizational changes over time.

**Acknowledgment.** We would like to thank all the participants and everyone who helped us with making this study possible, and we would like to acknowledge Jennifer Strand and Petra Boström specifically for their excellent support.

# References

1. Dybå, T., Dingsøyr, T.: Empirical studies of agile software development: a systematic review. Inf. Softw. Technol. **50**(9), 833–859 (2008)
2. Melnik, G., Maurer, F.: Comparative analysis of job satisfaction in agile and non-agile software development teams. In: Abrahamsson, P., Marchesi, M., Succi, G. (eds.) XP 2006. LNCS, vol. 4044, pp. 32–42. Springer, Heidelberg (2006). https://doi.org/10.1007/11774129_4
3. Serrador, P., Pinto, J.K.: Does agile work? - a quantitative analysis of agile project success. Int. J. Proj. Manag. **33**(5), 1040–1051 (2015)
4. Lenberg, P., Feldt, R., Wallgren, L.G.: Human factors related challenges in software engineering - an industrial perspective. In: Begel, A., Prikladnicki, R., Dittrich, Y., de Souza, C., Sarma, A., Athavale, S. (eds.) Proceedings of the 8th International Workshop on Cooperative and Human Aspects of Software Engineering, pp. 43–49. IEEE (2015)
5. Hogg, M.A., van Knippenberg, D.: Social identity and leadership processes in groups. Adv. Exp. Soc. Psychol. **35**, 1–52 (2003)
6. Hogg, M.A., Vaughan, G.M.: Social Psychology, 7th edn. Pearson, Harlow (2014)
7. Kozlowski, S.W., Watola, D.J., Jensen, J.M., Kim, B.H., Botero, I.C.: Developing adaptive teams: a theory of dynamic team leadership. In: Salas, E., Goodwin, G.F., Burke, C.S. (eds.) Team Effectiveness in Complex Organizations: Cross-Disciplinary Perspectives and Approaches, pp. 113–155. Routledge, New York (2009)
8. Hersey, P., Blanchard, K.H., Natemeyer, W.E.: Situational leadership, perception, and the impact of power. Group. Organ. Manag. **4**(4), 418–428 (1979)
9. Schein, E.: Organizational Culture and Leadership, 4th edn. Jossey-Bass, San Francisco (2010)
10. Northouse, P.: Leadership: Theory and Practice, 5th edn. Sage, Thousand Oaks (2010)
11. Tuckman, B., Jensen, M.: Stages of small-group development revisited. Group Organ. Manag. **2**(4), 419–427 (1977)

12. Gren, L., Torkar, R., Feldt, R.: Group development and group maturity when building agile teams: a qualitative and quantitative investigation at eight large companies. J. Syst. Softw. **124**, 104–119 (2017)
13. Hodgson, D., Briand, L.: Controlling the uncontrollable: 'agile' teams and illusions of autonomy in creative work. Work Employ Soc. **27**(2), 308–325 (2013)
14. Spiegler, S.V., Heinecke, C., Wagner, S.: Leadership gap in agile teams: how teams and scrum masters mature. In: Kruchten, P., Fraser, S., Coallier, F. (eds.) XP 2019. LNBIP, vol. 355, pp. 37–52. Springer, Cham (2019). https://doi.org/10.1007/978-3-030-19034-7_3
15. Millikin, J.P., Hom, P.W., Manz, C.C.: Self-management competencies in self-managing teams: their impact on multi-team system productivity. Leadersh. Q. **21**(5), 687–702 (2010)
16. Parris, D.L., Peachey, J.W.: A systematic literature review of servant leadership theory in organizational contexts. J. Bus. Ethics **113**(3), 377–393 (2013)
17. Wageman, R.: How leaders foster self-managing team effectiveness: design choices versus hands-on coaching. Organ. Sci. **12**(5), 559–577 (2001)
18. Wageman, R.: Critical success factors for creating superb self-managing teams. Organ. Dyn. **26**(1), 49–61 (1997)
19. Braun, V., Clarke, V.: Using thematic analysis in psychology. Qual. Res. Psychol. **3**(2), 77–101 (2006)
20. Dahlberg, K., Dahlberg, H., Nyström, M.: Reflective Lifeworld Research, 2nd edn. Studentlitteratur, Lund (2008)
21. Saldaña, J.: The Coding Manual for Qualitative Researchers, 3rd edn. Sage Publications, Thousand Oaks (2015)
22. Willig, C.: Introducing Qualitative Research in Psychology. McGraw-Hill Education, Berkshire (2013)
23. Gren, L., Goldman, A., Jacobsson, C.: Agile ways of working: a team maturity perspective. J. Softw. Evol. Process (in press)
24. Zieris, F., Salinger, S.: Doing scrum rather than being agile: a case study on actual nearshoring practices. In: Proceedings of the 8th International Conference on Global Software Engineering (ICGSE), pp. 144–153. IEEE (2013)
25. Rising, L., Janoff, N.S.: The scrum software development process for small teams. IEEE Softw. **17**(4), 26–32 (2000)
26. Adkins, L.: Coaching Agile Teams: A Companion for ScrumMasters, Agile Coaches, and Project Managers in Transition. Pearson Education, Boston (2010)
27. Smith, B., Sparkes, A.C.: Narrative inquiry in psychology: exploring the tensions within. Qual. Res. Psychol. **3**(3), 169–192 (2006)

# "This is Just a Prototype": How Ethics Are Ignored in Software Startup-Like Environments

Ville Vakkuri$^{(\boxtimes)}$ (ID), Kai-Kristian Kemell (ID), Marianna Jantunen (ID), and Pekka Abrahamsson (ID)

University of Jyväskylä, PO Box 35, 40014 Jyväskylä, Finland
{ville.vakkuri,kai-kristian.o.kemell,pekka.abrahamsson}@jyu.fi,
marianna.jantunen@gmail.com

**Abstract.** Artificial Intelligence (AI) solutions are becoming increasingly common in software development endeavors, and consequently exert a growing societal influence as well. Due to their unique nature, AI based systems influence a wide range of stakeholders with or without their consent, and thus the development of these systems necessitates a higher degree of ethical consideration than is currently carried out in most cases. Various practical examples of AI failures have also highlighted this need. However, there is only limited research on methods and tools for implementing AI ethics in software development, and we currently have little knowledge of the state of practice. In this study, we explore the state of the art in startup-like environments where majority of the AI software today gets developed. Based on a multiple case study, we discuss the current state of practice and highlight issues. The cases underline the complete ignorance of ethical consideration in AI endeavors. We also outline existing good practices that can already support the implementation of AI ethics, such as documentation and error handling.

**Keywords:** Artificial intelligence · AI ethics · AI development · Practices · Responsibility · Accountability · Transparency · Case study

## 1 Introduction

AI systems have become increasingly common in software engineering projects [1]. While much of the media attention is on flashier systems such as autonomous vehicles, less high-profile AI systems such as decision-making support systems have become increasingly widespread in various organizations. AI systems often operate under the surface in the form of e.g. recommendation algorithms, making the high-profile systems in the middle of the media hype only the tip of the iceberg.

Over the last two decades, progress on AI has been accelerating rapidly. AI systems are now widely used in various areas and for various purposes. Examples include medical systems [2], law enforcement [3], and manufacturing industries and industry 4.0 [4],

---

An early version of this paper was presented in the 20th International Conference on Product-Focused Software Process Improvement (Profes 2019)

V. Stray et al. (Eds.): XP 2020, LNBIP 383, pp. 195–210, 2020.
https://doi.org/10.1007/978-3-030-49392-9_13

among numerous others. As the field progresses, the already impressive potential of AI systems becomes even larger, including applications such as general AI systems, the likes of which are already being developed by the technology giants such as Alphabet. It is exactly because of this impressive potential and impact of these systems, especially in the future, that their potential negative impacts should also discussed more.

AI systems are ultimately still software. They are affected by largely the same requirements as any other software system. AI development projects are still for the most part conventional software engineering, with machine learning related tasks only comprising a small portion of these projects [5].

However, AI systems are unique in terms of their effects on various stakeholders to the point where they can even exert society-wide influence. Moreover, these stakeholders often have little power in opting out of using these systems. E.g. it is difficult to avoid having a firm filter your job application using AI or trying to avoid being monitored using AI-based surveillance systems if such systems are in place in the area.

Various system failures have already highlighted some of the potential issues these systems can have in practice. Past incidents that have received global media coverage, even smaller incidents can be costly for the affected organization(s). For example, the national Finnish broadcasting company, Yle[1], utilized AI for moderation purposes in its services. Having already changed its processes to suit the automation of the moderation, the organization ultimately ran into problems with the AI moderator system. Though the software was working fine on the technical level, the socio-ethical issues forced the organization to revert back to human moderators.

Many of these issues are ultimately rooted in ethics. AI ethics has thus become a new non-functional requirement to address; an -ility among the likes of quality, maintainability, and scalability. Existing methods have focused on tackling these functional and non-functional requirements. However, no such methods currently exist for AI ethics [6], with the existing tools and methods largely being technical and limited to narrow contexts in ML as opposed to being project-level methods.

In the absence of methods, how are ethics currently implemented? Much of the current literature in the area has been theoretical, and our understanding of the state of practice in AI ethics is currently lacking. [6] AI ethics literature discusses various aspects of AI ethics that should be taken into account, but bridging the gap between research and practice in the area remains an on-going challenge [7, 8]. Guidelines for implementing AI ethics exist, but their effect on the start of practice remains unknown.

Thus, to begin bridging this gap in the area, we conduct an empirical study to help us understand the current state of practice. We do so by means of a multiple case study of three projects focusing on healthcare systems. The goal of this study is two-fold: (1) to help us understand the current state of practice in AI ethics; and (2) to discover existing good practices that might help in implementing AI ethics. Out of these two goals, the first is a theoretical contribution while the second one is a practical one. The specific research question of the paper is as follows:

**RQ:** how are AI ethics taken into consideration in software engineering projects when they are not formally considered?

---

[1] https://yle.fi/uutiset/3-11158701.

## 2   Related Work: The Current State of AI Ethics

Ethics in software development and interactive systems design in general has a history of over 30 years. For example, Bynum [9] introduced the idea of adapting human values in design before the rise of human computer interaction and other human-centric paradigms. Theoretically grounded approaches such as Value Sensitive Design (VSD) and its variants have provided tools to design technology that takes into account human values in the design process [10, 11].

As more progress is made in the field of AI systems, old theoretical scenarios in AI ethics are slowly becoming reality. This calls for new methods to manage the ethical issues arising from these new systems [7, 12]. Indeed, Vallach and Allen [12] argue that AI and AI-based systems produce new requirements to consider. Specifically, they propose that designers implicitly embed values in the technologies they create [12]. AI and other complex systems force designers to consider what kind of values are embedded in the technologies and also how the practical implementation of these values could be carried out and how these systems could be governed [13].

Yet, little is currently known about software development practices and methods in the context of AI ethics, as empirical studies in the area are scarce. Our results from an existing study suggest that AI ethics are seldom formally implemented in SE projects, [14]. Similarly, there are currently no project-level methods that could aid in implementing AI ethics [6]. On the other hand, various tools that can support specific elements of AI ethics do exist, such as tools for managing machine learning [6]. However, they do not help developers implement AI ethics in general.

In this light, it can be said that AI ethics has hardly been incorporated into mainstream SE literature yet. The reason why AI Ethics has received little attention in the prior engineering literature is three-fold: 1) Prior research has been predominantly philosophical, 2) the field has not sensed the need to address ethical concerns and 3) thus it has not been part of the education system.

Though some practice-focused research does exist (e.g. [15]), most of the research on AI ethics has been conceptual and theoretical in nature. These studies have e.g. focused on defining AI ethics in a practical manner through various constructs in the form of values. For the time being, this discussion on defining AI ethics has come to center around four values: transparency [16, 17], accountability [8, 16], responsibility [16], and fairness (e.g. [18]). Not all four of these values are universally agreed to form the core of AI ethics, however, as we discuss in the following section while presenting our research framework.

Following various real-life incidents out on the field (e.g. Amazon's biased recruitment AI[2]), AI ethics has also begun to spawn public discussion. This has led to governments, standardization institutions, and practitioner organizations reacting by producing their own demands and guidelines for involving ethics into AI development, with many standards and regulations in the works. Countries such as France [19] and Germany [20] have emphasized the role of ethics in AI, and on an international level the EU began

---

[2] https://www.reuters.com/article/us-amazon-com-jobs-automation-insight/amazon-scraps-sec
ret-ai-recruiting-tool-that-showed-bias-against-women-idUSKCN1MK08G.

to draft its own AI ethics guidelines which were presented in April 2019 [21]. Moreover, ISO has founded its own ethical, trustworthy AI in ISO/IEC JTC 1/SC 42 Artificial intelligence subcommittee [22]. Finally, some larger practitioner organizations have also presented their own guidelines concerning ethics in AI (e.g. Google [23] and Microsoft [24] guidelines).

Thus far, these various attempts to bring this on-going academic discussion out on the field have been primarily made in the form of guidelines and principles. Out of these guidelines, perhaps the most prominent ones up until now have been the IEEE guidelines for Ethically Aligned Design (EAD), born from the IEEE Global Initiative on Ethics of Autonomous and Intelligent Systems alongside its IEEE P7000™ Standards Working Groups, which were branded under the concept of EAD [8].

Existing literature has shown us that guidelines and principles in the field of ICT ethics do not seem to be effective. Mittelstadt [25] argue that AI developers lack the professional norms and methods to translate principles into practice in successful way. To this end, McNamara et al. [26] also argue based on empirical data that the ACM ethical guidelines[3] had ultimately had very little impact on developers, who had not changed their ways of working at all. In this light, this is likely to be the case with the aforementioned AI ethics guidelines as well, as Mittelstadt suggest [25]. This notion is further supported by Morley et al. [6] who argue that developers focused on practicality are unlikely to adopt them when the competitive advantage of EAD is unclear.

## 3   Research Model

To assist in the data collection and analysis in this study, we devised a research framework based on prominent literature in the area. This research framework and the justifications behind it are further discussed in an existing paper [27] (Fig. 1).

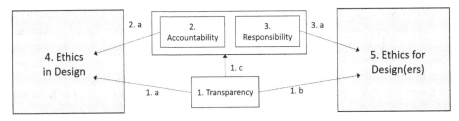

**Fig. 1.**  Research framework

As the basis of the framework, we utilized the ART principles of Dignum [16], which consist of Accountability, Responsibility, and Transparency. These have been central constructs in the area, having also been featured in the EAD guidelines of IEEE.

*Transparency* is required for accountability and responsibility (line 1.c), as we must understand why the system acts in a certain fashion, as well as who made what decisions during development in order to establish accountability [17]. Whereas accountability

---

[3] ACM Code of Ethics and Professional Conduct. https://www.acm.org/code-of-ethics.

can be considered to be externally motivated, closely related but separate construct responsibility is internally motivated. The concept of accountability holds a key role in aiming to prevent misuse of AI and in supporting wellbeing through AI [8].

*Accountability* refers to determining who is accountable or liable for the decisions made by the AI. Dignum [16] in their recent works defines accountability to be the explanation and justification of one's decisions and one's actions to the relevant stakeholders. In the context of this research framework, accountability is used not only in the context of systems, but also in a more general sense. We consider, e.g., how various accountability issues (legal, social) were considered during development.

Dignum [16] defines *responsibility* as a chain of responsibility that links the actions of the systems to all the decisions made by the stakeholders. We consider it to be the least accurately defined part of the ART model, and thus have taken a more comprehensive approach to it in our research framework. According to the EAD guidelines, responsibility can be considered to be an attitude or a moral obligation for acting responsibly [8] A simplified way of approaching responsibility would be for a developer to ask oneself e.g. "would I be fine with using my own system?".

In addition to the ART principles, we utilized the three AI ethics categories presented by Dignum [28] to make these constructs more practical. Dignum suggests that AI ethics can be divided into:

- Ethics by Design (integration of ethical reasoning capabilities as a part of the behaviour of artificial autonomous system, e.g. ethical robots);
- Ethics in Design (the regulatory and engineering methods supporting ethical implications of AI systems); and
- Ethics for Design: (codes of conduct, standards, and certification processes that ensure the integrity of developers and users) [28].

In this paper, we focus on the ethically aligned *development process*, and therefore the last two categories were included into the research framework.

Finally, aspects of commitment were utilized in the framework to aid data analysis. Specifically, we utilized the commitment net model of Abrahamsson [29] to approach the implementation of ethics into practice and have an explaining theoretical framework to examine ethics role to developers. From this model, we focused on concerns and actions. Concerns were analyzed to understand what ethical issues were of interest to the developers. Actions were then studied to understand how these concerns were actually tackled, or whether they were tackled at all.

In commitment net model, actions are connected to concerns because when actions are taken, they are always driven from concerns [29]. On the other hand, however, concerns can exist without any actions taken to address them. The dynamic between actions and concerns was considered a tangible way to approach the focus of this study: practices for implementing AI ethics. Developers actions could be likened to practices that were taking during the development. On the other hand, analyzing the concerns that developers have opens a view to understanding e.g. whether the developers perhaps wanted to implement ethics but were unable to do so.

# 4 Study Design

This section is split into three subsections. First, we discuss the cases of the case study. In the second and third ones we discuss the data collection and analysis, respectively.

## 4.1 Cases

We conducted a multiple case study featuring three case projects. In all of the case projects, AI systems were being developed for the healthcare sector. These cases are outlined in the table below (Table 1). We chose to utilize a qualitative case study approach due to the exploratory nature of the topic, as the research area is novel as far as empirical studies are concerned.

Healthcare cases were selected due to the assumption that ethical consideration would be more common in healthcare-related projects due to the nature of the area in closely dealing with human well-being (e.g. the tradition of bio and medical ethics). Indeed, healthcare systems can, for example, influence the decisions made by doctors or their patients related to the health of the patients. Moreover, due to the emphasis on tax-funded public healthcare in Finland, where the cases were from, the area is particularly regulated. These regulations impose some ethical requirements on software systems as well, especially in relation to handling patient data, which is considered particularly sensitive data from a legal point of view.

In the paper title, we characterize these case projects as being startup-like because the projects shared various characteristics typically associated with software startups. First, agile methods were commonly utilized in the projects. Secondly, the projects were all characterized by notable time pressure. Thirdly, the projects operated with scarce resources. Fourthly, the cases were centered around the development of functional prototypes, which were intended to as proof-of-concept type artifacts. However, the prototypes were being developed with real customers and tested in practice. Finally, the projects exhibited exploratory approaches that focused on experimentation.

Currently, much of the on-going AI development is happening in startups [1], even if the multinational organizations receive much media coverage in relation to AI. In characterizing them as startup-like, we consider them to be representative of the current AI development projects.

**Table 1.** Descriptions of each case

| Case | Example | Font size and style |
|------|---------|---------------------|
| A | Statistical tool for detecting social marginalization | Data Analyst [R1], Consultant [R2], Project Coordinator [R3] |
| B | Speech recognition and NLP based tool for diagnostics | Developer [R4], Developer [R5], Project Manager [R6] |
| C | NLP based tool for indoor navigation | Developer [R7], Developer [R8] |

## 4.2 Data Collection

Data from the cases were collected using semi-structured interviews [30]. This interview strategy enabled the interviews to be conducted in a way that allowed for flexibility from the interview questions, but without steering too far from the topic. The interview instrument used in the interviews can be found externally as a reference[4]. All interviews were conducted as F2F interviews and the audio was recorded for transcription. The analysis was conducted using the transcripts. The interviews were conducted in Finnish. This was done so that the respondents would not give shorter responses due to being uncomfortable with communicating in English, especially while being on record.

The respondents from the cases were either developers or managers. As we wanted to focus on development practices and project issues, we focused on the personnel directly involved with the practical development issues in the projects. The respondents are outlined in the table in the previous subsection. In terms of experience, respondents 4, 5, 7, and 8 were junior developers. Respondents 3 and 6, on the other hand, were senior developers. Respondent 1 was a junior data scientist.

## 4.3 Data Analysis

We analyzed the data in two phases. First, we utilized a grounded theory (Heath [31]) inspired approach to code the transcripts quote by quote for each interview. This process was carried out iteratively as the list of codes was updated during the process. This approach was chosen due to the lack of existing studies on the current state of practice in the area.

In the second phase, we utilized the commitment net model of Abrahamsson [29] to then further analyze and categorize the coded content. We utilized the model by focusing on the concerns and actions of the developers. The concerns and actions of each respondent were compared across cases in search of recurring concerns and actions between cases and respondents. By evaluating the relationships between the actions taken in development the development process and the concerns of the developers, we could better understand the motivation behind the actions. Similarly, we could also see which concerns did not lead to any actions, pointing to a lack of commitment towards tackling those concerns.

The data were then compared with the research framework again to evaluate how AI ethics were implemented in each project. Actions were the emphasis here, as the focus of this study was on tangible implementation of AI ethics and how it was carried out in terms of tools, practices, or methods. However, we also highlighted interesting findings in relation to the mere concerns related to AI ethics.

# 5 Empirical Results

This section is split into four subsections. The first three feature the analysis split between the accountability, responsibility and transparency constructs. The final subsection summarizes the analysis. We highlight our findings as Primary Empirical Conclusions (PECs). During the analysis, we use quotes from the interviews to elaborate on

---

[4] http://users.jyu.fi/~vimavakk/AIDevQuestionnaire.

the topic at hand. However, it should be noted that the conclusions are not drawn merely based on these individual citations.

## 5.1 Responsibility

The concerns of the developers related to responsibility were varied, but ultimately detached from practice as far as concerns related to AI ethics were considered. The concerns the developers discussed in relation to responsibility were simply very practical concerns related to internal project matters or delivering a high quality product:

"Responsibility on reporting and keeping the project on schedule" (R6)

**PEC1.** Developers feel most responsibility towards tackling problems related to software development, such as finding bugs, meeting project goals.

On the other hand, as the interviews progressed, the developers did also express some concerns towards various ethical issues. However, these concerns were detached from their current work. They did not affect the way they worked, and the developers felt that these types of concerns were not relevant during development. The presence of concerns in the absence of actions to address those concerns pointed towards a lack of commitment on this front.

"It is just a prototype" (R8)

"I do my best" (R5)

"But this is a prototype, an experiment, just to show people that you can do this type of thing. This doesn't really have any responsibility issues in it." (R1)

**PEC2.** On a personal level, developers are concerned about the ethical aspects of product development. However, little is done to tackle these concerns.

Furthermore, it was evident that in none of the cases had the hypothetical effects of the system on the stakeholders been discussed. To give a practical example, a system potentially affecting memory illness diagnoses clearly has various effects on its potential users, especially when the test can be taken without supervision. Yet, the developers of this particular tool also felt that their users would not be curious about the workings of the system. They considered it sufficient if the responsibility was outsourced to the user and it was underlined that the system does not make the diagnosis but simply advises doctors.

The developers did not consider the potential harm of the system past the tangible, physical harm potential of the systems. For example, stress or other negative effects on users and other stakeholders were not considered. In all three cases, the respondents did not consider the system to have had any potential of causing physical harm, and thus did not consider the system to have any notable harm potential at all.

"Nobody wants to listen to ethics-related technical stuff. No five hour lectures about it. It's not relevant to the users" (R5)

"I don't really understand what it [responsibility] has to do with product development. We developers are all responsible." (R7)

"What could it affect... the distribution of funds in a region, or it could result in a school taking useless action... it does have its own risks, but no one is going to die because of it" (R1)

PEC3. Responsibility of developers is unclear.

## 5.2 Transparency

Case A highlighted the potential importance of mathematical expertise. The team had internal mathematical capabilities that allowed them to develop their own algorithms, as well as to better understand third party components, in order to have achieve a higher standard of transparency. They utilized algorithms they were familiar with and which they understood on an in-depth level. Thus, the team considered themselves to be able to understand why the system made certain decisions in certain situations. This underlines the importance of mathematical skills in preventing the birth of black boxes in AI development.

"In that sense it's not really a black box as we can understand what's going on in there just fine, and we can show the nodes and what affects them. It's a very transparent algorithm." (R3)

The other two cases utilized existing AI solutions. They did not have an in-depth understanding of the technologies they were utilizing, which resulted in their systems being (partially) black boxes. They understood any components created by the team but did not have a full understanding of the third party components they had used as a base. This presents problems for feature traceability.

PEC4. Black box systems are a typical issue in AI development.

Even though transparency of algorithms and data was not present in two of the cases, the developers in case B nonetheless acknowledged its potential importance However, as it was not considered a formal requirement in the projects, the managers did not devote resources towards pursuing it. Even in case A, transparency was not produced as a result of ethical goals but out of business reasons.

"We have talked about the risks of decision-making support systems but it doesn't really affect what we do" (R5)

PEC5. Developers recognize transparency as a goal, but it is not formally pursued.

On the other hand, in relation to transparency of systems development, all three cases displayed transparency. By having formal decision-making strategies, they were able to keep track of higher-level decisions related to the system. Through proper documentation, they were able to keep track of decisions made on the code level. Version control also assisted in this regard, making it clear who made what changes and when in retrospect. There were thus various existing practices that produced transparency of systems development. Two of the cases also acknowledged the effects of team size on transparency of systems development. They noted that, in addition to documentation practices, the small team size itself made it easy to keep track of the actions of individual developers even in an ad hoc manner.

**PEC6.** Established SE practices, such as code documentation and code review, support transparency of systems development.

### 5.3 Accountability

Some aspects of accountability were clear points of focus in the projects, namely ones related to security in terms of general information security as well as data management. The respondents were aware of being in possession of personal data, given that they developed healthcare solutions, and were concerned with keeping it secure. They mentioned taking measures to keep the data secure from potentially malicious actors, and they were aware that they would have to take measures to act in accordance with laws and regulations in the area. However, in some cases they had not done so yet.

> "It's really important how you handle any kind of data, that you preserve it correctly, among researchers, and don't hand it out to any government actors. For example, many of the data packages have kind of interesting data and it can't get into the wrong hands. I personally can't see any way to harm anyone with the data we have though" (R2).

> "We haven't really paid much attention to the [data] safety aspects yet... it hasn't really been a main focus. There's probably a lot of things we have to take into account [eventually]" (R5).

The ethical concerns they had in relation to accountability were in general largely related to existing areas of focus in software development. For example, error handling was one aspect of accountability the respondents were particularly concerned with. This was tied with their goal of making quality software, which they considered their responsibility as professionals. The respondents could, to this end, discuss what tangible practices they utilized to deal with error handling.

**PEC7.** Developers feel accountable for error handling and have the means to deal with it.

However, error handling was largely considered from the point of view of writing code and testing it in a laboratory setting. I.e. the system was considered error free if there were no red lines in the code in the IDE during development. Only case company B discussed measures they had taken to monitor errors in use. Furthermore, potential misuse (e.g. a prankster drawing a horizontal white line on the pavement to intentionally confuse autonomous vehicles) and error scenarios during the operational life of the system had not been actively considered in any of the case projects.

> "The calculations are made in the algorithms, so it doesn't really make mistakes" (R2)

**PEC8.** Product misuse and error scenarios are only considered during development. They are not considered in terms of the future operational life of the system out on the field.

Due to the nature of machine learning, AI systems learn as they are taught with new data or as they collect it themselves while operating out on the field. From this arises the potential issue of unexpected behavior as a result of machine learning. None of the respondents had made plans to tackle potential unexpected behavior during the operational life of their system, should such behavior arise. In only one of the projects was the possibility directly acknowledged:

"We just put it up for end-users to test and note that this is still being developed" (R7).

**PEC9.** Developers do not have plans to deal with unexpected behavior of the system resulting from e.g. machine learning or the future expansion of the use context of the system.

### 5.4 Summary of Findings

Past the ART constructs, we highlight some commonalities between the cases on a more general level while summarizing our findings. In none of the cases were ethics implemented by following a formal method or tool, nor were ethical issues considered directly as ethical issues. Rather, any ethical issues tackled in the projects were tackled for practical reasons (e.g. error free software is beneficial from the point of view of customer relations). Nonetheless, some of the ethical issues such as error handling and transparency of systems development were tackled in a systematic manner through existing software engineering practices such as code documentation and version control.

On the other hand, though ethics were not taken into consideration on a project level, the respondents still exhibited some concern towards the potential socio-ethical issues in the systems. When prompted, they were able to come up with various negative effects the systems could have on different stakeholders. They considered these to be potential real issues, but did not have a way to address these concerns in the absence of tools, practices, and methods for doing so. Moreover, they seemed to realize these potential issues only after being directly asked about them in the interviews. This also points to a lack of tools to aid in ethical analyses.

## 6   Discussion

In this section, we have collected all the Primary Empirical Conclusions (PEC) outlined in preceding analysis section into Table 2. We relate each of these findings to existing literature and discuss their implications in this section. We classify each of these PECs based on their contribution into either novel findings, findings that (empirically) validated existing literature, or findings that contradict existing literature.

Many of our findings underline a gap between research and practice in the area. Whereas research on AI ethics alongside various guidelines devised by researchers [8] and practitioners [23, 24] alike has discussed various ethical goals for AI systems, these goals have not been widely adopted out on the field. In this sense, we consider some of our findings (PECs 4, 5, 8, and 9) to contradict existing literature.

For example, extant literature has highlighted the importance of transparency of algorithms and data [15–17]. Without understanding how the system works, it is impossible

**Table 2.** List of Primary Empirical Conclusions (PECs)

| # | Theoretical component | Description | Contribution |
|---|---|---|---|
| 1 | Responsibility | Developers feel most responsibility towards tackling problems related to software development, such as finding bugs, meeting project goals | Empirical validation |
| 2 | Responsibility | On a personal level, developers are concerned about the ethical aspects of product development. However, little is done to tackle these concerns | Novel |
| 3 | Responsibility | Responsibility of developers is unclear | Novel |
| 4 | Transparency | Black box systems are a typical issue in AI development | Empirical validation |
| 5 | Transparency | Developers recognize transparency as a goal, but it is not formally pursued | Contradicts existing literature |
| 6 | Transparency | Established SE practices, such as code documentation and code review, support transparency of systems development | Empirical validation |
| 7 | Accountability | Developers feel accountable for error handling and have the means to deal with it | Empirical validation |
| 8 | Accountability | Product misuse and error scenarios are only considered during development. They are not considered in terms of the future operational life of the system out on the field | Contradicts existing literature |
| 9 | Accountability | Developers do not have plans to deal with unexpected behavior of the system resulting from e.g. machine learning or the future expansion of the use context of the system | Contradicts existing literature |

to establish why it malfunctioned in a certain situation, which may e.g. be pivotal in understanding the causes of an accident that resulted in material damage [15]. Our findings point towards transparency being largely ignored as a goal (PEC5). Existing system components are utilized as black boxes, and developers do not see this as a notable problem (PEC4). We consider PEC5 to contradict existing literature in that existing literature has, on multiple occasions, highlighted the importance of transparency in AI systems. Yet, out on the field, this importance does not seem to be recognized to the point where it would result in changing development practices.

The situation is similar for tackling potential misuse of the systems, error handling during system operations, and handling unexpected system behavior (PEC8-9). These goals are included into the IEEE EAD guidelines [8]. However, none of the case companies took any measures to address these potential issues.

On a further note of transparency, however, the lack of emphasis placed on it is also curious in relation to feature traceability in SE. For decades, understanding the inner workings of the system was considered key in any SE endeavor. Yet, in the context of AI systems, the long-standing goal of feature traceability seems to be waning. Our findings point towards this being at least partially a result of a lack of mathematical understanding, as the one case company that considered their system to be fully transparent also noted that they fully understood the mathematics behind the algorithms they utilized. In using existing components in their systems, developers may not always understand the algorithms in these components. Indeed, in this vein, [32] noted that simply seeing the code is not enough if the algorithm is not understood, or the system is not understood as a whole.

Though we discovered various examples of ethics not being implemented, we also discovered that various existing and established SE practices can be used to implement AI ethics. Documentation, version control, and project management practices such as meeting transcripts produce transparency of systems development by tracking actions and decision-making (PEC6). Similarly, software quality practices help in error handling also in the context of AI ethics (PEC7), although they do not specifically account for the errors autonomous systems may face while operating out on the field. While discussing responsibility with the respondents, we also discovered that most of their responsibility was related to producing quality software and meeting project requirements. This validates existing literature in the area of SPI (e.g. Unterkalmsteiner, [33]).

Notably, we also discovered that the developers had ethical concerns towards their systems, which is a novel finding in this context (PEC2). Little is currently known about the state of practice out on the field, although a recent version of the EAD guidelines speculated about a gap in the area, which our findings support in relation to most aspects of AI ethics. Despite AI ethics largely not being implemented, our findings point towards it partially being a result of a lack of formal methods and tools to implement it.

In our data, the reason given by multiple respondents for not actively considering ethical issues was that they were developing a prototype. However, prototypes do influence the final product or service developed based by them, as shown by existing studies [34]. AI ethical issues should be tackled during earlier stages of development as well, seeing as many of them are higher-level design decisions (such as how to carry out machine learning in the system [15]), which can be difficult to undo later.

Following this study, as well as a past case study [14], we suggest that future research seek to tackle the lack of methods and tooling in the area. Though developers may be concerned about ethical issues, they lack the means to address these concerns. On the other hand, methods can also raise the awareness of developers in relation to AI ethics, creating concerns where there now are none. In creating these methods, we suggest exploring existing practices that can be used as is or tailored to implement AI ethics, as we have discussed here.

Given the amount of activity in AI ethics currently, with many governmental actors drafting their own AI ethics guidelines, likely followed by regulations, methods and tools will likely have practical demand in the future. Thus, even if one barrier to implementing AI ethics is currently the fact that it is seldom considered a requirement on a project level, regulations and laws can force organizations to take ethics into account. This would inevitably result in a demand for methods in this area, as well as the birth of various in-house ones.

Finally, in terms of limitations, the most notable limitations of the study stem from the data and the research approach. The qualitative multiple case study approach always poses problems for the generalizability of the data. We acknowledge this as a limitation, although we also refer to Eisenhardt [35] in arguing in favor of qualitative case studies, especially in the case of novel research areas. AI ethics, as far as empirical data goes, is a novel area of research. Moreover, the multiple case study approach adds some further validity to the data, as we do not base our arguments on a single case. Nonetheless, another limitation in the data is also that all the cases were based on Finland. For example, the implementation of AI ethics can be more of a focus in US-based companies, as much of the current discussion on AI ethics also originates from the US.

One other limitation in the data is that the interviews were conducted in Finnish. The constructs such as transparency may not carry the same connotations in Finnish as they do in English. This is especially the case with accountability and responsibility, which may not translate in a straightforward manner. However, during the interviews, we sought to clear any misunderstandings related to the constructs with the respondents.

The research framework can also be argued to be a limitation. As AI ethics is a currently active field in terms of theoretical discussion, the constructs in the area are constantly evolving. The ART principles and EAD chosen as a basis of the framework were, at the time of writing, some of the most prominent works in the area. The framework ultimately presents but one way of perceiving AI ethics.

# 7    Conclusions and Future Work

This paper furthers our understanding of the current state of practice in the field of AI ethics. By means of a multiple case study, we studied the way AI ethics is currently implemented in practice, if it is implemented at all, when it is not formally or systematically implemented in software engineering projects.

Our findings can be summarized through the following two key takeaways:

- Even when ethics are not particularly considered, some currently commonly used software development practices, such as documentation, support EAD. This is also the case with focusing on information security.
- While the developers speculate potential socioethical impacts of the resulting system, they do not have means to address them.

Thus, from the point of view of software engineering methods and practices, this highlights a gap in the area. While some of the existing common practices support the implementation of some aspects of AI ethics, there are no methods or practices that help implement it on a project-level.

Further studies on the topic should seek to assist in the practical implementation of AI ethics. Singular practices and especially project-level methods are needed to bridge the gap between research and practice in the area. This lack of higher-level methods was also highlighted in a review of tools and methods in the area [6].

# References

1. D'Onfro, J.: AI 50: America's Most Promising Artificial Intelligence Companies, Forbes https://www.forbes.com/sites/jilliandonfro/2019/09/17/ai-50-americas-most-promis ing-artificial-intelligence-companies/
2. Hamet, P., Tremblay, J.: Artificial intelligence in medicine. Metabolism **69**, 36–40 (2017)
3. Raaijmakers, S.: Artificial intelligence for law enforcement: challenges and opportunities. IEEE Secur. Priv. **17**(5), 74–77 (2019)
4. Lee, J., Davari, H., Singh, J., Pandhare, V.: Industrial artificial intelligence for industry 4.0-based manufacturing systems. In: Manufacturing Letters, vol. 18, pp. 20–23 (2018)
5. Sculley, D., et al.: Hidden technical debt in machine learning systems. Adv. Neural Inf. Process. Syst. **2**, 2503–2511 (2015)
6. Morley, J., et al.: From what to how: an initial review of publicly available ai ethics tools, methods and research to translate principles in-to practices. Preprint arXiv:1905.06876 (2019)
7. Charisi, V. et al.: Towards moral autonomous systems. Preprint arXiv:1703.04741 (2017)
8. The IEEE Global Initiative on Ethics of Autonomous and Intelligent Systems. Ethically Aligned Design: A Vision for Prioritizing Human Well-being with Autonomous and Intelligent Systems, First Edition, IEEE. https://standards.ieee.org/content/ieee-standards/en/ind ustry-connections/ec/autonomous-systems.html (2019)
9. Bynum, T.: Flourishing ethics. Ethics Inf. Technol. **8**(4), 157–173 (2006)
10. Friedman, B.: Value-sensitive design. Interactions **3**(6), 16–23 (1996)
11. Davis, J., Nathan, L.P.: Value sensitive design: applications, adaptations, and critiques. In: van den Hoven, J., Vermaas, P.E., van de Poel, I. (eds.) Handbook of Ethics, Values, and Technological Design: Sources, Theory, Values and Application Domains, pp. 11–40. Springer, Dordrecht (2015)
12. Allen, C., Wallach, W., Smit, I.: Why machine ethics? IEEE Intell. Syst. **21**(4), 12–17 (2006)
13. Etzioni, A.: Incorporating ethics into artificial intelligence. J. Ethics **21**(4), 403–418 (2017)
14. Vakkuri, V., et al.: Ethically aligned design of autonomous systems: industry viewpoint and an empirical study. Preprint arXiv:1906.07946 (2019)
15. Rudin, C.: Stop explaining black box machine learning models for high stakes decisions and use interpretable models instead. Nat. Mach. Intell. **1**, 206–215 (2019)
16. Dignum, V.: Responsible autonomy. Preprint arXiv:1706.02513 (2017)
17. Turilli, M., Floridi, L.: The ethics of information transparency. Ethics Inf. Technol. **11**(2), 105–112 (2009)
18. Flores, A.W., Bechtel, K., Lowenkamp, C.T.: False positives, false negatives, and false analyses: a rejoinder to "Machine bias: there's software used across the country to predict future criminals, and it's biased against blacks". In: Federal Probation, vol. 80(2), 38 (2016)
19. Villani, C., et al.: For a meaningful artificial intelligence: towards a French and European strategy. Conseil national du numérique (2018). https://www.aiforhumanity.fr/pdfs/Missio nVillani_Report_ENG-VF.pdf

20. German Federal Ministry of Transport and Digital Infrastructure: Automated and Con-nected Driving (2017). https://www.bmvi.de/EN/Topics/Digital-Matters/Automated-Connected-Driving/automated-and-connected-driving.html

21. AI HLEG: Ethics guidelines for trustworthy AI (2019) https://ec.europa.eu/digital-single-market/en/news/ethics-guidelines-trustworthy-ai

22. ISO/IEC JTC 1/SC 42 Artificial intelligence. https://www.iso.org/committee/6794475.html

23. Pichai, S.: AI at Google: our principles. Blog (2018). https://www.blog.google/technology/ai/ai-principles/

24. Microsoft (2018). Responsible bots: 10 guidelines for developers of conversational AI. https://www.microsoft.com/en-us/research/uploads/prod/2018/11/Bot_Guidelines_Nov_2018.pdf

25. Mittelstadt, B.: Principles Alone Cannot Guarantee Ethical AI. In: Nature Machine Intelligence (2019)

26. McNamara, A., Smith, J., Murphy-Hill, E.: Does ACM's code of ethics change ethical decision making in software development? In: Proceedings of the 2018 26th ACM Joint Meeting on ESEC/FSE, pp. 729–733 (2018)

27. Vakkuri, V, Kemell, K.K., Abrahamsson, P.: AI ethics in industry: a research framework. In: Rantanen, M., Koskinen, J (eds.) Tethics 2019: Proceedings of the Third Seminar on Technology Ethics, CEUR Workshop Proceedings, 2505. RWTH Aachen University (2019)

28. Dignum, V.: Ethics in artificial intelligence: introduction to the special issue. Ethics Inf. Technol. **20**(1), 1–3 (2018)

29. Abrahamsson, P.: Commitment nets in software process improvement. Ann. Softw. Eng. **14**(1), 407–438 (2002)

30. Galletta, A.: Mastering the Semi-structured Interview and Beyond: From Research Design to Analysis and Publication. NYU Press, New York (2013)

31. Heath, H.: Developing a grounded theory approach: a comparison of Glaser and Strauss. Int. J. Nurs. Stud. **41**(2), 141–150 (2004)

32. Ananny, M., Crawford, K.: Seeing without knowing: limitations of the transparency ideal and its application to algorithmic accountability. New Media Soc. **20**(3), 973–989 (2018)

33. Unterkalmsteiner, M., et al.: Evaluation and measurement of software process improvement—a systematic literature review. IEEE Trans. Softw. Eng. **38**(2), 398–424 (2011)

34. Duc, A.N., Abrahamsson, P.: Minimum viable product or multiple facet product? the role of MVP in software startups. In: International Conference on Agile Software Development, pp. 118–130 (2016)

35. Eisenhardt, K.M.: Building theories from case study research. Acad. Manag. Rev. **14**(4), 532–550 (1989)

# Hypotheses Elicitation in Early-Stage Software Startups Based on Cognitive Mapping

Jorge Melegati[(✉)] [ID] and Xiaofeng Wang [ID]

Free University of Bozen-Bolzano, Bolzano, Italy
{jmelegatigoncalves,xiaofeng.wang}@unibz.it

**Abstract.** Software startups develop innovative products for which there are typically no customers to refer to elicit requirements. Often, these companies develop a set of features without a better understanding of customer needs. An experiment-based approach to validate hypotheses about the customer and market could increase their chance of success or, at least, accelerate their realization of the product worthlessness. The first step of an experiment-based approach is to elicit hypotheses to guide experiments. Software startups base their products on business assumptions, but there is a lack of understanding of how these assumptions are formed and how teams could elicit hypotheses systematically. To fill this gap, we performed an empirical study consisted of two steps. First, we explored based on which assumptions startups define their products using a multiple case study. The results indicate that these companies developed their products based on founders' assumptions derived from their previous experience. Second, we investigated cognitive mapping as a tool to elicit hypotheses systematically with two software startups. The results indicate that this approach can serve as the basis of a method to elicit hypotheses in early-stage software startups.

**Keywords:** Hypotheses engineering · Software startups · Experimentation

## 1 Introduction

The use of experiments to understand the business value is a recent trend in software engineering [5,13]. In this context, experimentation is a process of continuously validating product assumptions, transforming them as hypotheses, prioritizing, and testing them following the scientific method to support or refute them [13]. This notion comprises several techniques like prototypes, controlled experiments [5], and problem or solution interviews [13].

In a recent position paper [15], we argued the need for Hypotheses Engineering to handle hypotheses in an experiment-driven approach in a similar way in which Requirements Engineering handles requirements in a traditional software development process. Hypotheses should be elicited, documented, analyzed, and

© The Author(s) 2020
V. Stray et al. (Eds.): XP 2020, LNBIP 383, pp. 211–220, 2020.
https://doi.org/10.1007/978-3-030-49392-9_14

prioritized to perform experiments efficiently. In this paper, we will use "assumption" as a personal or team-wise, generally implicit, understanding taken as truth without being questioned or proved, and "hypothesis" as an explicit statement that has not been verified yet, but an experiment could evaluate. That is, assumptions exist on a cognitive and abstract level, while hypotheses exist on a concrete level in experimentation.

Despite experimentation being a well-known approach for startups and serving as the basis of the Lean Startup methodology [6], software startups still focus on developing the product without testing critical assumptions [9]. In this paper, we targeted the problem of eliciting hypotheses in early-stage software startups, where experimentation is expected to be the primary way of working [17]. The following research question will guide the study: *How can early-stage software startups define hypotheses to support experimentation?*

To achieve our goal, we performed a two-phased empirical study. The first phase aimed to understand how the assumptions on which startups base their products are formed. The second phase investigated how to uncover these assumptions and elicit hypotheses to guide experiments. The first phase results indicated that products are based on the founder's assumptions about the market and the customer. In the second phase, we used cognitive mapping to make the founders' assumptions explicit. Our results indicated that this approach could underpin a method to elicit hypotheses systematically in software startups.

## 2   Background and Related Work

Although the term 'software startup' is still not a consensus among authors [1], a common set of characteristics has emerged in recent studies: innovation, lack of resources, uncertainty, time-pressure, small team, highly reactive, and rapid evolution [1]. Based on the literature, Klotins et al. [12] proposed a life-cycle model for startups with four stages: inception, stabilization, growth, and maturity. The first stage goes from idea conception until the first release. In the next stage, the startup prepares to scale regarding technical and operational aspects. On these two early-stages, teams focus on finding a relevant problem and solution. In the growth stage, the startup aims to reach the desired market participation, and, in the last stage, it progresses into an established company.

Usually, startups develop software in a market-driven context [1] and offer it to an open marketplace instead of a specific customer. In this latter situation, called specific-customer or bespoke development, one single customer covers the costs to produce the software according to its needs and wishes [16]. Klotins et al. [12] observed the similarities between market-driven development and software startups: mainly invented requirements, light-weight, and informal practices, and quick releases to get customer feedback.

Nevertheless, practices used in the market-driven context may not apply to software startups. In the former, requirements are generally gathered through observing a competing product or collaborating with key customers [16]. In software startups, the options are limited by the innovative nature of products.

What makes a product new and unique cannot be found elsewhere. It is typically not recognizable by potential customers, as the phrase attributed to Henry Ford says: "if I had asked people what they wanted, they would have said faster horses." This mismatch explains why teams in software startups still rely on their ideas or a product team [14] to elicit requirements, especially on how the founder views the market [19]. In such innovative contexts, experimentation has been promoted as an essential practice for new ventures (e.g., [3] and [11]).

In software engineering, experimentation has focused on testing hypotheses about the product and the market [5,13], and some models were proposed to systematize it [15]. These models extended and are similar to the Lean Startup's Build-Measure-Learn cycles [17]. In these cycles, startups should first take their assumptions as hypotheses and build the minimum solution to test one of them (Build). Based on metrics (Measure), the team should accept or reject the hypothesis (Learn), that is, persevering or pivoting.

These models provide an overview of the experimentation process, but they do not describe how to define hypotheses [15] and were not explicitly derived for startups. Regarding software startups, to elicit hypotheses, several industry practices have been suggested, such as Business Model Canvas (BMC) (e.g., [8]). Recently, Bland et al. [2] proposed the Assumption Mapping: a set of tools to help teams come up with hypotheses, highly inspired by BMC. But it was not derived from scientific work and did not focus on software startups. In summary, no scientific study focused on how assumptions, on which startups base their products, are formed and how they can inform hypotheses elicitation.

## 3    Research Method

We performed an empirical study divided into two phases, and each consisted of an exploratory multiple-case study. Following the rationale of typical cases [20], we selected software startups in the inception or stabilization phase and where founders had the initial ideas. Through our contact network, we selected four startups (A and B for the first phase, and C and D for the second phase).

The first phase aimed to understand how the assumptions on which startups based their products are formed. It consisted of semi-structured interviews following a defined guide. For both cases, we interviewed the founders and, for case B, also the software developer. The questions aimed to understand the interviewees' background, the startup idea, motivation to build the product, and how they changed throughout the company history. In the second phase, we evaluated a technique to elicit hypotheses based on the first phase results. It consisted of interviews with startup founders who had the initial ideas. Both founders interviewed in this phase recently did a course where several methodologies and techniques were presented, including Lean Startup and Business Model Canvas.

## 4    First-Phase Results

**Case A.** The startup was developing a software library to be added in projects which will detect run-time problems, like exceptions, observed or inferred based on data collected from the target system. A dashboard will show these problems live along with solutions from similar issues found on the Internet and a list of freelance developers that could help to solve the problem. In some cases, the system would be able to fix some issues automatically. The founder has worked as a software development consultant for an extended period. While working on third-party projects, he observed that such a tool could help him work more effectively. As another reason to develop the tool, he also believed that the technical level of software developers was decreasing nowadays.

**Case B.** The startup runs a website to help hotel owners and managers to find the best software solutions to their businesses. The interviewed founder had worked in a company that handled web marketing and websites before staying twelve years in a big web agency. Throughout his work life, he had extensive contact with the tourism sector, especially the hospitality industry. He claimed that the idea came to him based on the needs he observed from hotel owners, the fact that there are a lot of technological tools available in the market to run the business, and the needs that software vendors have to reach hotel owners. He was inspired by American software review websites and the lack of a specific one for the hospitality sector. Then, the original idea was to list available software with users' reviews, bring hotel owners to the website, and receive a fee for each lead (an interested customer that visited the vendor website) generated.

When the website went online, the use was below the expected. The team concluded that the hotel owners were not able to compare different solutions because these products rarely have the same set of features, and, often, hotels needed more than one to fulfill their needs. Then, the startup changed the website: now, the hotel owner fills a form giving details about her business, and the system would use a simple algorithm to match solutions with business needs.

**Cross-case analysis.** Based on the case descriptions above, the founder's background shaped beliefs about target customers and the market. Through these lenses, founders made sense about the specific business environment and its players, explaining their behavior and, in the last stance, trying to forecast it as illustrated in Fig. 1. Specifically, in startup B, the founder considered that hotel owners wanted to buy software solutions, and they were able to compare different alternatives and select the best for her case. Based on that, the founder foresaw the convenience for hotel owners of a website with the list of available software.

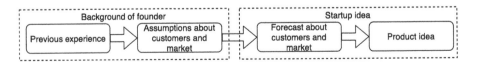

**Fig. 1.** The process of idea creation.

The assumptions the founder had about customers and market guided requirements elicitation. In startup B, it was possible to see what could happen next. After the software was ready and put into use, data showed that it was not working as predicted. Therefore, the founder had to update his assumptions and, consequently, change the product. This new understanding emerged from experiments and led to better results. Such rearrangement exposed an implicit process model (see Fig. 2) for development in software startups: the founder's assumptions guide the elicitation of requirements and the software usage data may impose changes on these assumptions. This updated world representation is used to elicit new requirements.

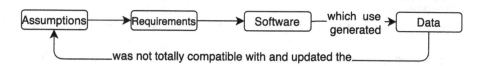

**Fig. 2.** The founder's assumptions being updated.

**Cognitive mapping.** To further explore the founders' assumptions, a valuable approach would be to make them explicit. For this task, an available tool is cognitive mapping. Cognitive maps are visual representations of causal aspects of a person's belief system as a graph where nodes represent the concepts individuals use and arrows, causal links between them [7] labeled according to its association: '+', positive; '−', negative, and '/o/' neutral.

We used case B to illustrate the approach. First, we elicited the founder's initial cognitive map (Fig. 3a). Then, through the relationships among concepts in the map, we derived hypotheses on which the product was based. They are (1) owners have several software options to run hotels; (2) because of that, they have difficulty to choose software; (3) a list of options would help owners to select the product; (4) software vendors have difficulty to reach hotel owners. Hence, the first product version acted as an experiment to test the usefulness of a list of available software to hotel owners, which results made the founders update their assumptions about the customers' behavior (Fig. 3b). Such analysis was performed *ex post* (after the product was developed). To verify if a cognitive map could be used *ex ante*, we performed a second phase for this study.

## 5    Second-Phase Results

In this phase, we performed a study with two other software startups, C and D. We interviewed the founders following the steps: (1) present the hypothesis concept and its relation to Lean Startup; (2) ask a summary of the startup idea, focusing on customer segments and value proposition; (3) ask on which hypotheses the founder believed his idea is based; (4) using a whiteboard and interacting with the founder, draw a cognitive map; (5) create a list of hypotheses based on the cognitive map and compare it with the initially created list; (6) ask feedback.

To draw the map, we adapted the approach proposed by Furnari [7]. First, we asked the interviewee to describe the business model. From that, we extracted concepts and causal relationships. Then, we dig on each concept to see if they

(a) Initial cognitive map on which the founder based the business idea.

(b) Cognitive map that emerged after the first failure. In bold, the learning obtained.

**Fig. 3.** Startup B founder's assumptions in different moments of the company life.

were, in reality, not based on an underlying assumption. The process ended when the interviewee said that the map represented her understanding of the problem. Throughout the process, we used the whiteboard to depict the current status of the mapping. Figure 4a and b display the cognitive maps obtained.

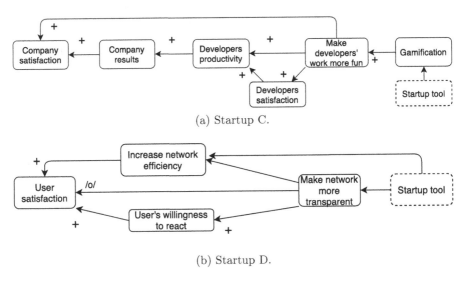

(a) Startup C.

(b) Startup D.

**Fig. 4.** Cognitive maps created during interview with the founders.

**Case C** is a startup where the founders plan to develop a digital mentor for software developers to increase their happiness and satisfaction. The product would try to adapt itself to each developer's needs. The paying customer would be companies interested in improving their developers' productiveness. When asked about hypotheses, the founder mentioned that the first was that software development teams could not organize themselves. Through some customer interviews, it got invalidated, and they pivoted the initial idea to the current one. The next hypothesis or, how the founder called, "exploration" is to understand if software developers care about soft skills. When asked about other hypotheses, the founder said that she is waiting for another round of tests.

In the interview, the founder stated that the main element to increase developers' productivity would be making their work more fun through gamification. The map implied six hypotheses: (1) developers productivity improves the company results; (2) developers satisfaction rises developers productivity; (3) making the development work more fun increases the developers' productivity and (4) the developers' satisfaction; (5) gamification could make developers' work more fun; (6) making the development work more fun would rise the company satisfaction. Although some identified hypotheses are trivial and may not demand an experiment, the founder recognized that "[they] have to see if the correlation between having fun and the productivity [exists], that is a major risk."

**Case D** is developing a solution to improve network connectivity, especially where the Internet quality is low. Through an innovative approach, suppressed here according to the interviewee's request, the solution will make the network status transparent to the user, allowing it to be adapted to the needs and, consequently, improving the quality of service. Initially, the founder answered that their main hypothesis regarded how large is the area where the quality is bad and if providers are willing to fix it soon. He mentioned that he talked to many potential customers, and most of them would want the solution.

The map implied four hypotheses: (1) increasing the network efficiency will improve user satisfaction, (2) making the network more transparent will not decrease user satisfaction, (3) making the network more transparent will increase the user's willingness to react, and (4) the users' willingness and ability to respond will increase user satisfaction. The founder mentioned they had considered these hypotheses before, but the process "made them explicit and more structured."

## 6  Discussion

Software startups elicit requirements on their own, based on assumptions regarding the customer or market. Since the founder is generally the sole owner of innovation [19], these assumptions are based on founders', not necessarily explicit beliefs. In other words, products are based on the founders' tacit knowledge about the customer and market. Yet, the delay in abandoning an unworthy idea could mean exhausting the resources and, consequently, failing the company. The possible reasons not to make these assumptions explicit include protecting them against criticism [4] or avoiding an uncomfortable situation of not being able to predict and control if they are invalidated [10]. Besides that, founders try to predict a distant event: the use of a product or a service after development. Thus, as we observed, it can take time for the founder to review her assumptions. Such an adjustment is more frequent when used to predict immediate happenings [10].

A hypothesis elicitation method should evidence assumptions that are guiding the startup product development. Then, the first step is to make explicit the founders' assumptions. Our study showed that cognitive mapping is a viable way to do it. This option is related to what Furnari [7] called "cognitive perspective" in business model research.

The value of a model cognitive map is two-folded. First, it allows the startup to check the business model for flaws. Second, the team can derive hypotheses from the cognitive map for experiment creation. Data collected from experiments will validate their understanding or update it. Once ideas are validated, they can be used to guide requirements elicitation.

To handle the threats to validity, we followed the definitions given by Runeson et al. [18]. Since the interview guide focused on the business model description and evolution, the threat to construct validity is minimal. Besides that, the triangulation of data with interviewing a different team member decreased the threat even more. Triangulation was also essential to mitigate threats to internal validity. Besides that, both authors discussed the results (peer debriefing). Concerning external validity, in case studies, it is not possible to draw statistical significance [18]. Then, the goal was analytical generalization through studying typical software startups where the founder is the main innovation owner. These companies generally focus on developing a solution instead of understanding the customer [9]. To improve reliability, we described all the performed steps.

## 7   Conclusions

Early-stage software startups have to evaluate if their ideas are worth pursuing. Developing experiments based on hypotheses about various aspects of a business model is essential to this task. In such a process, the first step is to define the hypotheses. There are some techniques in the literature to perform this, but they were not systematically obtained from scientific knowledge. To derive a basis for such a tool, we conducted a two-phased empirical study. First, we concluded that the founder's past experiences mold a set of assumptions used to predict the environment and how a new product would behave. Then, we had promising results using cognitive mapping to elicit hypotheses leading us to believe it could serve as the basis of a method for early-stage software startups. In order to develop such a method, future work should answer some questions, such as if the tool can elicit all hypotheses related to the product.

## References

1. Berg, V., Birkeland, J., Nguyen-Duc, A., Pappas, I.O., Jaccheri, L.: Software startup engineering: a systematic mapping study. J. Syst. Softw. **144**, 255–274 (2018)
2. Bland, D., Osterwalder, A.: Testing Business Ideas. Wiley, Hoboken (2019)
3. Eisenhardt, K.M., Tabrizi, B.N.: Accelerating adaptive processes: product innovation in the global computer industry. Adm. Sci. Q. **40**(1), 84 (1995)
4. Eraut, M.: Non-formal learning and tacit knowledge in professional work. Br. J. Educ. Psychol. **70**, 113–136 (2000)

5. Fabijan, A., Dmitriev, P., McFarland, C., Vermeer, L., Holmström Olsson, H., Bosch, J.: Experimentation growth: evolving trustworthy A/B testing capabilities in online software companies. J. Softw. Evol. Proc. **30**, e2113 (2018)
6. Frederiksen, D.L., Brem, A.: How do entrepreneurs think they create value? A scientific reflection of Eric Ries' Lean Startup approach. Int. Enterpren. Manag. J. **13**(1), 169–189 (2017)
7. Furnari, S.: A cognitive mapping approach to business models: representing causal structures and mechanisms. Adv. Strateg. Manage. **33**, 207–239 (2015)
8. Gutbrod, M., Münch, J.: Teaching lean startup principles: an empirical study on assumption prioritization. In: Software-intensive Business Workshop on Start-ups, Platforms and Ecosystems (SiBW 2018), pp. 245–253 (2018)
9. Gutbrod, M., Münch, J., Tichy, M.: How do software startups approach experimentation? Empirical results from a qualitative interview study. In: Felderer, M., Méndez Fernández, D., Turhan, B., Kalinowski, M., Sarro, F., Winkler, D. (eds.) PROFES 2017. LNCS, vol. 10611, pp. 297–304. Springer, Cham (2017). https://doi.org/10.1007/978-3-319-69926-4_21
10. Kelly, G.: The Psychology of Personal Constructs: Volume One: Theory and Personality. Taylor & Francis, Washington, DC (2002)
11. Kerr, W.R., Nanda, R., Rhodes-Kropf, M.: Entrepreneurship as experimentation. J. Econ. Perspect. **28**(3), 25–48 (2014)
12. Klotins, E., et al.: A progression model of software engineering goals, challenges, and practices in start-ups. IEEE Trans. Softw. Eng. **13**(9), 1 (2019)
13. Lindgren, E., Münch, J.: Raising the odds of success: the current state of experimentation in product development. Inf. Softw. Technol. **77**, 80–91 (2016)
14. Melegati, J., Goldman, A., Kon, F., Wang, X.: A model of requirements engineering in software startups. Inf. Softw. Technol. **109**, 92–107 (2019)
15. Melegati, J., Wang, X., Abrahamsson, P.: Hypotheses Engineering: first essential steps of experiment-driven software development. In: IEEE/ACM Joint 4th International Workshop on Rapid Continuous Software Engineering and 1st International Workshop on Data-Driven Decisions, Experimentation and Evolution (RCoSE/DDrEE), pp. 16–19 (2019)
16. Regnell, B., Brinkkemper, S.: Market-driven requirements engineering for software products. In: Aurum, A., Wohlin, C. (eds.) Engineering and Managing Software Requirements, pp. 287–308. Springer, Heidelberg (2005). https://doi.org/10.1007/3-540-28244-0_13
17. Ries, E.: The Lean Startup: How Today's Entrepreneurs Use Continuous Innovation to Create Radically Successful Businesses. The Lean Startup: How Today's Entrepreneurs Use Continuous Innovation to Create Radically Successful Businesses, Crown Business (2011)
18. Runeson, P., Höst, M., Rainer, A., Regnell, B.: Case Study Research in Software Engineering: Guidelines and Examples. Wiley, Hoboken (2012)
19. Seppänen, P., Oivo, M., Liukkunen, K.: The initial team of a software startup. In: 2016 International Conference on Engineering, Technology and Innovation (ICE) & IEEE International Technology Management Conference, pp. 57–65 (2016)
20. Yin, R.: Case Study Research: Design and Methods. Applied Social Research Methods. SAGE Publications, Thousand Oaks (2003)

# Agile and Testing

# Results from a Replicated Experiment on the Affective Reactions of Novice Developers When Applying Test-Driven Development

Simone Romano[1]([✉]), Giuseppe Scanniello[2], Maria Teresa Baldassarre[1],
Davide Fucci[3], and Danilo Caivano[1]

[1] University of Bari, Bari, Italy
{simone.romano,mariateresa.baldassarre,danilo.caivano}@uniba.it
[2] University of Basilicata, Potenza, Italy
giuseppe.scanniello@unibas.it
[3] Blekinge Institute of Technology, Karlskrona, Sweden
davide.fucci@bth.se

**Abstract.** Test-Driven Development (TDD) is an incremental approach to software development. Despite it is claimed to improve both quality of software and developers' productivity, the research on the claimed effects of TDD has so far shown inconclusive results. Some researchers have ascribed these inconclusive results to the negative affective states that TDD would provoke. A previous (baseline) experiment has, therefore, studied the affective reactions of (novice) developers—*i.e.*, 29 third-year undergraduates in Computer Science (CS)—when practicing TDD to implement software. To validate the results of the baseline experiment, we conducted a replicated experiment that studies the affective reactions of novice developers when applying TDD to develop software. Developers in the treatment group carried out a development task using TDD, while those in the control group used a non-TDD approach. To measure the affective reactions of developers, we used the Self-Assessment Manikin instrument complemented with a liking dimension. The most important differences between the baseline and replicated experiments are: *(i)* the kind of novice developers involved in the experiments—third-year vs. second-year undergraduates in CS from two different universities; and *(ii)* their number—29 vs. 59. The results of the replicated experiment do not show any difference in the affective reactions of novice developers. Instead, the results of the baseline experiment suggest that developers seem to like TDD less as compared to a non-TDD approach and that developers following TDD seem to like implementing code less than the other developers, while testing code seems to make them less happy.

**Keywords:** TDD · Affective state · Replication · Experiment

© The Author(s) 2020
V. Stray et al. (Eds.): XP 2020, LNBIP 383, pp. 223–239, 2020.
https://doi.org/10.1007/978-3-030-49392-9_15

# 1    Introduction

Test-Driven Development (TDD) is an incremental approach to software development in which unit tests are written before production code [1]. In particular, TDD promotes short cycles composed of three phases to incrementally implement the functionality of a software:

**Red Phase.** Write a unit test for a small chunk of functionalities not yet implemented and watch the test fail;
**Green Phase.** Implement that chunk of functionalities as quickly as possible and watch all unit tests pass;
**Refactor Phase.** Refactor the code and watch all unit tests pass.

Advocates of TDD claim that this development approach allows improving the (internal and external) quality of software as well as developers' productivity [8]. However, research on the claimed effects of TDD, gathered in secondary studies, has so far shown inconclusive results (*e.g.,* [15]). Such inconclusive results might relate to the negative affective states that developers would experience when practicing TDD (*e.g.,* [8]). For example, frustration due to spending a large amount of time in writing unit tests that fail, rather than immediately focusing on the implementation of functionality. Nevertheless, only Romano *et al.* [21] has studied through a controlled experiment the affective reactions of developers when applying TDD to implement software. In particular, they recruited 29 novice developers who were asked to carry out a development task by using either TDD or a non-TDD approach. At the end of the development task, the researchers gathered the affective reactions to the development approach, as well as to implementing and testing code. To this end, Romano *et al.* used Self-Assessment Manikin (SAM) [3]—a lightweight, but powerful self-assessment instrument for measuring affective reactions to a stimulus in terms of the pleasure, arousal, and dominance dimensions—complemented with the liking dimension [17]. The results highlight differences in the affective reactions of novice developers to the development approach, as well as to implementing and testing code. In particular, novice developers seem to like TDD less as compared to a non-TDD approach. Moreover, novice developers following TDD seem to like implementing code less than those developers following a non-TDD approach, while testing code seems to make TDD developers less happy.

The Software Engineering (SE) community has shown a growing interest in replications of empirical studies (*e.g.,* replicated experiments) and recognized the key role that replications play in the construction of knowledge [25]. To validate the results of the experiment by Romano *et al.* [21] (also called baseline experiment from here on), we conducted a replicated experiment with 59 novice developers. In the replication, we investigated the same constructs as the baseline experiment, but in a different site and with participants sampled from a different population—*i.e.,* 59 second-year vs. 29 third-year undergraduates in Computer Science (CS) from two different universities.

**Paper Structure.** In Sect. 2, we report background information and related work. The baseline experiment is summarized in Sect. 3. The replication is outlined in Sect. 4. The results of our replication are presented and discussed in Sect. 5 and Sect. 6, respectively. We discuss the threats to validity of our replication in Sect. 7. Final remarks conclude the paper.

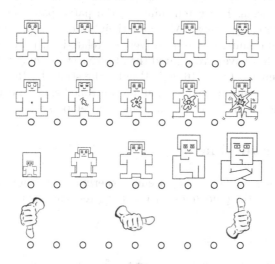

**Fig. 1.** From top down, the graphical representations of the pleasure, arousal, dominance, and liking dimensions. This figure has been taken from [21].

# 2 Background and Related Work

According to the PAD (Pleasure-Arousal-Dominance) model—a psychological model to describe and measure affective states—, people's affective states can be characterized through three dimensions: pleasure, arousal, and dominance [22]. The pleasure dimension varies from unpleasant (*e.g.*, unhappy/sad) to pleasant (*e.g.*, happy/joyful), the arousal one ranges from inactive (*e.g.*, bored/calm) to active (*e.g.*, excited/stimulated), and finally, the dominance dimension varies from "without control" to "in control of everything" [17]. To measure a person's affective reaction to a stimulus in terms of the pleasure, arousal, and dominance dimensions, Bradley and Lang [3] proposed a pictorial self-assessment instrument they named SAM. This instrument represents each dimension graphically with a rating scale placed just below the graphical representation of each dimension so that a person can self-assess her affective reaction in terms of that dimension (see Fig. 1). For instance, SAM pictures the pleasure dimension through manikins varying from an unhappy manikin to a happy one; thus the nine-point rating scale, placed just below the graphical representation of the pleasure dimension, allows a person to self-assess, from one to nine, that dimension of her affective reaction. Recently, Koelstra *et al.* [17] have complemented SAM with the liking dimension ranging from dislike—pictured through a thumb down—to like—pictured through a thumb up (see Fig. 1).

Both Human-Computer Interaction (HCI) and affective computing research fields have utilized SAM in their empirical studies (*e.g.,* [12,17]). Later, the SE research field has used SAM as well. For example, Graziotin *et al.* [11] conducted an observational study with eight developers who performed development tasks on individual projects. Every ten minutes, the participants self-assessed both their affective state, by using SAM, and their productivity. The results show that pleasure and dominance are positively correlated with productivity.

A few SE studies have investigated the affective states of developers through controlled experiments (*e.g.,* [16,26]). Besides the study by Romano *et al.* [21], which we summarize in the next section, no controlled experiment has been conducted to investigate the affective reactions of developers while practicing TDD.

## 3    Baseline Experiment

In this section, we summarize the baseline experiment by Romano *et al.* [21] by taking into account the guidelines for reporting replications in SE [6].

### 3.1    Research Questions

The baseline experiment aimed to answer the following Research Question (RQ):

**RQ1.** Is there a difference in the affective reactions of novice developers to a development approach (*i.e.,* TDD vs. a non-TDD approach)?

The aim of RQ1 was to understand the affective reactions that TDD raises on novice developers in terms of pleasure, arousal, dominance, and liking. To deepen such an investigation, two further RQs were formulated and studied:

**RQ2.** Is there a difference in the affective reactions of novice developers to the implementation phase when comparing TDD to a non-TDD approach?
**RQ3.** Is there a difference in the affective reactions of novice developers to the testing phase when comparing TDD to a non-TDD approach?

The aim of RQ2 and RQ3 was to understand the effect of TDD on the affective reactions of novice developers—in terms of the pleasure, arousal, dominance, and liking dimensions—with respect implementing and testing code, respectively.

### 3.2    Participants and Artifacts

The participants in the baseline experiment were 29 third-year undergraduates in CS at the University of Basilicata (Italy). According to previous work (*e.g.,* [13]), Romano *et al.* considered undergraduates in CS as a proxy of novice developers. The participants were taking the SE course when they voluntarily accepted to take part in the experiment. Once the students accepted to participate, they were asked to fill in a pre-questionnaire (*e.g.*, to collect information on their experience on unit testing). Based on the data gathered through this questionnaire, the participants had experience in both C and Java programming. No participant had experience with TDD at the beginning of the SE course.

The baseline experiment used two experimental objects—*i.e.*, Bowling Score Keeper (BSK) and Mars Rover API (MRA). Each participant dealt with either BSK or MRA. The participants, who received BSK, were asked to develop an API for calculating the score of a bowling game, while those who received MRA had to develop an API for moving a rover on a planet. In both cases, they had to code in Java and write unit tests by using JUnit. At the beginning of the experimental session, any participant was provided with: *(i)* a problem statement regarding the assigned experimental object; *(ii)* the user stories to be implemented (*i.e.*, 13 user stories for BSK and 11 user stories for MRA); *(iii)* a template project for the Eclipse IDE containing the expected API and an example JUnit test class; and *(iv)* for each user story an acceptance test suite to simulate customers' acceptance of that story. Both BSK and MRA had been previously used as experimental objects in empirical studies on TDD and could be fulfilled in a three-hour experimental session (*e.g.*, [9,10]).

To gather the affective reactions of the participants, Romano *et al.* exploited SAM [3] complemented with the liking dimension [17]. SAM allows measuring people's affective reactions to a stimulus over nine-point rating scales in terms of pleasure, arousal, dominance, and liking (see Sect. 2).

### 3.3   Variables and Hypotheses

The baseline experiment compared the affective reactions of two different groups of novice developers, namely *treatment* and *control*. The treatment group consisted of participants who were asked to use TDD to carry out a development task, while the control group consisted of participants who were unaware of TDD and had to perform a development task by using a non-TDD approach named YW (Your Way development)—*i.e.*, the approach they would normally utilize to develop [9]. Therefore, the main Independent Variable (IV), or main factor, manipulated in the baseline experiment was **Approach**, which assumed two values: TDD or YW. Within each group, some participants dealt with BSK, while others dealt with MRA. Thus, there was a second IV, namely **Object**, which had BSK or MRA as the value.

To measure the pleasure, arousal, dominance, and liking dimensions with respect to the development approach (*i.e.*, to answer RQ1), Romano *et al.* used the following four ordinal Dependent Variables (DVs): $APP_{PLS}$, $APP_{ARS}$, $APP_{DOM}$, and $APP_{LIK}$. These variables assumed integer values in between one and nine since each dimension could be assessed through a nine-point rating scale (see Sect. 2). Similarly, they measured pleasure, arousal, dominance, and liking with respect to the implementation and testing phases (*i.e.*, to answer RQ2 and RQ3) through the following four ordinal DVs each: $IMP_{PLS}$, $IMP_{ARS}$, $IMP_{DOM}$, $IMP_{LIK}$, $TES_{PLS}$, $TES_{ARS}$, $TES_{DOM}$, and $TES_{LIK}$.

To answer the RQs, the following parameterized null hypothesis was tested:

$\text{HO}_\text{DV}$. There is no effect of Approach on $\text{DV} \in \{\text{APP}_\text{PLS}, \text{APP}_\text{ARS}, \text{APP}_\text{DOM}, \text{APP}_\text{LIK},$ $\text{IMP}_\text{PLS}, \text{IMP}_\text{ARS}, \text{IMP}_\text{DOM}, \text{IMP}_\text{LIK}, \text{TES}_\text{PLS}, \text{TES}_\text{ARS}, \text{TES}_\text{DOM}, \text{TES}_\text{LIK}\}$.

### 3.4  Design and Execution

The design of the baseline experiment was 2 * 2 factorial [27]. Such a kind of between-subjects design has two factors (*i.e.*, two IVs) having two levels each. The two factors were Approach and Object. Each participant in the baseline experiment was randomly assigned to one development approach and to one experimental object—*i.e.*, no participant used both development approaches or dealt with both experimental objects. In particular, 15 participants were assigned to TDD—7 with BSK and 8 with MRA—, while 14 participants were assigned to YW—7 with BSK and 7 with MRA.

Before the experiment took place, the participants had undergone a training period. In the first part of the training period, all participants attended face-to-face lessons on unit testing, JUnit, Test-Last development (TL), and Incremental Test-Last development (ITL). They also practiced unit testing with JUnit in a laboratory session. In the second part of the training, the participants in the treatment group learned TDD and practiced it through two laboratory sessions and three homework assignments. The participants in the control group did not learn TDD, rather they practiced TL and ITL through two laboratory sessions and three homework assignments. Regardless of the experimental group, the assignments were the same. The researcher conducted the experiment in a single three-hour laboratory session at the University of Basilicata where, based on the experimental groups, the participants carried out the development task—*i.e.*, they tackled MRA or BSK—by using TDD or YW. At the end of the development task, the participants were asked to self-assess their affective reactions to the used development approach through SAM [3] complemented with the liking dimension [17]. Similarly, they self-assessed their affective reactions to implementing and testing code, respectively.

### 3.5  Data Analysis and Results

Romano *et al.* analyzed the effects of Approach, Object, and their interaction (*i.e.*, Approach:Object) by using ANOVA Type Statistic (ATS) [4], a non-parametric version of ANOVA recommended in the HCI research field to analyze rating-scale data in factorial designs [14] (like the case of the baseline experiment). In particular, for each DV, the following ATS model was built: $DV \sim Approach + Object + Approach : Object$. To judge whether an effect was statistically significant, the $\alpha$ value was fixed (as customary) at 0.05. That is, an effect was deemed significant if the corresponding p-value was less than $\alpha$. To quantify the magnitude of the effect of Approach, in case it was significant, Romano *et al.* used Cliff's $\delta$ effect size [7]. The size of an effect is deemed: *negligible*, if $|\delta| < 0.147$; *small*, if $0.147 \leq |\delta| < 0.33$; *medium*, if $0.33 \leq |\delta| < 0.474$; or *large*, otherwise [20].

In Table 1, we report the ATS results of the baseline experiment. These results show a significant effect of Approach on $APP_{LIK}$ (p-value = 0.0024), namely there is a significant difference between TDD and YW with respect to $APP_{LIK}$. This allowed rejecting $H0_{APP_{LIK}}$. The difference in the $APP_{LIK}$ values was in favor of YW and large ($\delta = 0.6048$).[1] Accordingly, Romano et al. concluded that developers using TDD seem to like their development approach less than those using a non-TDD approach (i.e., answer to RQ1). Table 1 also shows two further significant effects, one for $IMP_{LIK}$ (p-value = 0.0396) and one for $TES_{PLS}$ (p-value = 0.0178) so allowing rejecting $H0_{IMP_{LIK}}$ and $H0_{TES_{PLS}}$, respectively. Both effects were in favor of YW. The effect size was medium ($\delta = 0.4286$) for $IMP_{LIK}$, while large for $TES_{PLS}$ ($\delta = 0.5$). Based on these results, Romano et al. concluded that: developers using TDD seem to like the implementation phase less than those using a non-TDD approach (i.e., answer to RQ2); and the testing phase seems to make developers using TDD less happy as compared to those using a non-TDD approach (i.e., answer to RQ3). As for the effects of Object and Approach:Object, they were in no case significant—i.e., neither the experimental object nor the interaction with the development approach seems to influence the affective reactions of novice developers.

**Table 1.** Results, from statistical inference, of the baseline experiment.

| DV | IV | | | Cliff's $\delta$ | Outcome for $H0_{DV}$ |
|---|---|---|---|---|---|
| | Approach | Object | Approach:Object | | |
| $APP_{PLS}$ | 0.1615 | 0.7721 | 0.8998 | - | $H0_{APP_{PLS}}$ not rejected |
| $APP_{ARS}$ | 0.2774 | 0.7794 | 0.1816 | - | $H0_{APP_{ARS}}$ not rejected |
| $APP_{DOM}$ | 0.2796 | 0.8569 | 0.4296 | - | $H0_{APP_{DOM}}$ not rejected |
| $APP_{LIK}$ | 0.0024* | 0.165 | 0.6368 | 0.6048 (large) | $H0_{APP_{LIK}}$ rejected in favor of YW |
| $IMP_{PLS}$ | 0.2008 | 0.6663 | 0.9793 | - | $H0_{IMP_{PLS}}$ not rejected |
| $IMP_{ARS}$ | 0.6799 | 0.6881 | 0.5752 | - | $H0_{IMP_{ARS}}$ not rejected |
| $IMP_{DOM}$ | 0.3449 | 0.5614 | 0.4672 | - | $H0_{IMP_{DOM}}$ not rejected |
| $IMP_{LIK}$ | 0.0396* | 0.1862 | 0.2703 | 0.4286 (medium) | $H0_{IMP_{LIK}}$ rejected in favor of YW |
| $TES_{PLS}$ | 0.0178* | 0.65 | 0.7652 | 0.5 (large) | $H0_{IMP_{PLS}}$ rejected in favor of YW |
| $TES_{ARS}$ | 0.4147 | 0.4765 | 0.3406 | - | $H0_{TES_{ARS}}$ not rejected |
| $TES_{DOM}$ | 0.6341 | 0.2564 | 0.4738 | - | $H0_{TES_{DOM}}$ not rejected |
| $TES_{LIK}$ | 0.0504 | 0.1194 | 0.0547 | - | $H0_{TES_{LIK}}$ not rejected |

\* P-value indicating a significant effect.

**Further Analysis and Results.** To better contextualize the baseline experiment, Romano et al. also assessed participants' development performance. To this end, they used a time-fixed strategy [2]. In particular, they defined an additional DV, named STR, which was computed as follows: (i) count the number of user stories each participant implemented within the fixed time frame (i.e., three hours); then (ii) normalize the number of implemented user stories in [0, 100]—this is because the total number of user stories of MRA was different

---

[1] The descriptive statistics were used to determine if the difference was in favor of TDD or YW.

to that of BSK (*i.e.,* 11 vs. 13). It is ease to grasp that the higher the STR value is, the better the development performance of a given participant is. Romano *et al.* analyzed the effects of Approach, Object, and Approach:Object on STR by using ATS because the normality assumption to apply ANOVA [27] was not met. The results of ATS did not indicate a significant effect of Approach (p-value = 0.4765) on STR, namely the development approach seems not to influence the participants' development performance. The effects of Object (p-value = 0.2596), and Approach:Object (p-value = 0.0604) on STR were not significant.

**Table 2.** Summary of baseline and replicated experiments.

| Characteristic | Baseline experiment | Replication |
|---|---|---|
| Participant type | III-year undergraduates in CS taking the SE course at the University of Basilicata | II-year undergraduates in CS taking the SE course at the University of Bari |
| Participant number | 29 | 59 |
| Site | University of Basilicata | University of Bari |
| RQs | RQ1, RQ2, RQ3 | RQ1, RQ2, RQ3 |
| Experimental objects | BSK, MRA | BSK, MRA |
| Experimental groups | TDD, YW | TDD, YW |
| Environment | Java, Eclipse, JUnit | Java, Eclipse, JUnit |
| Design | 2 * 2 factorial | 2 * 2 factorial |
| Assignment to groups and objects | 15 participants assigned to TDD (7 BSK, 8 MRA), 14 participants assigned to YW (7 BSK, 7 MRA) | 28 participants assigned to TDD (14 BSK, 14 MRA), 31 participants assigned to YW (16 BSK, 15 MRA) |
| IV | Approach, Object | Approach, Object |
| DV | $APP_{PLS}$, $APP_{ARS}$, $APP_{DOM}$, $APP_{LIK}$, $IMP_{PLS}$, $IMP_{ARS}$, $IMP_{DOM}$, $IMP_{LIK}$, $TES_{PLS}$, $TES_{ARS}$, $TES_{DOM}$, $TES_{LIK}$ | $APP_{PLS}$, $APP_{ARS}$, $APP_{DOM}$, $APP_{LIK}$, $IMP_{PLS}$, $IMP_{ARS}$, $IMP_{DOM}$, $IMP_{LIK}$, $TES_{PLS}$, $TES_{ARS}$, $TES_{DOM}$, $TES_{LIK}$ |
| Null hypotheses | $H0_{DV}$ | $H0_{DV}$ |
| Statistical inference method | ATS to analyze the effects of Approach, Object, and Approach:Object | ATS to analyze the effects of Approach, Object, and Approach:Object |

## 4    Replicated Experiment

We conducted a replicated experiment to determine whether the results from the baseline experiment are still valid in a different site and with a larger number of participants sampled from a different population. Despite these differences, we designed and executed the replicated experiment as similarly as possible to the baseline experiment to determine, in case of inconsistent results with the baseline experiment, which factors could have caused those results. To this end, we used the replication package of the baseline experiment, which is available on the web[2] and includes experimental objects, analysis scripts, and raw data.

---

[2] https://doi.org/10.6084/m9.figshare.9778019.v1.

As shown in Table 2, the replicated experiment shares most of the characteristics of the baseline one. Therefore, in the following of this section, we limit ourselves to describe the replicated experiment in terms of participants, and design and execution. This is to say that RQs, artifacts, variables, hypotheses, and data analysis of the replication are the same as the baseline experiment; therefore, such information can be found in Sect. 3.

### 4.1 Participants

The participants in the replication were 59 second-year undergraduates in CS at the University of Bari who were taking the SE course. Participation was on a voluntary basis (*i.e.*, we did not pay the students for their participation). To encourage students to participate in the replication, we rewarded the participants with two bonus points in the final mark of the SE course (as had been done in the baseline experiment). The two bonus points were given regardless of the performance of the participants in the replication. Similarly to the baseline experiment, the participants were asked to fill in a pre-questionnaire. Based on the participants' answers, they had passed the exams of the Basic and Advanced Programming courses and had experience with C and Java programming. The participants were not knowledgeable in TDD.

### 4.2 Design and Execution

Based on the 2 * 2 factorial design used in the baseline experiment, the participants in the replication were randomly assigned to the experimental groups and objects: 28 participants were assigned to TDD—14 with BSK and 14 with MRA—; while 31 participants were assigned to YW—16 with BSK and 15 MRA.

All the participants in the replication attended face-to-face lessons on unit testing, JUnit, TL, and ITL. They also practiced unit testing with JUnit in a laboratory session. Later, the participants in the treatment group learned TDD and practiced it through two laboratory sessions and two homework assignments. The participants in the control group, who did not learn TDD, practiced TL and ITL through two laboratory sessions and two homework assignments. The material (*e.g.*, homework assignments) used to train the participants was the same as the baseline experiment, although the number of the homework assignments was different between the baseline and replicated experiments—*i.e.*, three vs. two. We were forced to give two homework assignments, rather than three, because the students could not carry out a third homework assignment during the training period due to deadlines that other courses requested in the same period. As so, we preferred not overloading students to avoid threat of dropouts from the experiment. We conducted the experiment in a single three-hour laboratory session in which the participants carried out the development task—*i.e.*, they tackled MRA or BSK—by using TDD or YW based on their experimental group. At the end of the development task, the participants self-assessed their affective reactions to the used development approach, as well as to implementing and testing code, by using SAM [3] complemented with the liking dimension [17].

## 5   Results

In Fig. 2, we summarize the values of the DVs (of the replicated experiment) by
using diverging stacked bar plots. These plots show the frequencies of the DV
values grouped by Approach. For each DV, the neutral judgment (*i.e.*, five) is
displayed in grey; while negative judgments (*i.e.*, from one to four) and those
positive (*i.e.*, from six to nine) are shown in shades of red and blue, respectively.
The width of a colored bar (*e.g.*, the grey one) is proportional to the frequencies
of the corresponding DV value (*e.g.*, five in the corresponding DV value for the
grey bar). The interested reader can find the raw data on the web.[3] The p-values
ATS returned for each DV are reported in Table 3.

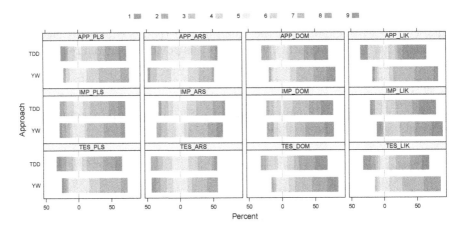

**Fig. 2.** Diverging stacked bar plots summarizing the DV values of the replication.
(Colour figure online)

**RQ1—Affective Reactions to the Development Approach.** The plots in
Fig. 2 (see the first row) do no show huge differences in the affective reactions
to the used development approach, namely TDD or YW, in terms of pleasure
($APP_{PLS}$), arousal ($APP_{ARS}$), dominance ($APP_{DOM}$), and liking ($APP_{LIK}$). However,
it seems that TDD has some negative frequencies more than YW as far as
the dominance and liking dimensions are concerned. The results of ATS (see
Table 3) indicate that there is no significant effect of Approach on the pleasure,
arousal, dominance, and liking dimensions of the participants' affective reactions
to the development approach. Accordingly, we cannot reject the corresponding
null hypotheses. Finally, we did not find any significant effect of the interaction
between Approach and Object, while the effect of Object is significant on the
liking dimension (p-value = 0.0324). That is, the used experimental object significantly influenced the affective reactions of the participants to the development
approach in terms of liking. However, the effect of the experimental object is
consistent within both experimental groups as there is no significant interaction.

---

[3] https://doi.org/10.6084/m9.figshare.12085821.v1.

**Table 3.** Results, from statistical inference, of the replication.

| DV | IV | | | Outcome for $H0_{DV}$ |
|---|---|---|---|---|
| | Approach | Object | Approach:Object | |
| $APP_{PLS}$ | 0.6937 | 0.0805 | 0.7001 | $H0_{APP_{PLS}}$ not rejected |
| $APP_{ARS}$ | 0.6421 | 0.9018 | 0.2817 | $H0_{APP_{ARS}}$ not rejected |
| $APP_{DOM}$ | 0.8295 | 0.1376 | 0.5235 | $H0_{APP_{DOM}}$ not rejected |
| $APP_{LIK}$ | 0.9211 | 0.0324* | 0.2571 | $H0_{APP_{LIK}}$ not rejected |
| $IMP_{PLS}$ | 0.904 | 0.2849 | 0.4421 | $H0_{IMP_{PLS}}$ not rejected |
| $IMP_{ARS}$ | 0.7781 | 0.9646 | 0.3198 | $H0_{IMP_{ARS}}$ not rejected |
| $IMP_{DOM}$ | 0.9529 | 0.2389 | 0.9411 | $H0_{IMP_{DOM}}$ not rejected |
| $IMP_{LIK}$ | 0.8048 | 0.1314 | 0.6618 | $H0_{IMP_{LIK}}$ not rejected |
| $TES_{PLS}$ | 0.5722 | 0.3083 | 0.7749 | $H0_{TES_{PLS}}$ not rejected |
| $TES_{ARS}$ | 0.7446 | 0.2281 | 0.4129 | $H0_{TES_{ARS}}$ not rejected |
| $TES_{DOM}$ | 0.509 | 0.1079 | 0.9945 | $H0_{TES_{DOM}}$ not rejected |
| $TES_{LIK}$ | 0.4588 | 0.3457 | 0.1566 | $H0_{TES_{LIK}}$ not rejected |

* P-value indicating a significant effect.

**Answer to RQ1.** We observed no significant difference in the affective reactions of novice developers to the used development approach, *i.e.*, TDD or YW.

**RQ2—Affective Reactions to the Implementation Phase.** As shown in Fig. 2, there is no huge difference between TDD and YW regarding pleasure ($IMP_{PLS}$), arousal ($IMP_{ARS}$), dominance ($IMP_{DOM}$), and liking ($IMP_{LIK}$) of the affective reactions to the implementation phase. We can also notice that, as for the liking dimension, TDD seems to have some negative frequencies more than YW. The results of ATS (see Table 3) do not show any significant effect of Approach on the four dimensions. Therefore, the corresponding null hypotheses cannot be rejected. The effects of Object and its interaction with Approach are not significant.

**Answer to RQ2.** With respect to the implementation phase, the results do not show a significant difference in the affective reactions of novice developers when they use TDD or YW.

**RQ3—Affective Reactions to the Testing Phase.** The plots in Fig. 2 show that the affective reactions of the control group to the testing phase in terms pleasure ($TES_{PLS}$), arousal ($TES_{ARS}$), dominance ($TES_{DOM}$), and liking ($TES_{LIK}$) are similar to the those of the treatment group. However, except for the arousal dimension, a slight trend in favor of YW can be observed since there are more negative frequencies for TDD as compared to YW. The results in Table 3 do not allow rejecting the null hypotheses. Finally, neither the effect of Object nor its interaction with Approach is significant.

**Answer to RQ3.** We did not observe a significant difference in the affective reactions of novice developers to the testing phase when they use TDD or YW.

**Further Analysis Results.** We used ATS to analyze STR because the normality assumption of ANOVA was not met (Shapiro-Wilk normality test p-value = 0.001). The results of ATS do not indicate a significant effect of Approach (p-value = 0.448) on STR, while the effect of Object (p-value < 0.001) was significant so suggesting that there was a difference in the development performance of the participants when dealing with BSK or MRA. However, the effect of the experimental object is consistent within both experimental groups since the interaction Approach:Object (p-value = 0.566) is not significant.

## 6  Discussion

Replications that do not draw the same conclusions as the baseline experiment can be viewed as successful, on a par with replications that come to the same conclusions as the baseline experiment [24]. Our replication falls into the former case since the outcomes of the replicated experiment do not fully confirm the outcomes of the baseline one. In particular, the baseline experiment found that participants seem to: *(i)* like TDD less as compared to YW; *(ii)* like less implementing code with TDD; and *(iii)* be less happy when testing code using TDD. The replication cannot support these findings because we did not observe any significant difference between TDD and YW. As for the other investigated constructs (*e.g.*, arousal due to the used development approach), the outcomes of the baseline experiment are confirmed by those of the replicated experiment (*i.e.*, the statistical conclusions are the same).

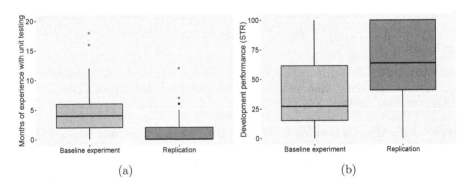

**Fig. 3.** Box-plots summarizing (a) months of experience with unit testing (at the beginning of the SE courses) of the participants and (b) development performance of the participants in the baseline and replicated experiments.

The question that now arises is why the replication fails to fully support the findings of the baseline one. We speculate that the inconsistent results between the baseline and replicated experiments are due to the type of participants (third-year vs. second-year undergraduates in CS from two different universities), rather than their number (29 vs. 59). Although the number of participants in the baseline experiment was not so high and less than that of the participants in the replication, the magnitude (*i.e.,* Cliff's $\delta$ effect size) of the three significant effects [5], in the baseline experiment, was either medium or large. Such a magnitude makes us quite confident that the inconsistent results between the baseline and replicated experiments are not due to the number of participants. This is why we ascribe them to the type of participants. In particular, the participants in the baseline experiment were more experienced with unit testing than those in the replication, who mostly had no experience (see Fig. 3a). Since the participants in the baseline experiment did not know TDD (at the beginning of the SE course in which the experiment was run), they were therefore used to practice unit testing in a *test-last* manner. That is, they were used to write unit tests after they had written production code—in contrast to TDD, where unit tests are written before producing code. This is to say that the participants in the baseline experiment were probably more conservative and therefore less prone to change the order with which they usually wrote production and testing code. Accordingly, their affective reactions, due to TDD, were more negative. This postulation suggests two possible future research directions: *(i)* replicating the baseline experiment with more experienced developers to ascertain that the greater the experience with unit testing in a test-last manner, the more negative their affective reactions, due to TDD, are; and *(ii)* conducting an observational study with a cohort of developers to investigate if the affective reactions caused by TDD change over time. The above-mentioned postulation could be of interest to lecturers teaching unit testing. In particular, they could start teaching TDD as soon as possible to lessen/neutralize the negative affective reactions that TDD causes; after all, there is empirical evidence showing that, with time, TDD leads developers to write more unit tests [9].

Another characteristic of the participants that varies between the baseline and replicated experiments is the academic year of the CS program in which the participants were enrolled—*i.e.,* third year vs. second one. This implies that the participants in the baseline experiment have learned to code in Java a few months before than those in the replication. Nevertheless, the development performance was better in the replication than in the baseline experiment (see Fig. 3b). Therefore, we are quite confident that the academic year did not cause the inconsistent results between the baseline and replicated experiments. On the other hand, we cannot exclude that the worse development performance of the participants in the baseline experiment could have somehow amplified the differences in the affective reactions of the participants who practiced TDD or YW. After all, past work (*e.g.,* [11,16]) has found that the affective states of developers are related to their performance in SE tasks, despite it is still unclear the role that TDD can play in such a relation. To better investigate this point, we suggest researchers to replicate the baseline experiment by introducing a change in the design, namely: allowing any participant to fulfil the development task (*i.e.,* no fixed time), rather than giving any participant a fixed time frame to carry the development task. Such a design choice should allow isolating the effect that the development performance could have on the affective reactions of developers.

# 7   Threats to Validity

The replicated experiment inherits most of the threats to validity of the baseline one since, in the replicated experiment, we introduced few changes. We discuss the threats to validity according to the guidelines by Wohlin *et al.* [27].

**Construct Validity.** Threats concern the relation between theory and observation [27]. We measured each DV once by using a self-assessment instrument (*i.e.,* SAM). As so, in case of measurement bias, this might affect the obtained results (threat of *mono-method bias*). Although we did not disclose the research goals of our study to the participants, they might have guessed them and changed their behavior based on their guess (threat of *hypotheses guessing*). To mitigate a threat of *evaluation apprehension*, we informed the participants that they would get two bonus points on the final exam mark regardless their performance in the replication. There might be a threat of *restricted generalizability across constructs*. That is, TDD might have influenced some non-measured constructs.

**Conclusion Validity.** Threats concern issues that affect the ability to draw the correct conclusion [27]. We mitigated a threat of *random heterogeneity of participants* through two countermeasures: *(i)* we only involved students taking the SE course allowing us to have a sample of participates with similar background, skills, and experience; *(ii)* the participants underwent a training period to make them as more homogeneous as possible within the groups. A threat of *reliability of treatment implementation* might have occurred. For example, a few participants might have followed TDD more strictly than others, somehow influencing their affective reactions. To mitigate this threat, during the experiment, we reminded the participants to use the development approach we assigned them. Although SAM is one of the most reliable instruments for measuring affective reactions [19], there might be a threat of *reliability of measures* since the measures gathered by using SAM, as well as the liking scale, are subjective in nature.

**Internal Validity.** Threats are influences that can affect the IVs with respect to the causal relationship between treatment and outcome [27]. A *selection* threat might have affected our results since the participation in the study was on a voluntary basis and volunteers might be more motivated to carry out a development task than the whole population of developers. Another threat that might have affected our results is *resentful demoralization*, namely participants assigned to a less desirable treatment might not behave as they normally would. To mitigate a possible threat of *diffusion or treatments imitations*, we monitored the participants during the execution of the replication and alternated the participants dealing with BSK to those dealing with MRA.

**External Validity.** Threats to external validity concern the generalizability of results [27]. In the replication, we involved undergraduates in CS to reduce the heterogeneity among the participants. This implies that generalizing the results to the population of professional developers might lead to a threat of *interaction of selection and treatment*. That is, while we mitigated a threat to conclusion validity like *random heterogeneity of participants*, we could not mitigate a threat to external validity. We prioritized a threat of *random heterogeneity of participants* to better determine, in case of different results between the baseline and replicated experiments, which factors might have caused such inconsistent results. However, it is worth mentioning that: *(i)* the use of students could be appropriate as suggested in the literature (*e.g.*, [13,18,23]) and *(ii)* the development performance of the participants in the replication was better than that of the participants in the baseline experiment (see Fig. 3b). The use of BSK and MRA as experimental objects might represent a threat of *interaction of setting and treatment* despite they are commonly used as experimental objects in empirical studies on TDD (*e.g.*, [9,10,23]). Moreover, both BSK and MRA can be fulfilled in a single three-hour laboratory session [9] so allowing better control over the participants.

## 8    Conclusion

We conducted a replicated experiment on the affective reactions of novice developers when applying TDD to implement software. With respect to the baseline experiment, we varied the experimental context and number of participants. The results from the replicated experiment do not fully confirm those of the baseline one. We speculate that the kind of developers can influence the affective reactions due to TDD. In particular, developers who have experience with unit testing in a test-last manner could have affective reactions, due to TDD, that are more negative than developers who have no/little experience with unit testing in a test-last manner. We also speculate that developers' performance in implementing software can influence the affective reactions of developers when applying TDD.

## References

1. Beck, K.: Test-Driven Development: by Example. Addison-Wesley, Boston (2003)
2. Bergersen, G.R., Sjøberg, D.I.K., Dybå, T.: Construction and validation of an instrument for measuring programming skill. IEEE Trans. Softw. Eng. **40**(12), 1163–1184 (2014)
3. Bradley, M.M., Lang, P.J.: Measuring emotion: the self-assessment manikin and the semantic differential. J. Behav. Ther. Exp. Psychiatry **25**(1), 49–59 (1994)
4. Brunner, E., Dette, H., Munk, A.: Box-type approximations in nonparametric factorial designs. J. Amer. Statist. Assoc. **92**(440), 1494–1502 (1997)
5. Caivano, D.: Continuous software process improvement through statistical process control, pp. 288–293 (2005)
6. Carver, J.C., Juristo, N., Baldassarre, M.T., Vegas, S.: Replications of software engineering experiments. Empir. Softw. Eng. **19**(2), 267–276 (2014)

7. Cliff, N.: Ordinal Methods for Behavioral Data Analysis. Psychology Press, London (1996)
8. Erdogmus, H., Melnik, G., Jeffries, R.: Test-driven development. In: Encyclopedia of Software Engineering, pp. 1211–1229. Taylor & Francis (2010)
9. Fucci, D., et al.: A longitudinal cohort study on the retainment of test-driven development. In: Proceedings of International Symposium on Empirical Software Engineering and Measurement, pp. 18:1–18:10. ACM (2018)
10. Fucci, D., et al.: An external replication on the effects of test-driven development using a multi-site blind analysis approach. In: Proceedings of International Symposium on Empirical Software Engineering and Measurement, pp. 3:1–3:10. ACM (2016)
11. Graziotin, D., Wang, X., Abrahamsson, P.: Are happy developers more productive? In: Heidrich, J., Oivo, M., Jedlitschka, A., Baldassarre, M.T. (eds.) PROFES 2013. LNCS, vol. 7983, pp. 50–64. Springer, Heidelberg (2013). https://doi.org/10.1007/978-3-642-39259-7_7
12. Herbon, A., Peter, C., Markert, L., Van Der Meer, E., Voskamp, J.: Emotion studies in HCI-a new approach. In: Proceedings of International Conference HCI (2005)
13. Höst, M., Regnell, B., Wohlin, C.: Using students as subjects–a comparative study of students and professionals in lead-time impact assessment. Empir. Softw. Eng. 5(3), 201–214 (2000)
14. Kaptein, M.C., Nass, C., Markopoulos, P.: Powerful and consistent analysis of likert-type ratingscales. In: Proceedings of International Conference on Human Factors in Computing Systems, pp. 2391–2394. ACM (2010)
15. Karac, I., Turhan, B.: What do we (really) know about test-driven development? IEEE Software 35(4), 81–85 (2018)
16. Khan, I.A., Brinkman, W.P., Hierons, R.M.: Do moods affect programmers' debug performance? Cogn. Technol. Work 13(4), 245–258 (2011)
17. Koelstra, S., et al.: Deap: a database for emotion analysis using physiological signals. IEEE Trans. Affect. Comput. 3(1), 18–31 (2012)
18. Lemos, O.A.L., Ferrari, F.C., Silveira, F.F., Garcia, A.: Development of auxiliary functions: should you be agile? an empirical assessment of pair programming and test-first programming. In: Proceedings of International Conference on Software Engineering, pp. 529–539. IEEE (2012)
19. Morris, J.D., Woo, C., Geason, J.A., Kim, J.: The power of affect: predicting intention. J. Advert. Res. 42(3), 7–17 (2002)
20. Romano, J., Kromrey, J.D., Coraggio, J., Skowronek, J.: Appropriate statistics for ordinal level data: should we really be using t-test and Cohen'sd for evaluating group differences on the NSSE and other surveys? In: Annual Meeting of the Florida Association of Institutional Research, pp. 1–3 (2006)
21. Romano, S., Fucci, D., Baldassarre, M.T., Caivano, D., Scanniello, G.: An empirical assessment on affective reactions of novice developers when applying test-driven development. In: Franch, X., Männistö, T., Martínez-Fernández, S. (eds.) PROFES 2019. LNCS, vol. 11915, pp. 3–19. Springer, Cham (2019). https://doi.org/10.1007/978-3-030-35333-9_1
22. Russell, J.A., Mehrabian, A.: Evidence for a three-factor theory of emotions. J. Res. Personal. 11(3), 273–294 (1977)
23. Salman, I., Misirli, A.T., Juristo, N.: Are students representatives of professionals in software engineering experiments? In: Proceedings of International Conference on Software Engineering, vol. 1, pp. 666–676. IEEE (2015)
24. Shull, F.J., Carver, J.C., Vegas, S., Juristo, N.: The role of replications in empirical software engineering. Empir. Softw. Eng. 13(2), 211–218 (2008)

25. da Silva, F., et al.: Replication of empirical studies in software engineering research: a systematic mapping study. Empir. Softw. Eng. **19**(3), 501–557 (2014)
26. Romano, S., Capece, N., Erra, U., Scanniello, G., Lanza, M.: The city metaphor in software visualization: feelings, emotions, and thinking. Multimedia Tools Appl. **78**(23), 33113–33149 (2019). https://doi.org/10.1007/s11042-019-07748-1
27. Wohlin, C., Runeson, P., Hst, M., Ohlsson, M.C., Regnell, B., Wessln, A.: Experimentation in Software Engineering. Springer, Heidelberg (2012)

# Examining the Current State of System Testing Methodologies in Quality Assurance

Rafaela Sophocleous and Georgia M. Kapitsaki$^{(\boxtimes)}$ (iD)

Department of Computer Science, University of Cyprus, Nicosia, Cyprus
rafaelas08@hotmail.com, gkapi@cs.ucy.ac.cy

**Abstract.** Testing is an important phase of every software system, as it can reveal defects early and contribute to achieving high software quality. In this process of quality assurance, organizations are usually relying on one testing technique. However, a combination of techniques may prove more beneficial to the organization, as it might give the chance to discover a larger number of defects early. In order to examine the above, in the current work we present a survey on the use of system testing methodologies. We have gathered data from 252 individuals that reveal current trends in testing, such as whether requirements are used in the test case definition and whether the testing techniques used are affected by parameters, such as years of experience, whereas we examine the combination of smoke testing and regression testing. We also demonstrate an industrial use case, where this combination was applied, reducing the number of defects identified by the customer.

**Keywords:** Software testing · Agile development · Regression testing · Smoke testing

## 1 Introduction

In Software Engineering, the testing phase can be defined as the process of validation and verification that a system meets the business and technical requirements of the customer and operates as expected. Through the phase of testing organizations are also trying to find defects with the purpose of resolving them and improving the system quality [5]. Developing a completely "error-free" software is almost impossible, but it is possible to produce very high quality software. Testing is moreover, the ability to test a specific process of the system and get every time the same result, verifying that the system behaves the same way.

Previous works surveyed testing techniques. Most approaches discuss the separation of the testing methodologies in different categories, such as dynamic and static testing, or focus on the best testing methodologies for specific programming languages [1]. Surveys that investigate the use of testing techniques in the software industry are also available, with one survey performed annually [6]. In this work, we examine how professionals are using system testing methodologies

© The Author(s) 2020
V. Stray et al. (Eds.): XP 2020, LNBIP 383, pp. 240–249, 2020.
https://doi.org/10.1007/978-3-030-49392-9_16

for Quality Assurance (QA) focusing on some of the choices they make (e.g. how defects are categorized), in an attempt to investigate how the combination of testing methodologies but also some choices performed during testing and the whole software engineering process can affect the testing success. Based on the results of the survey, we have applied the combination of testing methodologies in an industrial use case, specifically smoke testing and regression testing, to verify its usefulness. The main contribution of our work in relation to previous works are that: 1) we study the current state of adoption of basic testing techniques for QA, and 2) we have used a practical case to demonstrate that the combination of more than one testing techniques can decrease defect detection by the customer. Most of the participants of our study employ Agile methodologies, so our results are valid for Agile practices.

The rest of the paper is structured as follows. Section 2 presents related work in the area. Section 3 shows the process that we have followed in order to create the questionnaire and the data collection process. Section 4 presents the main results of the survey, whereas the results of the industrial use case and limitations of the study are also presented. Finally, Sect. 5 concludes the paper.

## 2  Related Work

Previous works present the available testing methods and tools, such as techniques for software functional testing [3] or regression testing [7]. Other works are dedicated to specific programming languages, such as techniques for dynamic program analysis and test generation for JavaScript [1]. Previous surveys have also addressed testing techniques in the industry. The State of Testing 2019 Annual Report gathered approximately 1,000 participants from more than 80 countries and studied various aspects of testing [6]. This study contains some similar questions with our survey, such as the size of the testing team, and the development lifecycle model used but focuses overall on more generic aspects, such as the tester's education, techniques and methodologies used and the tester's personal development. Its results are very useful and informative but have a different orientation from our work that aims mainly on identifying the usefulness of the combination of some testing techniques in quality assurance teams.

A survey of practices in software testing methods and tools (STMTs) focusing on capabilities, limitations, improvements and needs of the tools is presented in [4]. The main conclusions were that tool usage by the organizations was considerably lower than method usage, that there is limited tool support for testing methods and that there is a high demand for interoperability between methods and tools. In contrast to our work, this work focused on how well the software testing process and activities are supported by the existing methods and tools.

In relation to previous work, we present the current state of testing techniques and, although we have a smaller number of participants than the very useful State of Testing 2019 Annual Report, we also have a different focus with the aim of understanding test cases, connect testing techniques with other factors and identify combinations of testing techniques for the quality assurance team that assist in producing a lower number of defects. In addition, we have used an industrial use case, in order to examine whether combinations can provide better results in terms of defect detection before the system proceeds to production.

# 3    Study Design

The main aim of the current study is to understand the adoption of testing techniques with a focus on combining methodologies. Based on this aim, the survey questions were created in order to give emphasis on this combination and allow participants to provide information on their testing techniques and results. The main Research Questions (RQs) that our survey intended to answer are the following:

- **RQ1.** How are the test cases created, especially with relation to the requirements? How many defect categories does an organization use?
- **RQ2.** Which testing techniques do organizations employ? Are there any factors that affect the techniques used, such as the years of experience of the practitioner or the software lifecycle model used?
- **RQ3.** Are combinations of smoke and regression testing before the system goes to production usual? Do they provide better results in terms of defects detected by the customer?

The questionnaire[1] created for the purpose of the survey consists of 28 questions. The first part covers demographic data (e.g. country, age, years of experience), whereas the second part is dedicated to how testing is used within the organization, referring to generic techniques, their combination, the lifecycle model used and specific tools and environments adopted for testing purposes, building on the above research questions. The survey participants were informed about the purpose of the study and they had to agree to the consent form, in order to be able to proceed with answering the questionnaire. In order to reach a large number of participants, the survey questionnaire was distributed to local companies and was posted on social media in groups that are relevant to testing and testing practices, in an attempt to gather participation from different countries. Individual interviews with leaders of quality assurance teams from Cyprus (15 practitioners) were also performed and the main conclusions are included in the paper. However, no formal interview process was followed.

# 4    Results and Discussion

## 4.1    Demographics

252 responses were gathered, 56% of our respondents are male, 43.7% female, whereas 4% (1 participant) chose not to provide this information. Individuals of different age were reached: 23.4% are between 18 and 30, 51.2% between 31

---

[1] https://forms.gle/4jprqc2t2f4yq9fg8.

and 40, 23.8% between 41 and 60, and 1.6% above 60 years old. The individuals have various roles in the organization, including automation testers, test engineers, software engineers, performance testers, QA director and test leads, with most participants having more than one role. Most have a role in testing (90.9%), whereas the rest are developers, analysts or managers. Individuals from 11 countries took part in the study, although a large percentage of the participants are from Cyprus (25.79%), where the survey was designed, whereas many participants from Greece were also reached due to the proximity of the countries (23.02%). Figure 1 shows the participation per country.

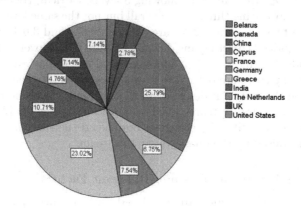

**Fig. 1.** Participation per country.

## 4.2   RQ1. Test Cases and Defects Categorization

**Test Cases and Requirements.** We asked the participants how much (%) of the requirements are covered by the test cases. Many companies are not using all system requirements, in order to design their test cases: 10.3% of the participants are not using the requirements at all, 29% are using 30% of the requirements, 8.3% are using them by 40%, the majority are using 50% of the requirements (39.7%), only 4.8% are using all requirements, and the remaining (almost 8%) are using 60–80% of them. This causes several problems because it means that the system is not tested properly in order to detect all errors before its delivery to the customer, as creating test cases from requirements to test the behavior of a software system is a main aspect of black-box testing [8].

Through the interviews with the leaders of QA teams of different companies about the results that we received for the specific question, participants commented that the team members of the QA team are not well trained to know some basic guidelines on how to write a test case or sometimes they do not have much time to execute these test cases. It has also been reported by most that they only use positive paths, in order to design their test cases. Through the interviews, it was identified that very few testing techniques are known or are used by the leaders of quality assurance teams in order to write their test cases:

functional, requirement, positive, stress and exploratory. However, this raises several problems regarding the software quality assurance team and ultimately the quality of the system that is delivered to the client, because negative testing is not used. It is important that a system is tested for both positive and negative paths to make sure that everything works as agreed with the client [2].

**Categories of Identified Defects.** We asked participants to indicate the defects categories they are using. We included indicative categories but allowed participants to mention more categories. The answers are shown in Table 1. Most participants (25.9%) are using the following 3 levels: Critical, Highest/High and Medium, with 53.6% using three levels overall but not the same levels in all cases. 39.7% are using two categories, 2.8% are using only one and 3.6% are using 4 or 5 different categories (1 participant did not provide any answer). Based on the interviews conducted, most of the companies tend not to pay enough attention to understand why there are defects that are categorized into the above specific categories, when the system is delivered to the customer. Also, most of the leaders of the quality assurance teams have been told that they simply collect the defects that can be identified by the client but they do not take into account the defects that are raised by the quality assurance team.

### 4.3   RQ2. Testing Techniques and Relevant Factors

Various testing methodologies are employed by the participants. Most are employing black box testing (87.3%), whereas some are using both black and white box (11.1%) and only 3 participants (1.2%) are only using white box testing. This is an expected result, as our survey targeted members of the QA team and the results we report concern primarily black box testing. Almost all participants are using both static and dynamic testing (96.8%) and almost all are relying both on functional and non-functional testing (94%). Figure 2 lists various specific techniques used by participants. Unit testing was also mentioned by a small number of participants but it is not considered, as we assume that it applies to almost all involved organizations, if we consider their development teams. 2 participants are using only one technique, most (35.7%) are using 3 different techniques, followed by 5 techniques in 21% of the participants, 4 techniques in 18.7% and 2 techniques in 14.7%. A small percentage (2.4%) is employing 8 or more techniques. Although automation testing appears in 56.3% of cases, in a more general question on automation, the use of some sort of automation was reported by 77% of the participants.

   We examined whether the testing techniques employed are affected by the years of experience of the engineer. We run one-way ANOVA and observed a statistically significant difference in the use of regression testing ($p = 0.000$), smoke testing ($p = 0.000$), system testing ($p = 0.000$), automation testing ($p = 0.001$), performance testing ($p = 0.009$), and usability testing ($p = 0.000$). From Table 2 we observe that there is a decrease in the use of system testing and performance testing by individuals with larger experience and also a slight decrease in the use of usability testing, whereas automation testing is used widely in all groups.

**Table 1.** Categories used to characterize defects.

| Categories | Use percentage | Categories | Use percentage |
|---|---|---|---|
| Critical, Highest/High, Medium | 25.9% | Highest/High, Medium, Low | 3.2% |
| Critical, Highest | 23.9% | Critical/Highest/High | 2% |
| Critical/Highest, High | 15.9% | Critical, High, Medium, Low | 1.6% |
| Critical/Highest/High, Medium | 14.3% | Critical, Highest, High, Medium, Low | 1.6% |
| Highest, High, Medium | 5.6% | Medium | 0.8% |
| Critical, Highest, High | 4.8% | Critical, High, Medium, Low, Block | 0.4% |

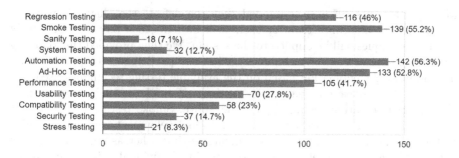

**Fig. 2.** Testing techniques used.

**Table 2.** Testing techniques with significant differences per years of experience.

| Experience (years) | Regression testing | Smoke testing | System testing | Automation testing | Performance testing | Usability testing |
|---|---|---|---|---|---|---|
| 1–3 | 47.5% | 67.5% | 20% | 52.5% | 42.5% | 60% |
| 3–5 | 51.7% | 41.4% | 37.9% | 55.2% | 65.5% | 27.6% |
| 5–10 | 26.8% | 70.1% | 2.4% | 48% | 35.4% | 20.5% |
| >10 | 86.3% | 17.6% | 11.8% | 82.4% | 33.3% | 25.5% |

We examined whether the adopted software development lifecycle model affects the testing techniques used, as for instance, automation testing is used mainly in Agile methodologies. 61.9% of the participants are using Agile or iterative incremental models (59.9% are using Agile methods). The next most frequent practice is DevOps (35.7%), followed by the waterfall model (2%), whereas V-shaped model was mentioned by 1 participant. We observed a statistically significant difference in the use of many testing techniques: sanity testing ($p = 0.000$), system testing ($p = 0.000$), automation testing ($p = 0.000$), performance testing ($p = 0.000$), usability testing ($p = 0.000$), compatibility testing ($p = 0.000$), security testing ($p = 0.000$) and stress testing ($p = 0.032$). In our dataset we observed that automation testing is used equally in Agile and waterfall methods (40.4% and 40% respectively), but it is used more in DevOps (85.6%). Sanity and system testing are far more common in the waterfall model (60% and 80% respectively), whereas they are used only in small percentages in

Agile and DevOps methods. Performance and usability testing are used more in Agile than in other techniques. Security testing is overall less common but more frequent in Agile (20%) than in other methodologies. Compatibility testing is used in Agile and waterfall methods (31.1% and 40% respectively), but is less common in DevOps (6.7%). Finally, stress testing is used overall less but is more common in the waterfall model (20%) and rare in DevOps (1.1%).

### 4.4    RQ3. Combination of Smoke and Regression Testing Before Production

Most participants (95.6%) responded that the defects that have been raised by the quality assurance team or client will be reduced if any combination of testing techniques will be applied to the system. We then provided the following specific choices of testing techniques asking the participants to provide their own additional combination based on the available testing techniques used also in other survey questions (e.g. sanity testing): 1) smoke testing and regression testing, 2) integration testing, 3) all the above. Smoke testing is generally a surface level testing to ensure that the build the development team has provided to the QA team can be accepted for further testing, whereas regression testing is testing on a deeper level. In integration testing, individual units are combined and tested together as a group. Most of the participants (91.67%) believe that the most effective combination of testing techniques before the system will be delivered to the production is the smoke and regression testing. Only 1.98% gave a positive answer for integration testing, and 6.35% would prefer a combination of all (smoke testing, regression testing and integration testing), with no participant providing any other specific combination. However, the majority of participants is currently not using this combination: 89.3% are not using smoke testing along with regression testing before production, 9.9% do and the remaining 0.8% were not sure or do not know.

### 4.5    Industrial Use Case

The combination of smoke and regression testing techniques was employed in the framework of an industrial use case in the local industry in Cyprus for a total duration of two months and a half. The use case concerns the testing of a web application in the healthcare domain. The organization uses development sprints and was initially employing only smoke testing. We are not providing however, more information on the organization and the specific system, as the organization asked for the anonymous use of the data. In order to examine the combination of techniques, both smoke and regression testing were used for 5 consecutive sprints. We run a t-test to examine whether there is any difference in the number of defects detected, when the system was delivered to the customer, before and after the use of the combined testing. In the total of 31 sprints, we observed that the difference in the results is statistically significant ($p = 0.000$) with considerably less defects being detected when the combination of testing techniques is used (Table 3). In order to examine whether the number of changes coming from development affects the number of defects detected (since some sprints contain more changes than others), we used Pearson correlation, but no correlation was detected ($r = 0.052$, $p = 0.782$), indicating that this is not a parameter that affects our results. Thus, this combination of testing techniques is very effective for the QA team, in order to identify the defects before the system will be deployed on production environment, that is an expected outcome as testing is strengthened.

**Table 3.** Difference in the number of defects in the industrial use case.

| Testing technique | N | Mean | Std. dev. |
|---|---|---|---|
| Smoke testing only | 16 | 263.81 | 90.385 |
| Smoke and regression testing | 5 | 55.2 | 13.989 |

### 4.6 Limitations

Our study is affected by *external validity*, referring to the extend we can generalize our findings. Our dataset is limited to 252 participants and expresses their views, whereas participants come from a limited number of countries (11 countries). Analyzing the state of testing techniques in other countries or populations may provide different results. *Construct validity*, i.e. the degree to which a test measures what it claims to be measuring, may have been affected by having specific views represented more in the data collected. More than one individuals from the same organization may have participated in the survey, affecting thus the overall results as they might contain in a larger degree the views of specific organizations. Although different testing techniques were mentioned in the questionnaire and were indicated by the participants (e.g. performance testing), we focused on the combination of specific testing techniques (i.e. smoke, regression and integration testing). Participants did not mention other combinations that could decrease the detection of defects, but mentioning specific techniques may have influenced their answer, having thus a negative effect on *conclusion validity* (the degree to which conclusions about the relationship among variables based on the data are correct). Finally, our study is not affected by *internal validity*.

## 5 Conclusions

In this paper, we have presented the main results on a survey on system testing methodologies that focused on identifying which testing techniques are used, whether they are affected by the experience of the participants or by the lifecycle model used, as well as observing other common testing parameters, such as whether requirements are used for the creation of the test cases and the levels used to categorize defects. We have applied some results of the survey that refer to the combination of smoke and regression testing by the QA team in the framework of an industrial use case. The main conclusions drawn can be summarized to the following:

- Not many organizations are using requirements to create their test cases. 39.7% of participants are using half of the requirements, but as revealed also via the interviews the test cases are restricted to testing positive paths that may not provide the optimal results, as negative paths are neglected.
- Most organizations are using three levels to categorize defects but there is still a large number of organizations not giving appropriate importance to using more than one levels for the defects.
- In terms of testing techniques, various are being used in different phases of the development process. Ad-hoc testing is used by the majority of participants (52.8%), although it is usually not the only technique used. Some important types of testing, such as security testing and stress testing, appear to be less common (used by 14.7% and 8.3% of participants respectively).
- The choice of some testing techniques is affected by the years of experience of the expert or by the lifecycle model used, but since the participants number in each category is relatively small the observations drawn about these factors cannot be regarded conclusive.
- The combined use of smoke and regression testing can have a positive influence on the decrease of the number of defects detected by the customer and one main take-away message for organizations is to introduce this combination in their testing process by the QA team.

# References

1. Andreasen, E., et al.: A survey of dynamic analysis and test generation for javascript. ACM Comput. Surv. (CSUR) **50**(5), 1–36 (2017)
2. Causevic, A., Shukla, R., Punnekkat, S., Sundmark, D.: Effects of negative testing on TDD: an industrial experiment. In: Baumeister, H., Weber, B. (eds.) XP 2013. LNBIP, vol. 149, pp. 91–105. Springer, Heidelberg (2013). https://doi.org/10.1007/978-3-642-38314-4_7
3. Kobrosly, W., Vassiliadis, S.: A survey of software functional testing techniques. In: Proceedings of the IEEE Southern Tier Technical Conference, pp. 127–134. IEEE (1988)
4. Lee, J., Kang, S., Lee, D.: Survey on software testing practices. IET Softw. **6**(3), 275–282 (2012)
5. Myers, G.J., Sandler, C., Badgett, T.: The Art of Software Testing. Wiley, Hoboken (2011)
6. PractiTest: State of testing survey 2019. https://www.practitest.com/resource/state-of-testing-report-2019/
7. Rosero, R.H., Gómez, O.S., Rodríguez, G.: 15 years of software regression testing techniques—a survey. Int. J. Softw. Eng. Knowl. Eng. **26**(05), 675–689 (2016)
8. Whalen, M.W., Rajan, A., Heimdahl, M.P., Miller, S.P.: Coverage metrics for requirements-based testing. In: Proceedings of the 2006 International Symposium on Software Testing and Analysis, pp. 25–36 (2006)

# Author Index

Printed in the United States
By Bookmasters